No Wealth but Life

This book re-examines early-twentieth-century British welfare economics in the ~~~~~~~ ~~ ~~~ ~~lfare state. There are fresh
views
and |
Daun
welfa
phy (
expo
this :
polic
on C
Kon
the (
and

Rog
the
in 1
Ecc
Uni
ics,
he
of
Eu
A
Ec
Th
as
Th
ha
Ec
of

Ta
C
ha
R
fr
tl

~~~~~~~~. ~~~~~~~~~~
(1994, in Japanese) and *Economic Thought of Alfred Marshall and the Historical School* (2007, in Japanese). He has edited several books, including *Marshall and Schumpeter on Evolution: Economic Sociology of Capitalist Development* (with Y. Shionoya, 2009). He was the editor of the *Journal of the Society of the History of Economic Thought in Japan.*

No Wealth but Life

*Welfare Economics and the Welfare
State in Britain, 1880–1945*

Edited by

ROGER E. BACKHOUSE

University of Birmingham and Erasmus University Rotterdam

TAMOTSU NISHIZAWA

Hitotsubashi University, Tokyo

CAMBRIDGE
UNIVERSITY PRESS

CAMBRIDGE
UNIVERSITY PRESS

University Printing House, Cambridge CB2 8BS, United Kingdom

Cambridge University Press is part of the University of Cambridge.

It furthers the University's mission by disseminating knowledge in the pursuit of education, learning and research at the highest international levels of excellence.

www.cambridge.org
Information on this title: www.cambridge.org/9781107569430

© Cambridge University Press 2010

First published 2010
First paperback edition 2015

A catalogue record for this publication is available from the British Library

Library of Congress Cataloguing in Publication data
No wealth but life : welfare economics and the welfare state
in Britain, 1880–1945 /
edited by Roger E. Backhouse, Tamotsu Nishizawa
p. cm.
Includes bibliographical references and index.
ISBN 978-0-521-19786-1 (hardback)
1. Public welfare – Great Britain – History.   2. Welfare state – Great Britain – History.
3. Welfare economics – History.   I. Backhouse, Roger, 1951–   II. Nishizawa, Tamotsu,
1950–   III. Title.
HV245.N668 2010
361.6′5094109041–dc22   2009051344

ISBN 978-0-521-19786-1 Hardback
ISBN 978-1-107-56943-0 Paperback

Contents

Contributors

Roger E. Backhouse, University of Birmingham and Erasmus University Rotterdam

Martin Daunton, University of Cambridge

Peter Groenewegen, University of Sydney

Atsushi Komine, Ryukoku University, Kyoto

Maria Cristina Marcuzzo, University of Rome "La Sapienza"

Steven G. Medema, University of Colorado, Denver

Tamotsu Nishizawa, Hitotsubashi University, Tokyo

Yuichi Shionoya, Hitotsubashi University, Tokyo

Richard Toye, University of Exeter

Preface

Starting in 2002, Hitotsubashi University in Tokyo acted as host to a series of workshops, generously funded by the Japan Society for the Promotion of Science and the Ministry of Education, on the Cambridge School of Economics. One of the themes that emerged was welfare economics, and in 2005 and 2006, workshops were held on the theme of 'welfare economics and the welfare state'. We soon realised that if Cambridge welfare economics was to be placed in its proper context, the discussion needed to be broadened to permit a comparison of developments at Cambridge with those at Oxford and the London School of Economics.

Our starting point, partly symbolic as elements of the story go further back, is the 1880s, when Alfred Marshall was writing his *Principles of Economics*, first published in 1890. This was the decade when the demonstrations in the East End of London brought the problem of poverty to the fore. Though Bismarck's Germany, an example with which Marshall would have been very familiar, had introduced welfare reforms earlier, the moves towards the British welfare state took place only over the ensuing decades, the heyday of Cambridge welfare economics. Though historians are well aware of Marshall's concern with the problem of poverty, the development of Cambridge welfare economics has generally been considered not against this background but against that of theoretical developments internal to the discipline of economics.

By the 1940s, both the welfare state and welfare economics had entered a different era. The Second World War, the Beveridge Report, and the election of the first Labour government to have a working majority in the House of Commons led to the creation of a welfare state that went beyond anything that was feasible in previous decades. At the same time, academic welfare economics became more technical, dealing with abstract questions concerning the measurement of welfare. Though they might be applied to problems relating to the welfare state, these techniques were independent, developed by economists whose attitudes had become very different from those of their nineteenth-century counterparts. The result was that when economists turned to write the history of welfare economics, they focused on developments within economic theory, divorcing the story from that of the emergence of the welfare state. Our contention is that the conventional history of welfare economics, focusing on the contrast between Pigovian and Paretian welfare economics, is a stylized account based on selective memory that needs to be questioned.

A concomitant of placing welfare economics in this broader context was the need to turn to discussions of welfare (whether or not it should be called welfare economics is a matter for debate) outside Cambridge, for the drivers of welfare reform (including Beatrice and Sidney Webb, Bernard Bosanquet, Llewellyn Smith, William Beveridge, and John A. Hobson) were connected not with Cambridge, but with Oxford and the fledgling London School of Economics. They are absent from conventional histories of welfare economics, with their focus on Pigovian versus Paretian methods, because they are not seen as significant economic theorists. What we came to realise is that, whilst this may have been the view at Cambridge, it was not the view of contemporaries. Moreover, when the story was broadened to include them, a different history began to emerge, in which legitimate ways to analyse welfare were contested in ways that went beyond the very narrow concerns about the measurability of utility that dominate traditional accounts. This revised history has dramatic consequences for the way we should see the developments, associated with Lionel Robbins and the New Welfare Economics, out of which modern welfare economics emerged.

The essays in this book are based on presentations at these workshops in 2005–6. They do not offer a complete history of the development of British thought on welfare economics during this period: far from it – the gaps are too obvious even to need listing. As we have come to realise, the history of welfare economics is, in the manner of much intellectual history, a story in which economics is entangled with philosophy, politics, and that amorphous concept, public opinion, during a time of dramatic transformation in British society, the institutions of government, and the university system. A comprehensive study cannot yet be written. However, we believe that the essays brought together in this volume shed fresh light on important parts of that history and help establish what is currently known: though they do not provide a comprehensive history of welfare economics, we believe that they not only establish that the history of welfare economics needs to be rewritten but they also provide some of the blocks out of which a new history will have to be built.

R. E. B.
T. N.

ONE

Introduction

Towards a Reinterpretation of the History of Welfare Economics

Roger E. Backhouse and Tamotsu Nishizawa

I. PLACING WELFARE ECONOMICS IN CONTEXT

Towards the end of the 19th century, the laissez-faire ideology that had dominated Victorian Britain was increasingly called into question. There was great prosperity yet poverty remained endemic. London's poor East End was, for the middle classes, a dangerous foreign world quite unlike the areas in which they lived. Socialism was in the air. This term could denote a wide spectrum of positions, from Marxism and other forms of revolutionary socialism at one end to municipal socialism, centred on local authority provision of public goods and services, from sewers to street lighting, at the other. There were also important national initiatives in areas such as education. Such concerns were given impetus by the extension of the franchise to the working class, in 1867, 1884 and 1918, and by the rise of organised labour and the Labour movement, culminating in the displacement, in Parliament, of the Liberal Party by the Labour Party. Questions about the functioning of a capitalist economy became even more acute with the economic turmoil of the inter-war period, culminating in the Great Depression, when capitalism seemed, to many, to have failed. After 1917 there was, in the Union of Soviet Socialist Republics, an alternative with which comparisons could be made. However, as in the late 19th century, the issue facing most economists was not whether capitalism was so flawed that it needed to be overthrown but whether its faults could be put right by measures that fell far short of a Soviet-style command economy. John Maynard Keynes, in his *General Theory* (1936), pointed to one apparent limitation of capitalism – its inability to keep workers and resources fully employed and suggested ways in which it could be made to work better.

1

This was the background to two developments that have hitherto been considered separately. One was the emergence of what, after 1945, came to be called the welfare state: a state-provided system of universal health care, old age pensions and provision for support of those who were unemployed or incapable of work, funded by moderately progressive taxation. The other was the development of a body of principles for evaluating policies that the government might pursue: what was labelled by its most influential proponent, 'the economics of welfare', or welfare economics. By 1945, this had developed as a widely agreed upon and well understood set of principles, which from the 1950s were formalised in a series of textbooks.

There is a sense in which economists had always been concerned with welfare (see Myint 1948). Rising incomes meant rising living standards, and political economists could explain why allowing people to pursue their own interests would produce outcomes that were generally in the public interest. It was also possible to provide convincing arguments that individuals acting individually through markets (the key feature of capitalism) would fail to ensure certain goods were produced, the classic statement being that of John Stuart Mill in the final chapter of his *Principles* (1848). However, it is misleading to call this welfare economics, because economists had no techniques for analysing welfare as anything different from production. The framework for the analysis of welfare as something different from total production was provided only towards the end of the century. In 1871, William Stanley Jevons, strongly influenced by contemporary experimental psychology, took up Jeremy Bentham's ideas about utility maximisation. When combined with mathematical methods taken from physics, the result was a mathematical theory of individual behaviour, focusing on utility, which could be taken as a measure of individuals' welfare. If different individuals' utilities could be added up (something Jevons was very cautious about doing) the result was a measure that could be used, as Bentham had argued, to measure welfare.

The person who applied this most systematically to problems of welfare was the Cambridge philosopher, Henry Sidgwick. In his *Principles of Political Economy* (1883 [1901]) he used utilitarian arguments to argue that there were two ways of measuring wealth: goods could be valued using prices or according to the utility they created. Because the price of a good is not related to its average utility, the two measures would not be the same. Though he did not use this terminology, Sidgwick drew a clear distinction between wealth (understood as income) and welfare. Furthermore, marginal analysis provided tools with which the limitations of free markets could be analysed. He went on to draw up a much longer list of cases where government intervention was required than could be found in Mill. Cambridge welfare economics was then developed by his Cambridge colleagues and successors, notably Alfred Marshall (1920) and A. C. Pigou (1920), who provided the tools that could be used to analyse the limitations of the capitalist system much more effectively than Sidgwick had been able to do. Though they moved away from utilitarianism, either as an account of behaviour or as an ethical system, their analysis retained many utilitarian characteristics. In Pigou's hands, Cambridge welfare economics, as it came to be known, provided arguments for an extensive programme of government intervention.

Conventional accounts of welfare economics proceed from Cambridge welfare economics to the attack that was mounted on it in the 1930s. A simplified account of this runs as follows. Up to 1930, welfare economics was, in Britain, virtually synonymous with Pigovian welfare economics. In his *Essay on the Nature and Significance of Economic Science* (1932), Lionel Robbins argued that the inter-personal utility comparisons implicit in the adding together of different individuals' utilities, as required by the Cambridge method, were matters of individual judgement, for which there was no scientific basis. They should, therefore, be banished from economic science. At the same time, two of Robbins's young colleagues at the London School of Economics (LSE), John Hicks and Roy Allen, had shown that it was possible to base a theory of individual behaviour on nothing more than assumptions about preferences, dispensing with the notion of utility altogether. One might use 'ordinal' utility, attaching numbers to different levels of well-being, but these numbers had no significance beyond indicating how different bundles of goods were to be ranked. It was meaningless to add them together.

Faced with this challenge, Cambridge welfare economics was no longer tenable. Attempts were therefore made to reconstruct welfare economics on foundations that did not include utility. Hicks and other young theorists turned instead to the continental tradition that flowed from Jevons's French contemporary, Léon Walras, to the Italians, Enrico Barone and Vilfredo Pareto. Welfare criteria were developed that relied on knowing only individuals' preferences. If making a change made one person better off, but made no one worse off, that must be an improvement, says the criterion eventually named after Pareto. The problem was that this was a very weak welfare criterion indeed because, in practice, virtually any change that made someone better off would make someone else worse off. Because it was impossible to measure how much better or worse off people were, it was impossible to say anything in such cases without an additional criterion. John Hicks, Nicholas Kaldor and others sought this in compensation tests, an idea floated by Pareto, that a change was an improvement if the winners could compensate the losers and still remain better off.

Much of the history of welfare economics is correct. However, it is seriously incomplete in ways that have dramatic implications for how these developments should be interpreted. The conventional story fails to look outside academic welfare economics, paying no attention to economists' awareness of social problems. Yet this is a period when social problems were at the forefront of economists' concerns. The Cambridge view of the relation between academic economics and social reform can be represented by Marshall. As is well known, he came into economics because of a desire to understand and deal with the problem of poverty. Though they might as individuals become involved in the Settlement Movement or the Charity Organisation Society (COS), the Cambridge economists, from Marshall onwards, sought to create a scientific economics, set apart from the political process. Their relation to the political process was typically that of advisers, giving evidence to Royal Commissions or publishing analyses on which policy makers could draw.

At Oxford, on the other hand, the relation between academic ideas and involvement in social and political reform was different. The home of the Oxford Movement, with its integration of High Church Anglican Christianity and social involvement, produced economists who became directly involved in politics. The generation that included L. T. Hobhouse, J. A. Hobson, Bernard Bosanquet and William Beveridge left Oxford to become civil servants, journalists and politicians, actively involved in creating some of the institutions that developed into the welfare state. They provided much of the intellectual framework for the reforms that came with the Liberal government of 1906, the first to include Labour representatives. Within the space of a few years, the government introduced a range of radical measures from progressive income tax to labour exchanges and unemployment benefits.

Given that Marshall moved into economics because he wanted to address the problem of poverty, and that many other economists were concerned with these issues, it is surprising that the links between welfare economics and the welfare state have been neglected. The reason this changes the history so significantly is that it brings in Oxford, where the intellectual basis for reform was very different from that offered by Cambridge. The background common to both universities was the perceived inability of Christianity, any longer, to provide an acceptable foundation for ethics and the resulting need to find an alternative. However, whereas Cambridge largely developed the utilitarian tradition, Oxford turned instead to idealism. Where Cambridge had Sidgwick, Oxford had T. H. Green and John Ruskin. Though none went so far as to argue against the existence of capitalism, many of those who came out of Oxford, such as Hobson and R. H. Tawney, held much more radical views on the limitations of capitalism than did their Cambridge counterparts. There was no rigid divide (Marshall, for example, was influenced by his brief experience at Oxford and paid great attention to Kant)[1] but the Oxford–Cambridge divide provides a useful way of characterising two attitudes to the study of social problems and responses to them.

To set the scene for the chapters that follow, the first theme that needs to be clarified concerns the location of thinking about welfare at the interface between academic economics and the policy process. This problem is addressed in the next section. The argument then turns, in Section 3, to the contrast between utilitarianism and idealism as foundations for the analysis of welfare and the welfare state. Sidgwick is compared with Green, and the key features of Ruskin's critique of capitalist society are outlined. Section 4 then outlines the subsequent chapters.

2. ECONOMISTS, THE ACADEMY AND POLITICS

The story of welfare economics from the 1870s to the First World War centres on two figures: Henry Sidgwick (at Cambridge) and Thomas Hill Green (at Oxford). They were friends from an early age, whose careers had much in common. Both contributed to establishing ethics as an academic discipline: Sidgwick through his *Methods of Ethics* (1874) and Green through his teaching at Balliol and, to a lesser extent, through his posthumous *Prolegomena to Ethics* (1883).[2] In their different ways, both were inspirational figures for their generation.[3] However, their careers also diverged in ways that, quite apart from their philosophical differences, considered in detail in Section 3, help explain the difference between the welfare economics that came out of Cambridge and Oxford.

---

[1] Though note that Groenewegen (in Chapter 2) argues that the influence of Oxford on Marshall should not be exaggerated. On Marshall's attitude to Kant, see Cook (2009).

[2] See Richter (1964).

[3] See footnotes 2 and 5.

Sidgwick and Green were both members of the group of 'academic Liberals' who sought to enter politics in the 1860s. Faced with the extension of the franchise to the working class, a process started with the 1867 Reform Act, they believed that academics had an obligation both to help educate the new electorate and to provide enlightened leadership. Education for newly enfranchised adults was provided by the university extension movement. Leadership was to be provided by academics standing for Parliament. They were radicals, successors to the earlier Philosophic Radicals, wanting reform of society, in particular to reduce the role of the church and the aristocracy. In 1868, 19 of their number were elected and they were full of hope that Gladstone's administration would fulfil this aim of reforming society on a rational basis. However, these hopes were rapidly dashed when it became clear that religious interests were still sufficiently strong to prevent the educational reforms that were needed. An Education Act was passed in 1870, but the radicals felt let down because it left the churches in a strong position in providing education. When Gladstone regrouped the Liberal Party, it was on the basis of foreign policy. The new electorate was revealed as conservative, and a barrier to reform. It was necessary to find a new way forward.

Another of the academic Liberals, Leslie Stephen, assessed the problem in the following terms:

For a solid reform therefore we must look to the gradual infiltration of sound beliefs through the whole social organism, which must end by bearing the fruit of an intelligent loyalty to trustworthy leaders. The change must be inward before it can be outward: no shuffling of the cards can make them all turn up trumps; it is a new force that is required, not a new machinery; and all constitution-mongering is thrown away till a new spirit has been breathed into the dead bones. (Stephen [1875], quoted in Harvie 1976: 198)

The relation between academia and politics needed to be re-assessed. In order to bring about this 'inward' change, many Liberals retreated from Parliament, and resorted to single issue politics – the temperance movement, public health, public education and poor relief.

Sidgwick's response was to explore the foundations of ethics, political economy and politics in a series of weighty tomes, each offering a meticulous analysis of the problem in hand. In response to Marshall's comment that his lectures failed to attract more than a handful of students (in contrast to the hundreds who were inspired by Green), Sidgwick responded that he could not do anything to make his philosophy more popular (Sidgwick and Sidgwick 1906: 394–6). Though it was Marshall, whose work rested on philosophical foundations that were different from Sidgwick's,[4] who established the Cambridge school, the process whereby economists became academic experts, distancing themselves from direct political involvement, can arguably be traced back to Sidgwick. One could not say the same of Green's influence. Sidgwick's *Principles of Political Economy* (1883 [1901]) used utilitarian arguments to make a case for government intervention that went beyond what his predecessors, such as Mill, had advocated, but he remained conservative in his outlook, with views that were largely those of traditional Liberalism. Thus he was involved in the COS, an organisation established in 1869 to tackle the problem of poverty by ensuring that poor relief was not handed out inappropriately: it would harm its recipients' moral character and hence undermine their ability to help themselves.

Green also 'retreated' to academia, and shared many of Sidgwick's classical Liberal views. However, his teaching in Balliol had a very different effect. Unlike Sidgwick, Green remained within the Church of England, seeking to reinterpret Christianity as an ethical creed. Students might come away from his lectures without having understood a word, but inspired by the call of duty. This consciously moral outlook on social problems was reinforced by John Ruskin, who became Professor of Fine Arts in 1869, offering a denunciation of the life-threatening values of commercial society and political economy. Perhaps their most influential student was Arnold Toynbee whose lectures on the Industrial Revolution used history to reinforce the moral critique of capitalist society, though, like his teacher, Green, he resisted socialism: reform was to come about through improvement of character. He threw himself into the university settlement movement, and after his death, in 1883, at the age of 30, he was lionised as if a martyr. The combination of Green, Ruskin and Toynbee inspired a generation of students, including many historically-minded economists whose careers were dominated by questions of social reform. Even more than their Cambridge counterparts, many of them went into the extension and settlement movements, exemplified by Toynbee trust and Toynbee Hall. Some retained Green's liberal values, but others moved in a more collectivist direction, especially after the 'bitter cry of outcast London' came to their attention in the 1880s (see Stedman Jones 1984). Bernard Bosanquet and J. H. Muirhead, like Sidgwick, were

---

[4] This brief summary glosses over much. For a detailed discussion of Marshall's differences from Sidgwick, see Raffaelli (2003), Cook (2009) and the essays by Raffaelli and Cook in Raffaelli, Becattini and Dardi (2006). See also Backhouse (2006).

supporters of the COS. John Atkinson Hobson, Leonard Hobhouse and Graham Wallas moved towards the Fabians (though Hobson remained a Cobdenite Liberal in many respects). Of these, 'the two Hobs' became the leading intellectual spokesmen for a New Liberalism of social reform (Clarke 1996: 43).

In contrast, the Cambridge welfare economists became professional academic economists in the modern sense. Marshall sought to professionalise economics. Pigou did for the economics of welfare, whose 'official' history starts with his *Wealth and Welfare* (1912), what Marshall did for economics in general with his *Principles.* The latter begins by trying to show that what is good for economic man is normally good for 'total man'; Pigou's *Wealth and Welfare* begins by postulating this. They sought to observe the positive-normative distinction and engaged in economic analysis that was separate from their policy advice. This analysis might comprise dry logical dissection of problems (as in Sidgwick's major books) or technical mathematical arguments such as used by Marshall, or Pigou, or it might be analysis of specific problems of policy. A major exception was the Tariff Reform Campaign of 1903, where Marshall, Pigou and others sought to enter political controversy directly. Even here, however, they were seeking (with disastrous consequences) to impose the authority of an economic science that lay above the political arena.

In contrast, the Oxford economists and their students became involved much more in organisations designed to have a direct influence on policy or social reform. They might not seek to enter Parliament, but they did not retreat into academia. Some went into journalism (e.g., Hobson and Hobhouse) and many became involved in groupings such as the New Liberals and the Fabian Society. Hobson and Hobhouse worked alongside politicians such as Samuel and Haldane (both Ministers in Asquith's 1908 government) and Ramsey McDonald (later Labour prime minister). Sydney Olivier and Graham Wallas (both Oxford products) founded the Fabian Society with George Bernard Shaw and Sidney Webb. Perhaps more significant, there was no demarcation between the economic and the political; they were political economists in a fairly literal meaning of the term. This overlap of the political and the economic is shown more clearly in Hobson's writing, where his ideas on welfare were developed not only in books that addressed the problem specifically, such as *Work and Wealth* (1914), but also in clearly political writings, such as *The Crisis of Liberalism* (1909) or *The Social Problem* (1901), or in the close cooperation that developed between him, Hobhouse and Wallas. A similar difference in attitude is also found in economic and social history. In the hands of John and Barbara Hammond or R. H. Tawney, history could, in the tradition of Toynbee's *Lectures on the Industrial Revolution*, be used to make a clearly political point. In contrast, Cambridge's J. H. Clapham wrote economic history that served purely academic purposes.

The contrast was not absolute. From Oxford, Llewellyn Smith, Michael Sadler and Beveridge became bureaucrats, as did the Cambridge economists Sydney Chapman and Walter Layton, whereas Keynes falls into a category of his own, so varied were his activities. There was, however, a significant difference in emphasis. In the inter-war years, many from Oxford became associated with LSE. Wallas became Professor of Political Science, Hobhouse Professor of Sociology, Tawney Professor of Economic History and Cannan Professor of Economics. Hobson had no permanent position but undertook some teaching there.

This group constituted the core of the group that the American Walton Hamilton (1919: 318) labelled 'the English school of welfare economics'. Although this clearly suggests a parallel with Pigovian welfare economics, the similarities should not be pushed too far. Though Marshall and Pigou used different methods, they were engaged in the same enterprise – developing and applying a set of techniques that could identify beneficial changes in the way economic activity was undertaken. This was also the goal of the new (Paretian) welfare economics that was developed in the 1930s and 1940s. Hamilton's 'English school of welfare economics', on the other hand, hardly merited being described as a school given the variety within it. What united them was a willingness to apply to the problem of evaluating economic activities a more detailed and stronger ethical criteria than those the Cambridge economists were willing to employ, leading them all to adopt an approach to welfare economics that was very different from that found in the Cambridge School. Beyond that, the differences among, for example, Hobson, Cannan and Tawney were profound both as regards specific judgements made and as regards the extent to which they sought to develop new conceptual tools. As Maloney (1985, 183–4, 232) has expressed it, the battle to professionalise economics was primarily a battle between those who saw it as a discipline comparable to the natural sciences and those who saw it as an adjunct to immediate social reform. The former inclined to an absolutist method involving 'scientific' tools where the latter inclined to a historical-relativist method.

There are further explanations that must be appended to the claim that the crucial distinction that needs to be made in this context is between

Cambridge and Oxford. The first is that, though it can be argued that ideas coming out of Oxford had more effect on politicians, and hence on the movement towards the welfare state, influence is hard to establish. The changes that led to the creation of the welfare state were not the result of directly applying economic theory – it was not 'welfare economics in action'. They were political events that were dependent on the broad range of social factors that typically underlie major historical changes. It is often very difficult to establish clear links between ideas and the resulting policies. For example, it has been argued that Hobson's arguments about the surplus had more effect on the move towards progressive taxation in Lloyd George's 'People's budget' of 1908 than more orthodox utilitarian arguments. Hobson did move in the circles frequented by decision makers, and his views were certainly more important in influencing the climate of opinion on taxation, than would be suggested by his almost complete neglect among historians of academic economics. However, the evidence is speculative and circumstantial, as is often the case. Apart from the problem that political events typically have multi-layered causes, there is the problem that politicians pick up ideas from surprising sources. Toye, in Chapter 8, illustrates this by showing that Churchill and Lloyd George may have been persuaded to adopt certain welfare policies, not as a result of arguments by economists (whether defined to include Hobson or not) but by H. G. Wells. Wells, of course, was associated with the Fabians and thereby with the Oxford side of the division discussed here, but he was by no stretch of the imagination an Oxford economist. In his hands, ideas were given new twists. In the same way, Sidney and Beatrice Webb, who had even stronger connections, through LSE, with Oxford economists, and of whom Sidney was classified by Hamilton as a welfare economist, were not themselves from that tradition.

3. IDEALISM, UTILITARIANISM AND MORALITY

The two men who lie at the roots of the ideas discussed in this book, Sidgwick and Green, offered contrasting philosophical foundations for the subject: utilitarianism and idealism. However, despite this difference, they were both responding to the mid-Victorian loss of religious faith caused by the results of biblical criticism emanating from Germany and the evolutionary ideas associated with Charles Darwin and Herbert Spencer. They both struggled with this crisis of faith, the problems they faced resonating with those of their friends and students. Sidgwick is renowned for, in Keynes's words, never doing anything but 'wonder whether Christianity was true and prove that it wasn't and hope that it was'.[5] He sought, through his involvement in spiritualism, to recover the supernatural element lost with traditional Christianity; in his philosophy he sought to find a secular basis for ethics. Green, in contrast, sought to accommodate Christianity to the new developments: to reinterpret the Christian religion as a system of ethics that could stand independently of Christian dogma. In doing this, Sidgwick turned to the utilitarianism of Bentham and Mill, and Green, to the idealism of Kant and Hegel.

Sidgwick's great work on utilitarianism was *The Methods of Ethics* (1874), a book which arguably changed the direction of moral philosophy away from discussion of ethical judgements themselves to discussion of the principles on which ethical judgements should be based.[6] Though it argued the case for utilitarianism, it posed clearly the dilemma that dominated his ethical thought. He could not find a decisive reason why utilitarianism was better than egoism as a criterion for moral judgement. This meant that utilitarianism, the purpose of which was to provide a justification for ethical judgements, rested on an intuition. He might claim that this was an intuition shared by the relevant community – that there was a consensus among experts – but he had not provided a rational argument that should persuade a sceptic who did not share this intuition.

In contrast, Green was known as much for the ethics he espoused as for the philosophical basis on which he sought to ground them. It was not unusual for students attending his lectures to be baffled by the technical arguments, but to come away impressed with the speaker's sincerity and passion: Green 'transmitted earnestness with a charismatic force' (Clarke 1978: 13). His ethics was one of social reform: challenging the Evangelical claim that faith was a matter of personal piety. This social gospel, to use an anachronistic term, was not new, but Green, unlike earlier Methodists and High Church figures, was dissociating it from traditional theological doctrines. In one of his highly influential lay sermons, one of the few things published before his death, Green concluded that though criticism had invalidated much traditional Christian doctrine, 'it is not the reality of God or of the ideal law of conduct that is in question, but the adequacy of our modes of expressing them' (Green 1888: 276). He went on to claim that 'Faith in God and duty will survive

---

[5] Quoted by Harrod (1951: 116–7). Cf. Richter (1964: 138).
[6] This has been discussed in much more detail in Backhouse (2006), which contains further references. The principal ones are Schultz (2004) and Schneewind (1977). See also Collini (2001).

much doubt'. It was an ethic of self-sacrifice, for 'if once we have come
to acquiesce in such a standard of living as must make us wish God and
duty to be illusions, it must surely die'. The pairing of God and duty
(twice in the last two sentences of his sermon) reflected a sense of duty
that Sidgwick would wholeheartedly have endorsed, but such language
was far from anything Sidgwick would have used.

The philosophical basis on which Green sought to base this
Christianity-as-ethics was idealism, taken from Kant and Hegel. In
Hegel's hands, idealism was a conservative doctrine, but Green sought to
turn it around and use it to ground social reform.

Green adapted idealism to the needs of those who wanted justification for the
moral code of their parents; he gave conscience a social and political meaning,
and gave an outlet to the strong sense of duty and obligation to serve, so characteristic of his generation. (Richter 1964: 12)

For Green, the world was the realisation of a spiritual principle: an eter-
nal consciousness (God) was realising itself gradually but imperfectly in
the human organism. Moral good was the realisation of moral capability.[7] Because the process was imperfect, people had a duty to help bring
it about. In so doing, people were realising their true freedom, doing not
simply what they wanted to do, but fulfilling their capabilities according
to the divine plan, or doing what was rational to do.

This view of freedom in terms of identification with an ultimate end
has been seen as justifying totalitarianism (cf. Popper 1945). What
freed Green from this charge is the values he placed at the centre of
this process. He was committed to democracy and freedom; he argued
that one had to recognise the rights of others and that the community
had obligations to its members; he believed in social harmony. A major
flaw in his philosophy is that these ethical principles were arguably not
based on reason so much as on a will to believe. This will to believe was
characteristic of men of his generation for whom traditional Christian
doctrines had become untenable. The idea that freedom meant freedom
to do something worthwhile – that duty called for self-sacrifice – was
what many of them wanted to hear. One of those who picked up this
message was Arnold Toynbee, a student at Balliol from 1875 to 1878,
and who was on the verge of taking up a fellowship there when he died.
The spirit of Green's religion was captured in the settlement movement,
in which Toynbee had become involved, which involved middle class

[7] This and the following two paragraphs draw very heavily on Richter (1964).

people moving into the slums and working alongside people there. The most influential such settlement was Toynbee Hall, in the East End of London, named in his memory.

Some of Green's students took up his idealistic philosophy, R. L. Nettleship, J. H. Muirhead, Bernard Bosanquet and F. H. Bradley being the most prominent. However, what was more important was that although it was a philosophical doctrine, its influence was felt far more widely than most philosophical ideas. One of the remarkable aspects of Green's influence was its breadth. It lay beneath the substantially secular London Ethical Society, as well as the Christian Social Union and the Anglo-Catholic *Lux Mundi* movement. Politically, Green's influence was also diverse. Bosanquet, C. S. Loch and the COS focused on the reform of character: the aim of the COS was to make sure poor relief did not harm character by going to the undeserving poor. In contrast, for others such as the New Liberals, Hobhouse and Hobson, the effect of Green's philosophy was to liberate them from the individualism of the Manchester School and nonconformist religion. Though the Cambridge School never took up Green's idealistic philosophy, they shared many of his ideals. Sidgwick and Green were close friends. Marshall was exposed to Green's lecturing in his year at Oxford and spent significant time studying Kant and Hegel. Marshall himself was an admirer of Toynbee and was a trustee of Toynbee Hall. Students from Cambridge as well as Oxford flocked into the settlement movement.

A vital additional ingredient added to the intellectual and emotional stimulation coming from Sidgwick and Green was provided by Ruskin. His influence was so strong that one historian had gone so far as to claim that 'it would be difficult to overestimate Ruskin's position as cultural hero at Oxford in the 1870s' (Kadish 1982: 32). Ruskin was neither a Liberal (many of his views were extremely conservative) nor a philosopher, at least in the technical sense, but the moral values found in his analysis of culture and society could be used to offer a profound challenge to the values of political economy. *Unto This Last*, which first appeared in 1860 as 'four essays on the first principles of political economy', had as its stated aim to give 'a logical definition of WEALTH' for the first time in plain English. Its second aim was to show that the acquisition of wealth was possible under certain moral conditions of society (Ruskin 1994: vii–ix). Ruskin defined value as 'to avail towards life' and declared that it was an intrinsic quality of things. What varied greatly was the ability to appreciate and to use what was valuable: Wealth was 'the possession of the valuable by the valiant'

(Ruskin 1994: 118, 125).[8] He summed this up in one of his best known remarks: 'There is no wealth but life. Life including all its powers of love, of joy, and of admiration' (Ruskin 1994: 156).

4. WELFARE ECONOMICS AND THE WELFARE STATE

This book brings together chapters that place the history of welfare economics in this context, which is broader than that usually considered. The movement from Cambridge (Pigovian) welfare economics to the 'new' welfare economics of the 1930s is placed alongside the competing approach to the analysis of social welfare centred on Oxford and LSE, and the movement towards the welfare state. The three parts focus respectively on Cambridge, Oxford and the policy arena. The coverage is different, reflecting the different attention that has been paid to these three aspects of the history.

Cambridge welfare economics is well known and the transition from Sidgwick to Marshall and Pigou hardly needs to be analysed in detail.[9] There remains, however, the task of placing it in a broader context. Chapter 2 by Peter Groenewegen juxtaposes Marshall's well-known theoretical case for welfare provision with his less well-known statements about the welfare state. Of key importance is the difference between his unpublished views and the more cautious views expressed in his published work. In his early writing, there is a contrast between the bolder statements in his unpublished work on ethics and the statements made in the articles on poor relief that he contributed to the early volumes of the *Economic Journal* and expressed in evidence to the Royal Commission on the Aged Poor in 1893. In his later work his writing on economic chivalry, both in his *Economic Journal* article of 1907 and in later editions of the *Principles*, was more guarded than views he expressed in correspondence.

As Groenewegen points out, Marshall, in his early unpublished writing on ethics, was clear in supporting all measures that we now think of as comprising the welfare state, with the exception of providing health care. What gave his published statements a much more cautious tone was his emphasis on individual responsibility, as befits a supporter of the COS. He went so far as to say that problems such as poverty were less important than they appeared to be, except as regards their effects

[8] The entire phrase is capitalised in the original.
[9] See Backhouse 2006, which provides further references.

on human character. He attached importance to economic growth and, though cautious, was optimistic about prospects for tackling poverty.

Pigou, Marshall's successor, is also known for his theoretical case for measures that make up the welfare state. Steven Medema (Chapter 3) draws attention to a little-known pamphlet, 'State Action and Laisser-Faire' (1935), in which Pigou wrote about how these ideas might work out in practice, which sheds a different light on the subject. The key point was that there was no sharp division between state action and laissez-faire, the reason being that the beneficial effects of the market were dependent on man-made institutions, in the creation of which the state played a significant role. When it came to practice, it was necessary to pay attention to the quality of the decision-making bodies, not merely to the desirability or otherwise of policies considered in the abstract. Politicians and bureaucrats might have private interests that caused their decisions to differ from those that were in the public interest. This comes back to Pigou's earlier point about the desirability of policies depending on man-made structures, for there was a need to create government structures that minimised conflicts between private and social interests. Medema's claim is that, when viewed in this light, Pigou is much less vulnerable to the criticisms associated with Ronald Coase, and found in much of the public choice literature, than if attention is confined to *The Economics of Welfare*.

Daunton (Chapter 4) focuses on one aspect of the welfare state, taxation, making arguments that reinforce those of Groenewegen and Medema. One of the influences on the 1908 budget, he argues, was the literature on earned and unearned income associated with Henry George, Sidney Webb and J. A. Hobson. Though his published writings were more cautious, when he was approached by opponents of progressive income tax, Marshall refused to support their campaign. Poverty crushed character and progressive taxation might make it easier for people to improve themselves. This may have fallen short of Hobsonian arguments about unproductive surplus but, though coming with the proviso that it must not be pushed too far, it worked in the same direction. When he turns to Pigou, Daunton points out that Pigou, in the same way that he did not trust politicians or bureaucrats to pursue the public interest, did not trust the poor, who would not necessarily use resources effectively. His focus was on the efficiency of state intervention, directing resources to those with the ability to make best use of them, and away from the moral side of the problem. This concern with the practicality of reform, and scepticism about grand schemes of reform, was also characteristic of Keynes, the other Cambridge economist considered by Daunton.

If the philosophical foundations of Cambridge welfare economics are well known, the same cannot be said of its Oxford counterpart, comprising a seemingly disparate group of thinkers (not all economists), united as much by what they disagreed with as by what they believed. In the first chapter in Part II, Yuichi Shionoya (Chapter 5) addresses this problem. The roots of the Oxford approach, he argues, go back to German *Sozialpolitik*, represented by Gustav Schmoller, whose work was ethical as well as historical and aimed at solving practical problems of reform in the German state. Green drew on German sources to develop a specification of the relations between economics, ethics and ideology that contrasted with that of his Cambridge friend and counterpart, Sidgwick. Shionoya identifies a philosophical framework in which virtue had priority over good. He then uses this rational reconstruction of the Oxford approach to make sense of recent scholarship on Green and to relate Green's ethics to the ideas of Ruskin and Hobson, thereby defending the notion that it makes sense to talk of an Oxford approach to problems of welfare.

One characteristic of the Oxford approach, as identified by Shionoya, is that it encompassed political ideology as well as academic philosophy (the latter exemplified by Green's idealist followers, the philosophers R. L. Nettleship and J. H. Muirhead). The New Liberalism, often thought of simply as a political philosophy, modifying traditional liberalism in response to the late-Victorian move towards collectivist ways of thinking, can be seen as a response to this different ethical framework that focused, not on good but on virtue, community and civic solidarity. The theme of community is found in the writings of many Oxford thinkers (such as Green, Hobson, Hobhouse, Ruskin and Tawney) whose work is otherwise very different in its origins.

One of the most prolific and influential thinkers in this group was Hobson, the subject of Roger Backhouse's chapter (Chapter 6). Backhouse argues that, rather than thinking of Hobson simply as a social philosopher and one of the creators of the New Liberalism, he should be taken more seriously as a welfare economist. Surprisingly, given the common association of utilitarianism with the Cambridge school, Hobson portrayed himself as a utilitarian, albeit one whose utilitarianism was pervaded by ideas taken from Ruskin. In the same way that Green had taken Hegelian idealism and turned it into a radical doctrine, so Hobson created a radical welfare economics and social philosophy out of ideas that Ruskin used with a more conservative purpose. Ethical judgements influenced by Ruskin offered valuations of different activities that could be placed in a broadly utilitarian framework to justify a radical critique of capitalism. This view of Hobson also casts a new light on Pigou, for it can be argued that what Hobson was doing was taking seriously arguments about divergences between wealth and welfare that Pigou acknowledged, only to minimise their importance. The significance of Hobson's work in this area, though recognised by some contemporaries, was lost, perhaps because he never separated economic analysis from political philosophy. Furthermore, it was unfashionable to attack, as he did, the idea that economics should be scientific.

British economics was dominated, for much of this period, by Marshall's Cambridge, where the attempt was being made to create a scientific economics. This task was later taken up by Lionel Robbins at LSE. In such an environment, the Oxford approach was not well received and was generally ignored. Outside Britain, however, it encountered a better reception, notably in the United States, among the institutionalists (Rutherford 2007). Chapter 7 by Nishizawa broadens the context further by considering a Japanese scholar Fukuda. Fukuda was one of the major Japanese economists of the period and author of a substantial work on welfare economics. His starting point, stemming from his association with Lujo Brentano, who wrote the preface to the German translation of Marshall's *Principles*, was the ethico-historical approach of the German historical school. Fukuda learned welfare economics from Marshall and Pigou, and he had worked closely with Brentano, with whom he wrote his first book, on labour economics. Yet it was Hobson's welfare economics that he believed came closest to his own. His integration of these various strands involved a belief that though the German historical school's emphasis on nations and communities captured an essential aspect of welfare problems, it was Marshall who, with his individualistic approach, had progressed furthest. Fukuda no doubt saw in Hobson the attempt to further the community-centred approach that the German historical school had barely begun to develop, partly through a failure to appreciate the role to be played by theory.

These three chapters do not make the case that there is a case for speaking of an Oxford welfare economics to parallel that of Cambridge, though some American contemporaries did see things this way. However, they make the point that what is perhaps best called the Oxford approach should be seen as providing a significant alternative, or group of alternatives, to the welfare economics that came out of Cambridge. Shionoya shows that it is possible to discern a different philosophical foundation, centred on the idea of virtue, and that the origins of this lay in German thought. This and Nishizawa's chapter serve as a reminder that, in discussing British economics, it is essential to remember the wide international influence of the German historical school, the work of which had a very broad influence on countries ranging from the United States to Japan. The Japanese economist Fukuda shows how, within a framework established by the German historical school, it was possible to integrate approaches ranging from Marshall to Hobson, which in Britain were seen as fundamentally different: that, even when discussing British work, it is important to bear in mind the international context.

The Oxford approach was characterised by a refusal to acknowledge any fundamental divide between academic economics and involvement in the political process. The thinkers under discussion may have been actively involved in the political process but the focus has been on the development of ideas, whether the academic welfare economics of the Cambridge school or the welfare analysis involved in the political philosophy of New Liberalism. The three chapters in Part III focus on the involvement of economists and social theorists in the policy process. The first, by Richard Toye (Chapter 8), considers the reforms introduced by Lloyd George and Winston Churchill, radical members of Asquith's Liberal government, to argue that it can be remarkably difficult to identify the intellectual origins of policy changes and that the ideas that influence policy can come from surprising places.

The New Liberals, such as Green, Hobhouse and Hobson, clearly contributed to the climate of opinion out of which the Liberal reforms emerged. Toye does not dispute this, but argues that the evidence that these thinkers had a direct influence on the thinking of politicians is circumstantial: that it is very difficult to show how the ideas of 'opinion forming intellectuals' translated into concrete political action. Just as Hobson, Hobhouse and the New Liberal thinkers moved in the same circles as Liberal and later Labour politicians, with whom they undoubtedly discussed their ideas, so too did Wells. Furthermore, it is possible to find clear parallels between statements made by Wells, very probably read by Churchill and Lloyd George, and decisions made soon after. This may be circumstantial evidence for a link, but no more so than the evidence that their policies were directly influenced by those with more widely acknowledged social–scientific credentials such as Hobson or Hobhouse.

Two economists who clearly did engage directly with policy and the emergence of the welfare state were Keynes and Beveridge, the subjects of the other two chapters, by Maria Cristina Marcuzzo (Chapter 9) and Atsushi Komine (Chapter 10). Marcuzzo explores the relationship between Keynes and Beveridge in two stages. The first is to examine discussions of the Beveridge Report, seeking to resolve some of the puzzles that confronted the biographers of these two men. The main feature of this is the 'shattering encounter' of Beveridge, largely self-taught in economics, with Keynes's *General Theory*. Beveridge sought assistance from Keynes and some of his disciples in the work that led to *Full Employment in a Free Society* (1944). Marcuzzo then reviews the Keynes–Beveridge correspondence, which spanned the period from the First World War, concerned with Beveridge's articles in the *Economic Journal*, edited by Keynes, to the discussions that followed *Full Employment in a Free Society*.

Komine is instead concerned with the relationships between the works that he describes as Beveridge's trilogy: the Beveridge Report (*Social Insurance and Allied Services*) (1942), *Full Employment in a Free Society* and *Voluntary Action* (1948). These were concerned, respectively, with the problems of social security, full employment and the establishment of a civic society. The Beveridge Report clearly has strong links with Beveridge's previous work and to ideas such as the Webbs' proposals for a national minimum. The second owed much to Keynesian economics. And yet, for all the differences, there is, Komine claims, a unity underlying the three works. It is the last volume that echoes most strongly the Greenian themes of community and duty that Beveridge would no doubt have picked up in his youth at Oxford.

These three chapters point, in very different ways, to the complexity of the links between ideas and policy. Toye's example illustrates the difficulty that can arise in linking policy decisions to specific opinion formers and the likely significance of thinkers who, from the perspective of academia, are decidedly unorthodox. Marcuzzo and Komine show that, even where policies can readily be linked to individuals, such as Beveridge, the problems do not disappear. Beveridge's ideas evolved and reflected his long-accumulated knowledge of unemployment and the practical problems involved in designing policy as well as, after 1942, his exposure to Keynesian ideas. However, Keynesian ideas did not displace earlier ones, the overall framework for his thinking about welfare, owing much to the Oxford of Green.

5. CONCLUDING REMARKS

These chapters offer a reappraisal of welfare economics during the period when the British welfare state was being established. They make the case that to understand what was going on, it is necessary to adopt a perspective that is much broader than is conventionally adopted, encompassing both the ethico-historical approach that became associated with

20 *Roger E. Backhouse and Tamotsu Nishizawa*

Oxford and the welfare state. The latter is relevant not only because the most prominent thinkers associated with Oxford refused to draw a sharp divide between welfare economics and welfare policy but also because the attitudes of the Cambridge school towards policy reflected considerations that, even if present, were far from prominent in their scientific economics. The chapters in this book does not provide a comprehensive history of welfare economics – on the contrary, much is left out – but it establishes that the subject needs to be considered as part of a broader tradition of social thought that transcends present-day disciplinary boundaries.

Though this volume does not venture far into the period after the Second World War (or perhaps we should say after *Full Employment in a Free Society*) it clearly has implications for the way that the subsequent history of welfare economics is viewed. A postscript (Chapter 12) amplifies the account provided of welfare economics in the 1920s sufficiently to show how the re-interpretation of the history of welfare economics offered in this book alters our perspective on the emergence of the new welfare economics and what might be called the Robbinsian approach that has dominated modern economics.

References

Backhouse, R. E. 2006. Sidgwick, Marshall and the Cambridge School of Economics. *History of Political Economy* 38 (1):15–44.
Beveridge, W. H. 1942. *Social Insurance and Allied Services*, Cmd. 6404. London: HMSO.
1945. *Full Employment in a Free Society.* London: George Allen & Unwin.
1948. *Voluntary Action: A Report on Methods of Social Advance.* London: George Allen & Unwin.
Clarke, P. 1978. *Liberals and Social Democrats.* Cambridge: Cambridge University Press.
1996. *Hope and Glory: Britain 1900–1990.* London: Penguin Books.
Collini, S. 2001. My Roles and Their Duties: Sidgwick as Philosopher, Professor, and Public Moralist. In *Henry Sidgwick.* Proceedings of the British Academy, 109. Ed. R. Harrison, 9–49. Oxford: Oxford University Press.
Cook, S. 2009. *The Intellectual Foundations of Alfred Marshall's Economic Science: A Rounded Globe of Knowledge.* Cambridge: Cambridge University Press.
Green, T. H. 1883. *Prolegomena to Ethics.* Ed. A. C. Bradley. 5th edition 1907. Oxford: Clarendon Press.
1888. *Works of Thomas Hill Green*, Volume III. Ed. R. L. Nettleship. London: Longmans Green.
Hamilton, W. H. 1919. The Institutional Approach to Economic Theory. *American Economic Review* 9 (1): 309–18.
Harrod, R. 1951. *The Life of John Maynard Keynes.* London: Macmillan.

Harvie, C. 1976. *The Lights of Liberalism.* London: Allen Lane.

Hobson, J. A. 1901. *The Social Problem.* London: Nisbet.

1909. *The Crisis of Liberalism.* Brighton: Harvester Press. Edited with an introduction by P. F. Clarke, 1974.

1914. *Work and Wealth.* London: Macmillan.

Kadish, A. 1982. *The Oxford Economists in the Late Nineteenth Century.* Oxford: Oxford University Press.

Keynes, J. M. 1936. *The General Theory of Employment, Interest and Money.* London: Macmillan.

Maloney, J. 1985. *Marshall, Orthodoxy and the Professionalization of Economics.* Cambridge: Cambridge University Press.

Marshall, A. 1920. *Principles of Economics,* 8th edition. London: Macmillan.

Mill, J. S. 1848. *Principles of Political Economy.* London: Parker.

Myint, H. 1948. *Theories of Welfare Economics.* Cambridge, MA: Harvard University Press.

Pigou, A. C. 1912. *Wealth and Welfare.* London: Macmillan.

1920. *The Economics of Welfare.* London: Macmillan.

1935. State Action and Laisser-Faire. In *Economics in Practice: Six Lectures on Current Issues,* London: Macmillan, 107–28.

Popper, K. R. 1945. *The Open Society and Its Enemies.* 2 vols. London: Routledge.

Raffaelli, T. 2003. *Marshall's Evolutionary Economics.* London: Routledge.

Raffaelli, T., Becattini, G., and Dardi, M., eds. 2006. *The Elgar Companion to Alfred Marshall.* Cheltenham: Edward Elgar.

Richter, M. 1964. *The Politics of Conscience: T. H. Green and His Age.* London: Weidenfeld and Nicolson.

Robbins, L. C. 1932. *An Essay on the Nature and Significance of Economic Science.* London: Macmillan.

Ruskin, J. 1994 [1860]. *Unto This Last: Four Essays on the First Principles of Political Economy.* London: Routledge/Thoemmes Press.

Rutherford, M. 2007. Institutionalism and Its English Connections. *European Journal of the History of Economic Thought* 14(2): 291–323.

Schneewind, J. B. 1977. *Sidgwick's Ethics and Victorian Moral Philosophy.* Oxford: Clarendon Press.

Schultz, B. 2004. *Henry Sidgwick: Eye of the Universe.* Cambridge: Cambridge University Press.

Sidgwick, A., and Sidgwick, E. M. 1906. *Henry Sidgwick: A Memoir.* London: Macmillan.

1883 [1901] *Principles of Political Economy.* London: Macmillan.

Sidgwick, H. 1874. *The Methods of Ethics.* London: Macmillan.

Stedman Jones, G. 1984. *Outcast London: A Study in the Relationship Between Classes in Victorian Society.* 2nd ed. New York: Pantheon Books.

PART ONE

CAMBRIDGE WELFARE ECONOMICS
AND THE WELFARE STATE

TWO

Marshall on Welfare Economics and the Welfare State

Peter Groenewegen

It is well known that Marshall's *Principles of Economics* contained a number of innovations in economics which became part of the toolbox of welfare economics and that some of these had their roots in his early writings. The notion of consumer's surplus is a good instance (see Myint 1948 for a classic treatment of this subject). Moreover, Marshall's broad hint at a tax/bounty policy designed to favour increasing returns industries and to penalise those working under diminishing returns was a policy for enhancing growth of output through a state induced shift in resource allocation of productive factors. For Marshall, of course, output growth was advantageous to all classes of society and of particular benefit to the poor. Such an emphasis on output in welfare policy was part of Marshall's classical heritage, since as Myint (1948) has also pointed out in his still very authoritative historical treatment of welfare economics in the 19th and early 20th centuries, the classical approach to welfare economics was heavily output orientated.

On the other hand, it is less well known that some of Marshall's perspectives on social progress, including those that remain unpublished from the material housed in the Marshall papers, embrace aspects of what later became known as the welfare state. In fact, some of his later published views, particularly his 1907 excursus into economic chivalry (Marshall 1907) and the final chapter on progress in the later editions of the *Principles* (Marshall 1961, Book VI, chapter XIII) contain support for state initiatives to enhance the welfare of society, with special reference to the welfare of the poorest sections of the community. These views not only mark out Marshall as a grand, albeit generally conservative, social reformer (Whitaker 2004) but also as someone who in specific planks of his social policy resembles the perspectives of 'new labour' in their concern for the environment, housing, education, redistributive tax policy and 'social policing' or, as I put it in my 1995 Marshall biography, the views of the small 's' socialist (Groenewegen 1995, p. 571).

In this chapter, I wish to examine briefly these two strands of Marshall's economic perspectives on how to enhance economic welfare. Section 1 looks at the classical welfare economics aspects of his work, embodied in the doctrine of the surpluses. Section 2 briefly reviews the social policy planks of his thought on desirable state intervention to enhance individual and social welfare, captured in his reinterpretation of a restrictive laissez-faire policy through the more progressive slogan, 'let the state be up and doing' (Marshall 1907, p. 336). The chapter says nothing about the impact of Marshall's year at Oxford on his notion of welfare economics and economic welfare. This is because the influence of either Toynbee or T. H. Green thereon can be easily overstated, as I have discussed in some detail elsewhere (Groenewegen 1995, pp. 294–5). Section 3 presents the conclusions of this inquiry into Marshall's welfare views including some comments on how the formal welfare economics and his views on the welfare state may be linked.

I. CLASSICAL WELFARE ECONOMICS ANALYSIS: THE DOCTRINE OF THE SURPLUSES

Marshall's pioneering excursions into welfare economics relied heavily on his doctrine of the surpluses (consumers' and producers' surplus) elaborated quite early during his economics career. These excursions, he later claimed, had been reached quite independently of any acquaintance with Dupuit's work of which, he recalled in 1910, 'he knew nothing' by 1873. (Marshall to John Maynard Keynes, 4 December 1910, cited in Groenewegen 1995, pp. 162–3.) The concept of consumer's surplus, or as Marshall more generally mentioned it, consumers' surplus, made an early appearance in the draft for a volume on international trade prepared in the mid-1870s. It was then called 'consumers' rent', a name which Marshall continued to use until the fourth edition of the *Principles* (when it became consumers' surplus). It was used in this argument to shed light on the welfare burden (excess burden) of indirect taxes on specific commodities (in Whitaker 1965, II pp. 77–8). The concept, however, appears to have been first developed in a very succinct manner in a mathematical notebook Marshall used from 1867 to 1872 (in Whitaker II pp. 279–80) and in the associated 'abstract theory of a general uniform tax' most likely written during 1873 or 1874 (Whitaker 1965, II pp. 285, 289–302). These unpublished items undoubtedly formed the basis for the welfare argument on taxes (and bounties) which Marshall included in the *Pure Theory of Domestic Value* (Marshall 1879, chapter 2), printed in 1879, at Sidgwick's urging, for private circulation. This version in turn formed the foundation for the doctrine as exposited in the *Principles* from the 1890s onwards, in an increasingly cautious manner. The reasons for such caution, according to Whitaker (1965, II pp. 287–8), seem to have been apparent to Marshall from the very beginning, though they may have been partially forgotten in the long process of turning his early economic theory into the detailed exposition it received in the pages of the *Principles* (for a discussion of this drawn-out process, see Groenewegen 1995, chapter 12).

In what follows, the discussion of Marshall's welfare economics will be taken almost exclusively from the pages of the *Principles*, particularly from its eighth definitive edition. The exception to this practice is to alert readers to Marshall's changing views on the subject as it moved through the eight editions. Neither the notion of the surpluses, nor their association with individual and social well-being, were ever eliminated from the *Principles*. Generally speaking, both their definition and Marshall's position on their application remained substantially the same from when they were first developed, though his faith in the practicality of their application to real problems grew somewhat weaker with the passing decades from the 1890s.

The surpluses were most concisely defined in Appendix K of the *Principles* where their relationship with the concepts of rent and quasi-rent was also discussed. The wording in that Appendix originated with the third edition, but it was shifted elsewhere in the fourth edition and did not find its more permanent 'home' in Appendix K until the fifth edition. The need for such a concise definition came undoubtedly from the criticism the concept had received at the time of the first two editions from J. S. Nicholson and from Leslie Stephen, both people whose judgement Marshall respected. This was partly attributable, Marshall feared, to the lack of clarity in his 'initial' exposition of 'consumer's rent' (see the summary of this discussion in Groenewegen 1995, pp. 424–5).

At the start of Appendix K, Marshall warned that its subject matter, the interdependence of the various concepts of surplus was difficult, and had only 'academic attractions' rather than a 'practical bearing' on real problems. Consumer's surplus was simply defined as 'the excess of total utility to him of the commodity over the real value to him of what he paid for it, ... A true net benefit which he, as consumer, derives from the facilities offered to him by his conjuncture' (Marshall 1961, I p. 830). Producer's surplus, in a similar way, was derived from the utility obtained from intra-marginal units of labour (or waiting) which are paid at the same wage (or interest rate) as the final unit which is equated to the relevant rate of remuneration. Marshall conceded that producer's surpluses were difficult to estimate, if only because so much of the wage rate was in fact remuneration for the expense of preparing a person for work, which costs may in fact have been met by either his parents or by the state (Marshall 1961, I pp. 830–1). The problem of estimation was compounded by the fact that these two types of surplus were not independent and could only be aggregated with a high risk of double counting. Estimating producer surplus was easier for material appliances of production, Marshall maintained. In their case, however, this could only be done over the short run, since in the long run such surpluses (like quasi-rents) disappeared. Land, a non-man-made agent of production, secured a permanent surplus (or rent), however, 'from the social point of view'. The analysis of this surplus was of particular value because 'it affords of a great principle that permeates every part of economics', namely that the rent of land is but 'the leading species of a large genus'. This also explains why the two surpluses (consumer's and producer's) were initially described as types of rent (Marshall 1961, I p. 832, and for the dictum pp. 412, 421, 629).

Book III chapter VI defined the notion of consumer's surplus in a manner similar to that given in Appendix K. It could be used to 'estimate roughly some of the benefits which a person derives from his environment' (Marshall 1961, I p. 125), whereas consumers' surplus (the aggregate concept) was useful for estimating the excess burden of an increase in tax on a specific commodity, provided that 'statistical knowledge' was sufficiently advanced (Marshall 1961, I p. 133 n.1). This passage dated from the third edition, as did the earlier warning that aggregation of consumer surplus (total utility) of all commodities would be so complicated, that the 'results' from such calculations, based as they had to be on 'many hypotheses', would be 'practically useless'. Only by assuming that expenditure on the commodity in question was not very important in the household budgets of consumers, that there were no close substitutes for the commodity in question, that the price changes induced by a tax rise, for example, were small, and that the marginal utility of money income was equal for everyone, could reasonable estimates of such excess burdens be made in Marshall's view. Since few of these assumptions were to be met with in actual life, the theorem was somewhat of an 'empty box'. Its practical significance therefore continued to be minimised in the subsequent editions of the *Principles*.

The more famous application of the surpluses was in the context of Marshall's tax/bounty policy on commodities produced under diminishing/increasing return as a means of raising social welfare, provided in Book V, chapter XIII, 'Theory of Changes of Normal Supply and Demand in Relation to the Doctrine of Maximum Satisfaction'. This chapter dealt with shifts in demand and supply schedules, or the effects of new schedules caused by changes in tastes, technology, new raw materials or like changes of such magnitude (Marshall 1961, I p. 462). Marshall's argument had been present from the first edition, even if that edition gave the chapter a slightly different title. Marshall conducted the supply side part of the analysis in terms of commodities produced under either diminishing, constant, or increasing returns. An increase in demand for commodities produced under diminishing returns would raise its price if it generated increased production; for commodities produced under constant returns, more would be produced but at the same price; while under conditions of increasing returns, much more would be produced as a result of the falling prices increased output generated (Marshall 1961, I pp. 463–4). Moreover, improved facilities of supply (lowering the supply schedule) would invariably lower normal price from an increase in demand; least in diminishing returns industries, and extensively, if not cumulatively, in increasing returns industries. The more elastic the demand, the greater the output and price consequences in the increasing returns case and Marshall suggested that such a result could be obtained either by removing a tax from such commodities or granting a bounty on their production (Marshall 1961, I p. 466).

The next step taken by Marshall in this analysis is the one of particular relevance to this paper. What was the impact on consumers' surplus (N.B. Marshall's use of the aggregate concept in this context) from such changes in the conditions of supply, of which a tax change or the introduction of a bounty were taken as representative examples (Marshall 1961, I p. 467).

In the case of commodities produced under conditions of constant returns, imposition of a tax would lower consumers' surplus by more than the gross receipts of the tax. The reasoning was as follows. On the part of consumption continuing after the introduction of the tax, society loses in consumers' surplus what the state receives; but on the part of the consumption which disappears as a result of the tax, consumers' surplus is completely eliminated and the state gains nothing in tax revenue. In the same way for the case of constant returns, the gain in consumers' surplus from the introduction of a bounty is less than the cost of the bounty. This was easily explained. On that part of consumption existing before the bounty, consumers' surplus is increasing by just the amount of the bounty, while for the new consumption induced by the bounty, consumers' surplus is less than the cost of the bounty, a theorem Marshall illustrated geometrically (Marshall 1961, I pp. 467–8 and notes 1).

By similar reasoning, Marshall showed that a tax may raise supply price by something less than the full amount of the tax for commodities produced under conditions of diminishing returns. Hence gross tax receipts in this case *may* be greater than loss of consumers' surplus. The uncertainty of the result arose from the fact that the relevant elasticities determine the precise quantitative consequences of the change. A bounty in the diminishing returns case will increase consumers' surplus by much less than its cost. Likewise, a tax on a commodity produced under conditions of increasing returns decreases consumers' surplus by a great deal more than the revenue from the tax, while a bounty will raise consumers' surplus far in excess of its cost, especially if these increasing returns 'act ... sharply' (Marshall 1961, I pp. 468–90). For Marshall, these results suggested two things. First, they informed some principles of public finance policy, but only when they were fully elaborated; second, and related to the purpose of the chapter as shown by its title, they enabled more precise examination of the doctrine that a position of stable equilibrium of demand and supply was a position of *maximum satisfaction* (Marshall 1961, I p. 470).

Marshall argued against the general proposition that a position of stable equilibrium of normal supply and demand was one of maximum satisfaction in the sense that departures from that position necessitated a loss of aggregate satisfaction for the parties concerned. For a start, the argument ignored differences in wealth (and income) of the parties which generated quantitatively different welfare consequences from departures from equilibrium for the relevant parties. For example, if consumers 'as a class' were much poorer than producers, 'aggregate satisfaction must be increased by extending the production beyond the equilibrium amount and selling it at a loss'. However, Marshall intended to ignore this aspect of the problem, important though it was for demonstrating the potential for welfare gains from forced (or voluntary) redistribution of wealth or income (Marshall 1961, I p. 471).

More importantly, the association between maximum satisfaction and equilibrium need not hold if increases in output (supply) generated the benefits of increasing returns from, say, improvements in industrial organisation. In this case, losses by producers were more than offset by substantial gains in consumers' surplus. A bounty on goods produced under conditions of increasing returns may therefore be highly welfare improving, particularly if consumers devoted part of their gain to compensate producers for their possible losses (Marshall 1961, I p. 472).

This conclusion led Marshall to enunciate his 'simple plan' of levying a tax on diminishing returns industries and devoting the revenue to paying a bounty on increasing returns industries. Such a plan, Marshall warned, needed to take full account of administrative and collection costs of bounty and tax; equitable distribution of the tax burden and gains from the bounty; the potential for undesirable side effects such as 'openings for fraud and corruption' and the diversion of entrepreneurial energy from the management of their business to the lobbying for bounties from the appropriate authorities. Nor should the potential effects on landlord be ignored, particularly if they owned land essential to the production in either the taxed diminishing returns industries or the subsidised increasing returns industries (Marshall 1961, I pp. 472–3).

More generally, Marshall concluded that the specific direction of consumption and production played a role in determining whether a stable position of equilibrium was one of maximum welfare. Opportunities for the rich to direct their consumption expenditures to commodities and services created by the poor were another example of an exception to this proposition; directing consumption to products from diminishing returns industries and away from those of increasing returns industries likewise had the potential for influencing the welfare of others by detrimentally affecting price and supply, and lowering the real purchasing power of incomes, and hence the degree of satisfaction that could be derived from such incomes, ceteris paribus. Moreover, the tax/bounty welfare argument based on the effects on diminishing and increasing returns industries, destroyed the welfare case for uniform, general commodity taxation (as least interfering with consumer sovereignty in spending decisions). Marshall's final paragraph warned that 'by themselves' these considerations did not appear as 'a valid ground for government interference'. They only suggested that with the availability of the requisite information on supply and demand, society was able to redirect advantageously 'the economic actions of individuals into those channels in which they will add the most to the sum total of happiness' (Marshall 1961, I p. 475).

Marshall's tax/bounty welfare argument was taken over by Pigou in a significantly amended form, and it was quite severely attacked by some of his other students. Clapham, Marshall's favourite economic historian, devastatingly heaped scorn on the likelihood that the relevant information would ever become available by describing the actual possibility of classifying industries into increasing and diminishing returns producers as an 'empty economic box' (Clapham 1922). The concept of consumers' surplus, based as it was on additive utility functions, was severely criticised by Knight (1921), by Robbins (1938) and by many others (including Myint 1948, chapter IX, which remains one of the better accounts of Marshall's welfare economics). Marshall himself had been quite aware of the force of many of these objections, but he was apparently unable to jettison this policy completely, presumably because it once again highlighted the crucial importance to him of the presence of increasing returns for generating economic progress. Such increasing returns-based progress was crucial for eliminating, or at least reducing, the levels of poverty so prevalent in his times (and still so in ours). Eliminating poverty had of course been a major motive for steering Marshall into economic studies. Hence Marshall would never have capitulated in the face of criticism that increasing returns, as a dynamic factor, was completely irrelevant to the essentially static nature of stable equilibrium analysis.

2. MARSHALL'S PERSPECTIVES ON THE WELFARE STATE

Marshall mentioned many of the essential features of a welfare state in point 4 of a series of brief observations on the interrelationship between ethics and economics, preserved as an undated fragment among his bundle of jottings on social progress. It can be quoted in full, if only to indicate the rather tentative and hesitant manner with which Marshall raised these types of issue:

Ought the community to interfere to secure (i) steadiness of work; (ii) comfort in old age; (iii) comfort and necessities for children (training, e.g. free meals); (iv) fresh air; (v) good homes for all or good and cheap homes. (Marshall Library, Red Box 1(5), undated)

For Marshall, a case could therefore be mounted for government interference to secure steady employment for everyone; a comfortable existence for the aged; assurance to all children that they would obtain the necessary goods and services for a life in reasonable comfort, including the provision of suitable education and training; and that all were entitled to enjoy fresh, unpolluted air and to secure satisfactory shelter at a reasonable price. It may be noted here that the urban development aspects of this policy had been proposed by Marshall as long ago as 1884 (Marshall 1884, 1925), whereas aspects of provision for the poor under the old poor laws were also raised by him around this time (they are comprehensively discussed in Groenewegen 1995, pp. 353–60).

The poor law issue had been first addressed by the Marshalls (Alfred Marshall and Mary Paley Marshall 1879, pp. 31–5) in their *Economics of Industry*, in which they stressed the growing value of charity work by voluntary organisations in alleviating poverty, and in particular praised the work of Octavia Hill. During 1892, Marshall published two articles on poor law reform in the *Economic Journal* (Marshall 1892a, 1892b) in which he supported the case for a state-funded pension scheme for the aged, largely, but not totally, supporting Charles Booth's pension scheme for those who had passed their 65th birthday (Marshall 1892a, p. 451). Moreover, Marshall raised the need to ensure that those 'who bring up children under conditions incompatible with health and physical and moral life' were to be 'coerced', if at all possible, 'into better habits' of living. In addition, Marshall brought up the question whether private welfare, financed from state tax revenue, would not yield better results in targeting needy cases among the aged than Booth's 'brilliant' aged pension scheme. That scheme, Marshall conceded, had considerable practical difficulties, not least that many aged poor did not know their age, 'and if pensions were granted only to those who could prove themselves to be more than 65 years of age, ... [a] great part of the poverty resulting from old age [would] remain untouched' (Marshall 1892a, p. 453). Marshall prefaced these remarks by introducing the possibility that welfare expenditure (private or public) could be self-financing:

It is doubtful whether we spend fifty millions a year on all forms of public and private charity, including hospitals and asylums. Suppose that, by spending fifty millions more, we could so raise the character of the people that they would on average do one-twelfth more work, we should add a good deal more than it cost to our real national income. This is one 'ethico-economic' fact. (Marshall 1892a, pp. 447–8)

Marshall (1892a) was attacked by several persons, and the next issue of the *Economic Journal* contained his response to these criticisms. As part of this response, Marshall argued that in the previous article, he had only 'advocated' a 'cautious, tentative and slow' expansion of the scope of poor relief, and had indicated that 'able-bodied men would not receive outdoor relief under ordinary circumstances' (Marshall 1892b, p. 457). Marshall then argued against the opponents of 'outdoor relief' (i.e. relief given without forcing the persons receiving it into the poor house) on the ground of *'justice'* to the working class (who after all had contributed to the poor rate); 'the point [in poor law reform] which interests me most' (Marshall 1892b, pp. 459–60), and that, moreover, there was considerable room for 'public relief' (Marshall 1892b, p. 461). A major reason for this was that England had advanced enormously since 1834, the year the Poor Law had been drastically reformed, a reform which still provided the basis for the contemporary poor law legislation. National income was four times greater, but spending on the poor law was less than in that year. The problem of poor relief continued to manifest many practical difficulties, but Marshall insisted that if a new commission was established to inquire into the operations of the poor law, its potential clients among the poor should be consulted, as well as 'experts in the art of raising the poor [to higher standards]' (Marshall 1892b, pp. 458, 464).

When a Royal Commission on the Aged Poor was set up in November 1892, Marshall submitted a preliminary memorandum on which he was questioned (Marshall 1893). Much of this elaborated on some of the issues he had raised in his two articles for the *Economic Journal.* In his preliminary memorandum for the Commission, Marshall indicated that the problem of poverty was changing and that opportunities were therefore increasing for genuinely improving the lives of the poor. For the relief of poverty, he supported both public and private initiatives and argued that the 1834 Poor Law Report was not as relevant as it had been, due to changes in economic and social conditions. Some of its underlying principles were, however, universals, including the proposition that personal or private charity could be more discriminating than public charity. Marshall also denied that outdoor relief would lower wages, a frequently held belief in private charity circles and one vigorously argued in the 1834 Poor Law Report. Marshall strongly praised the role of the private Charity Organisation Society, with which he (to a small extent) and his wife (to a larger) were both involved, and suggested that poor law reform should draw on both public and private initiatives. Marshall's evidence followed on similar lines. After declaring his long interest in poverty issues, he expanded on his views on private and public charity, both in connection with their respective drawbacks and advantages, and their scope for cooperation. An instance of the last was his suggestion, attributed to Sidgwick, that the Charity Organisation

Society could assist in the distribution of public money, particularly since it had far more experience in investigating the merits of individual cases for relief (Marshall 1893, p. 210). Much of the questioning was designed to test Marshall's knowledge of the facts of the situation, but he was also able to push his claim for greater working class involvement in the issue, and his own, admittedly small, attempts at doing so. He also discussed practical tests for eligibility for relief such as thrift (Marshall 1893, pp. 214–18). A great deal of Marshall's evidence was designed to strengthen the importance of the Charity Organisation Society as part of his 'constantly fighting against those tendencies of socialism that are towards increased bureaucracy' (Marshall 1893, p. 261). His evidence shows Marshall to be frequently on the defensive because he knew less about the details than his preliminary memorandum to the commission appeared to suggest.

In contrast with his contributions on (aged) poor relief in the 1890s, however, the undated fragment on economics and ethics quoted at the start of this section, echoed, or foreshadowed, the much more extensive demands of a Charles Booth or a William Beveridge. These indicated that all citizens of a modern state have a moral right to expect that during their lives they will be able to earn their living through regular work, and that both before and after their working lives, they will in addition be assured of reasonable subsistence and essential education and training in pleasant surroundings. Through these demands, Marshall implicitly portrayed a world without poverty, designed to guarantee satisfactory living standards and, more importantly, a good standard of life for everyone from the cradle to the grave. Only the provision of adequate health care as a right for all citizens was omitted from this succinct Marshallian blueprint for almost as thorough a welfare state as Britain instituted in the immediate post–World War II period. It must also be said, however, that much of the detail was left out from Marshall's prognostications. Examples include the age to which children were entitled to obtain free education and training and the age (presumably 65) at which people could retire from work in the expectation of a government provided pension. Moreover, it should be added, Marshall was quite willing to make such general remarks in the privacy of his study (and therefore not for outside critical scrutiny), whereas in public (as clearly shown by the earlier account of his published views in 1892 and 1893), he tended to be much more cautious and aware of the views of those who knew more about the fine points relevant to this intricate subject than he did.

Marshall's *Principles*, in its final chapter 'Progress in Relation to
Standards of Life', nevertheless reiterated such a programme, initially for
the 'residuum' or the poorest, and least 'deserving', of the poor (Marshall
1920, 1961, I p. 714, n.1) but, more generally, a few pages later, as a
state responsibility to ensure the well-being of the whole of 'the poorer
working class' (Marshall 1920, 1961, I pp. 718–19). Marshall explicitly
linked this discussion to his wish to generate 'a wider understanding
of the social possibilities of economic chivalry', succinctly summarised
as a state scheme of redistribution through taxation of the rich. Such a
scheme would turn their resources 'to high account in the service of the
poor, ... [to] remove the worst evils of poverty from the land' (Marshall
1920, 1961, I p. 719). The basic social aim of abolishing extreme poverty required special attention by government to the new generations
of children, giving them 'long continued freedom from mechanical toil;
together with abundant leisure for school and for such kinds of play as
strengthen and develop character' (Marshall 1920, 1961, I, p. 720). In
Marshall's opinion, such a transformation of society would bring about
that 'economic chivalry [dominated] ... [l]ife even under existing institutions of private property' so that the good life and hopefully a high standard of life were obtainable by all without any need to resort to utopian
schemes of socialism (Marshall 1920, 1961, I, pp. 721–2).

Marshall's discussion in the final editions of the *Principles* drew
heavily on the contents of his 1907 *Economic Journal* article, 'Social
Possibilities of Economic Chivalry'. This had dealt with progress in
economics and progress in general, though Marshall was clearly aware
that the latter's record was rather mixed. Too many persons, including
the poor, were still spending their hard-earned incomes 'on things that
do them little good and some ... that do them harm' (Marshall 1907,
1925, p. 324). There also remained a great deal of poverty in England,
even if Charles Booth's statistics to that effect were rather exaggerated
(Marshall 1907, 1925, p. 328) but 'economists generally desire increased
intensity of State activity for social amelioration' (Marshall 1907, 1925,
p. 333), more particularly in city planning. In that domain, Marshall
argued 'the State should be up and doing' (Marshall 1907, 1925,
pp. 336–7) in providing green belts around cities on the plan of Octavia
Hill (Marshall 1907, 1925, p. 345), by bringing 'the beauties of nature and
of art within the reach of ordinary citizens', and on providing assistance
to make everyone 'so well nurtured and so truly educated' that life all
around would be better lived without the need to introduce collectivist
schemes of drastic redistribution of wealth through high taxation or of

creating much state enterprise. The social aims Marshall presented in that paper incorporated and elaborated on the short social welfare programme he had so succinctly summarised in his notes on economics and ethics, from which they were quoted at the start of this section.

Marshall also elaborated on his social welfare aims in some of his correspondence. Writing to Bishop Wescott in early 1900, Marshall indicated that his social programme was one for the long run and in no way could be conceived as a short run remedy. It can be quoted in full:

> to improve the education of home life, and the opportunities for fresh-air joyous play of the young; to keep them longer at school; and to look after them, when their parents are making default, much more paternally than we do. Then the Residuum should be attacked in its strongholds. We ought to expend more money, and with it more force, moral and physical, in cutting off the supply of people unable to do good work, and therefore unable to earn good wages. And as private individuals, I think we can do much more. We can find out people who, because they are old, or broken, or perhaps a little stupid, would be avoided by the money-making employer, even if he could get them a good deal below the 'standard' wage: and we can pay them a good deal more than the market value of their labour; and help them up. After a while they will often find themselves worth good wages and steady employment; and will leave the rest where they have been sheltered, making room for others. This happens in fact. (Marshall to Bishop Wescott, 24 January 1900, in Whitaker 1996, II, pp. 263–4)

A few years later, Marshall succinctly restated his social welfare philosophy in a letter to his former student, Helen Dendy Bosanquet. 'I have always held that poverty & pain, disease & death are evils of much less importance than they appear, except in so far as they lead to weakness of life & character; & that true philanthropy aims at increasing strength more than at diminishing poverty' (Marshall to Helen Dendy Bosanquet, 28 September 1902, in Whitaker 1996, II, p. 399). Self help, encouraged if necessary with initial assistance, was the main thrust of Marshall's views on social welfare and poverty relief; hence the need for the building of character and a desire for independence, most easily implemented if a start was made with the young through providing them with adequate sustenance, shelter, education and a healthy environment. These Marshallian foundations for the welfare state greatly resemble the current philosophy on this subject met with in much of the English speaking world, as is briefly mentioned in Section 3.

There is somewhat of a dichotomy in Marshall's preserved jottings on issues pertaining to what would now be simply called the welfare state. When writing on these in detail for publication, Marshall tended to be cautious and rather restricted on the extent of the relief which could be justified on sound principles. In the privacy of his study, he showed himself to be far more generous and optimistic on welfare policies, as indeed he seemed to be when writing for the general (economic) reader (as in the *Principles*). There he could indulge his strong beliefs into growth and progress, often based on the presence of increasing returns, which were superior instruments for removing the scourge of poverty from the face of the earth. The last possibility was raised more moderately in his evidence to the Commission on the Aged Poor where he argued that the fourfold increase in national income (at least partly explicable in terms of increasing returns) had effectively made much of the 1834 Poor Law Report more or less redundant.

3. 'LET THE STATE BE UP AND DOING': AN OPTIMISTIC MARSHALL ON WELFARE ECONOMICS AND THE WELFARE STATE

What other conclusions can be drawn from this discussion, more particularly, what can be said on the interrelationship between Marshall's views on welfare economics and his position on the welfare state? Marshall's welfare economics and the Marshallian position on the welfare state come together on at least two points. First of all, both in their different ways emphasised the importance of growth. Marshall's tax/bounty policy, impractical though it was, was intended to draw maximum benefits from the output consequences of increasing returns. Likewise, Marshall's 'utopian' vision of a future welfare state, and even his cautious support for 'outdoor relief' to the aged poor over 65, relied on high growth in income and output to bring them about. In that way, the tax/bounty policy had the potential in theory of advancing the welfare state, even if Marshall himself never went so far as to draw such a conclusion. Secondly, if a welfare state was financed by taxation, as any such scheme inevitably had to be, Marshall's welfare economic analysis of taxation policy indirectly shed light on aspects of that policy. If the taxation used to finance a welfare initiative entailed a large excess burden, the concomitant welfare losses could wipe out all the welfare gains derived from the social welfare schemes it financed. However, if that taxation was progressive by levying tax at higher rates according to income levels of the taxpayers, the positive welfare implications of the implied income redistribution would add to the gains from the welfare initiatives its revenue had financed. Although in the *Principles*, Marshall avoided the direct use of his welfare economics tools in this way, there were enough hints in that discussion to make this type of cost/benefit analysis of a tax-financed welfare scheme something that he could have easily contemplated.

By way of a second conclusion from this discussion, Marshall's schemes for a welfare state in so far as they were enunciated, may be briefly compared with its 20th century counterparts as introduced after World War II. The Marshallian programme for adequate social welfare contained in his undated fragment on the subject, and partly elaborated in the 1907 'Social Possibilities of Economic Chivalry' article (its contents repeated in the final chapter of the *Principles*), foreshadowed the introduction of aged and disability pensions, financial support for children and widows, as well as the public housing initiatives that arrived with the onset of the British welfare state in 1945–50. As noted previously, Marshall's outlines of a welfare programme said nothing about the health provision aspects so prominent in the post-1945 welfare state. As far as I know, Marshall was silent on topics such as the free provision of hospital care, visits to medical practitioners at no (or a minimal) cost to the patient, and subsidised, if not free, medicines and pharmaceutical products. These were of course part of the British welfare state with the introduction of the National Health Service. Health is a large omission from Marshall's preserved thought as a social welfare reformer.

Moreover, various parts of Marshall's programme that resemble social policies introduced with the welfare state, do so less when his times are compared with the situation in the late 1940s, let alone the start of the 21st century. Child support, for example, as also previously noted, did not come with an explicit age limit in Marshall's outline; if it had, it was more likely to have been set at the age of 12 than at the age of 16, let alone 21. Similarly, Marshall's advocacy of education and training assistance for the young would not have gone much beyond that provided by an elementary school training and extensions of industrial apprentice schemes. It probably would have excluded higher education altogether, whether at secondary school level or university. Furthermore, Marshall's definition of eligibility at age 65 for the aged pension was far less generous in the 1890s than it is now, given the substantial difference in life expectancy then as compared with that currently prevailing, particularly for those actively engaged in physical labour. A far smaller proportion of the working class would have survived to 65 in Marshall's time, as compared with today, if only because industrial work has become far less physically arduous and schemes of industrial safety are much more extensively enforced. Not that Marshall would have disapproved of such measures. Improvements of this type were part and parcel of his, admittedly, long-term social aims for the future and formed part of his vision of economic and social progress.

One final comment needs to be made in bringing this discussion to a close. How compatible with the cautious and tentative Marshall on social reform issues is the picture of a welfare state legislated within the life of one parliament? Here there is no simple answer. It fits in poorly with the Marshall visible in his appearances before the conservative Charity Organisation Society, some of whose leaders dominated his questioning before the Royal Commission on the Aged Poor, where he was on the defensive and at his least adventurous in spirit. Compatibility is greater, however, if we contemplate the optimistic and enthusiastic Marshall addressing his public on the possibilities of social chivalry and encouraging them to endorse as the slogan for the new century, 'Let the State be up and doing!' The fact that both a cautious and an adventurous and optimistic Marshall exist makes his views on the welfare state, and on welfare economics, all the more interesting.

References

Clapham, J. H. 1922. "Of Empty Economic Boxes." *Economic Journal* 32: 305–14; reprinted in American Economic Association, *Readings in Price Theory*. London: Allen and Unwin, 1953, pp. 119–30.

Groenewegen, Peter. 1995. *A Soaring Eagle: Alfred Marshall 1842–1924*. Cheltenham: Edward Elgar.

Knight, F. H. 1921. *Risk, Uncertainty and Profit*. Boston and New York: Houghton Mifflin Company.

Marshall, Alfred. 1879. *Pure Theory of Domestic Values*. London: The London School of Economics and Political Science, Reprints of Scarce Tracts in Economics and Political Science, No. 1, 1949, pp. 1–37.

1884, 1925. "Where to House the London Poor." In A. C. Pigou, ed., *Memorials of Alfred Marshall*. London: Macmillan, pp. 142–51.

1892a. "The Poor Law in Relation to State-Aided Pensions." *Economic Journal* 2. Reprinted in Peter Groenewegen, ed., Alfred Marshall, *Collected Essays*. Bristol: Overstone Press, 1997, vol. 2, pp. 447–54.

1892b. "Poor-Law Reform." *Economic Journal* 2. Reprinted in Peter Groenewegen, ed., Alfred Marshall, *Collected Essays*. Bristol: Overstone Press, 1997, vol. 2, pp. 455–65.

1893. "Royal Commission on the Aged Poor: Preliminary Memorandum and Minutes of Evidence." In J. M. Keynes, ed., *Official Papers of Alfred Marshall*. London: Macmillan for the Royal Economics Society, 1926, pp. 199–262.

1907. "Social Possibilities of Economic Chivalry." In A. C. Pigou, ed., *Memorials of Alfred Marshall*. London: Macmillan, 1925, pp. 323–46.

1961. *Principles of Economics.* Ninth (variorum) edition, C. W. Guillebaud, ed., London: Macmillan for the Royal Economic Society, 2 volumes.

Marshall, Alfred, and Marshall, Mary Paley. 1879. *The Economics of Industry.* London: Macmillan & Co.

Myint, Hla. 1948. *Theories of Welfare Economics.* London: Longmans, Green & Company for the London School of Economics.

Robbins, L. C. 1938. "Interpersonal Comparisons of Utility: A Comment." *Economic Journal* 48: 635–41.

Whitaker, J. K., ed. 1965. *Early Economic Writings of Alfred Marshall 1867–1890.* London: Macmillan for the Royal Economic Society, 2 volumes.

1996. *The Correspondence of Alfred Marshall: Economist.* Cambridge: Cambridge University Press for the Royal Economic Society, 3 volumes.

2004. "Alfred Marshall and Grand Social Reform." In Tony Aspromourgos and John Lodewijks, eds., *History and Political Economy: Essays in Honour of P.D. Groenewegen.* London: Routledge, pp. 167–78.

THREE

Pigou's "Prima Facie Case"

Market Failure in Theory and Practice

Steven G. Medema

I. INTRODUCTION

The idea that the pursuit of private interests may not redound to the larger social interest has a long history in economic thinking,[1] but it was not until the second half of the 19th century that this line of thought began to coalesce into an analysis of market failure. The first stage of this process culminated in A. C. Pigou's analysis of private and social net products, beginning with his *Wealth and Welfare* and then, more expansively, in *The Economics of Welfare*. *The Economics of Welfare*, in turn, laid the foundation for the second stage: the development of the orthodox theory of market failure in the middle third of the 20th century. Indeed, Pigou's work has been cited by supporters and critics alike as the basis for a neoclassical approach to market failures that dominated economic thinking from the 1940s onward.[2] The resulting advances showed the restrictive nature of the conditions for optimality and, as a result, the pervasiveness of market failure. With this came demonstrations of how governmental policies could be put in place to achieve optimality. The last third of the century witnessed a series of challenges to this received view, catalyzed by the Chicago and Virginia schools. The work of James

---

[1] See Medema (2003, 2009) for surveys.

[2] The first edition of *The Economics of Welfare* was published in 1920.

I would like to thank Roger Backhouse for the many insights that have come out of several years of conversations on this related subject. The comments of Geoff Harcourt, Cristina Marcuzzo, Tamotsu Nishizawa, participants at the "International Conference on the Cambridge School" held in Tokyo in March 2006, participants in sessions at the 2005 meetings of the History of Economics Society and the European Society for the History of Economic Thought have been most useful in the preparation of the final version of this chapter.

Buchanan, Ronald Coase, Milton Friedman, Robert Lucas, George Stigler, and Gordon Tullock both challenged the traditional view and led to a larger reexamination by economists of the relations between state and economy at both the micro and macro levels.

The "micro" side of this challenge was aimed squarely at Pigou and the Pigovian tradition, and it reflected what amounted to a universally held view that the theory of market failure,[3] circa 1960, was built on the foundation laid by Pigou in *The Economics of Welfare*. This take was nicely summed up by Stanislaw Wellisz's (1964, 347) remark that "The Pigovian tradition, accepted by modern welfare economists, claims that whenever private and social costs diverge, steps should be taken to equalize the two."[4] There can be no doubt that *The Economics of Welfare*, with its extensive array of market failures and prescribed government policies for correcting them, inspired much of the literature that followed. But this evolution, and thus the history of the theory of market failure, rested on a particular view of Pigou's contribution in *The Economics of Welfare*, and a good case can be made that this literature represents a significant departure from Pigou's perspective.

Specifically, when read against the background of Pigou's little-known essay "State Action and Laisser-Faire" (1935d), one gets a very different picture of what Pigou intended in *The Economics of Welfare*[5] – one rather at odds with both the subsequent Pigovian tradition and the characterization of Pigou's approach by critics such as Ronald Coase.[6] In the pages that follow, we shall attempt both to juxtapose Pigou's position on the economic role of government as reflected in his 1935 essay with that in *The Economics of Welfare* and to shed a bit of light on how the Pigovian (as distinct from Pigou's) theory of market failure came to diverge so significantly from this. The answer, as it happens, has a great deal to do with Pigou's distinction between theory and practice,

---

[3] When we speak of "market failure" here, we are referring to what is traditionally called "allocation" failure, as reflected in the theories of externalities and public goods in particular. For a discussion of the larger welfare approach of Pigou and the Cambridge tradition, see the several recent works on this subject by Roger Backhouse.

[4] In addition to Wellisz (1965), see also Meade (1952), Bator (1958), Mishan (1971), Coase (1960), Buchanan and Stubblebine (1962), and Baumol (1972).

[5] While one may argue that Pigou's position in 1935 may have been different than that elaborated in a book written in 1920 and revised in 1932, the revisions undertaken in editions published after 1935 do not contradict the basics of the earlier analysis. Moreover, Pigou's *Study in Public Finance* (1928) evidences a similar perspective to that of his 1935 essay.

[6] See Baumol (1972), Coase (1960), and the discussion of Coase and Pigou in Aslanbeigui and Medema (1998).

and the attribution of "practice" to Pigou's "theory" by those who later built upon his work in the process of constructing the neoclassical theory of market failure.

2. MARKET FAILURE IN THEORY

When Pigou succeeded Marshall as Professor of Political Economy at Cambridge in 1908, it was his mission to champion the economics of his mentor. This, however, was a difficult task, as Marshall had analyzed a wide range of problems in both static and dynamic contexts. For new and non-trivial contributions, Pigou turned to areas suggested by Henry Sidgwick, whose work had influenced Pigou's views on both ethics and economics,[7] and to the question of how far it was "desirable that the action of free competition should be restrained or modified" (Sidgwick 1901, 23).

The result was the construction of a system of welfare economics, a subject which, for Pigou, consists in the study of the "many obstacles that prevent a community's resources from being distributed among different uses or occupations in the most effective way" – that is, the study of market failures. The purpose of his welfare analysis, in turn, was "to bring into clearer light some of the ways in which it now is, or eventually may become, feasible for governments to control the play of economic forces in such wise as to promote the economic welfare, and, through that, the total welfare, of their citizens as a whole" (Pigou 1932, 129–30). While Pigou claimed to build his welfare economics on Marshall, and Marshall had certainly opened up a couple of important lines of inquiry on this front,[8] the line of descent actually runs more strongly from Sidgwick to Pigou. Pigou's welfare measure has content far broader than Marshall's consumer surplus, and the breadth and scope of Pigou's analysis corresponds far more to Sidgwick than to Marshall. In fact, the most accurate characterization of Pigou's work here would be to say that he put Sidgwick's ideas into a Marshallian theoretical framework.

Pigou, like Sidgwick (1901) before him, was critical of what he saw as a tendency among classical economists and their followers to ascribe to the free play of self-interest a maximum of economic welfare. He rejected Marshall's consumer surplus as a welfare measure on several

---

[7] See O'Donnell (1979), Aslanbeigui (1995), and Backhouse (2006).
[8] On Marshall and welfare economics, see Medema (2006), Groenewegen (Chapter 2), and Daunton (Chapter 4).

grounds, choosing instead to focus on what he called the "national dividend": "that part of the objective income of the community ... which can be measured in money" (Pigou 1932, 31).[9] The national dividend, then, is the social product or the value of output – the same measure used by many of the classical economists.[10] This was to be Pigou's measuring stick – the criterion upon which he assessed economic outcomes.

Pigou saw the problems of laissez-faire rooted in certain base effects of self-interested behavior, effects that the system of natural liberty could not overcome. Writing in 1913, LSE economist Edwin Cannan (1913, 333) said that "the working of self-interest is generally beneficent, not because of some natural coincidence between the self-interest of each and the good of all, but because human institutions are arranged so as to compel self-interest to work in directions in which it will be beneficent." Pigou seems to have concurred with Cannan's assessment and quoted him approvingly. But Pigou went on to say that in spite of all of the efforts made to create institutions that will channel self-interest toward the larger social interest, there remain "failures and imperfections," even in the most advanced of nations (Pigou 1932, 129). And these, in turn, serve among other things to negatively impact the size of the national dividend.

Pigou's evaluation of the workings of self-interest was grounded in the concept of the dividend, and the task that he set for himself was to examine, in part, "how far the free play of self-interest, acting under the existing legal system, tends to distribute the country's resources in the way most favourable to the production of a large national dividend, and how far it is feasible for State action to improve upon 'natural' tendencies" (Pigou 1932, xii). To get at these issues, Pigou utilized the concept of the margin, which was so central to the Marshallian analytical system, and which enabled Pigou to put his analysis in a marginal benefit–marginal cost framework. The two key analytical constructs here were marginal

---

[9] Pigou also used a broader measure, "economic welfare," which included the dividend, but accounted for distributional effects as well. For example, in Pigou's system, an increase in the national dividend will increase economic welfare, all else equal, *if* the portion of the dividend accruing to the poor is not reduced in the process (1932, 82). This broader notion of economic welfare was soundly thrashed by Robbins and the Paretians, though the Paretian measure, too, for all its theoretical elegance was found untenable.

[10] Malthus (1798) was an exception here. He argued that increases in national output that did not result in an increase in the means of subsistence (particularly the food supply) could not necessarily be considered wealth-enhancing given the importance of the food supply vis-à-vis population pressures.

social net product and marginal private net product. Pigou defined the former as "the total net product of physical things or objective services due to the marginal increment of resources in any given use or place, not matter to whom any part of this product may accrue" (134). The marginal private net product is similar, but consists of the portion that "accrues in the first instance ... to the person responsible for investing resources" in the process or activity in question (134–5). Each of these constructs measures net benefits, with these net benefits accruing to society as a whole in the one case and to the resource owner alone in the other. They are also simply the physical measures; the *value* of these net products is the amount of money that they are worth in the market (135).

As Marshall, W. S. Jevons, and others had shown, self-interested behavior on the part of economic agents brings about the equality of *private* net products. However, the national dividend is maximized when marginal *social* net products are equalized across the various uses of society's resources (Pigou 1932, 136). The implication of these two conditions is that the national dividend will only be maximized when marginal private net products are equal to marginal social net products. This, then, led Pigou to examine the extent to which market forces generate these coincidences and the circumstances that determine whether and to what extent private and social net products diverge. It is when such divergences arise, said Pigou, that a potential role for government corrective action arises, as "certain specific acts of interference with normal economic processes may be expected, not to diminish, but to increase the dividend" (172).

The first class of divergences between private and social net products pointed to by Pigou are those where agents with the potential to invest in socially beneficial capital improvements fail to do so in optimal amounts because there is some positive probability that they will not be able to recoup the necessary share of associated benefits (1932, 174–83). This type of situation can arise in agricultural tenancy relationships, where tenants will have little incentive to invest in improving the land if there is a strong probability that they will not be able to recoup this investment when the tenancy arrangement comes to an end. Likewise, when private firms are given concessions to operate "public utilities," the incentive for them to make capital improvements is reduced in proportion to the probability that the plant may, at the expiration of the concession contract, pass into the hands of government without compensation. Pigou points out that the resultant under-investment problem can be mitigated to some extent via negotiation – that contractual terms can be specified to mandate compensation. In reality, though, Pigou finds these private measures less than adequate to ensure the optimal level of investment and suggests that a more adequate adjustment can come via laws that mandate compensation for capital improvements made, whether between government and concessionaire or between landlord and tenant.

The second class of divergences that Pigou examined was perhaps the most important, in terms of long-run impact on the literature – situations of externality. These divergences arise in situations where,

one person A, in the course of rendering some service, for which payment is made, to a second person B, incidentally also render services or disservices to other persons (not producers of like services), of such a sort that payment cannot be exacted from the benefited parties or compensation enforced on behalf of the injured parties. (Pigou 1932, 183)

This, of course, is the classic situation of externality, and Pigou distinguishes between two general types. The first, now commonly referred to as positive externalities, involve situations where marginal private net product is less than social net product, "because incidental services are performed to third parties from whom it is technically difficult to exact payment" (183–4). Pigou lists a number of examples, including lighthouses, parks, roads and tramways, afforestation, street lighting, pollution abatement, and scientific research. Each of these provides benefits to society beyond those to the agent directly engaged in providing the good or service, thereby generating a social net product in excess of the private one and causing an underproduction of those goods and activities through the market. The second category is negative externalities, where, "owing to the technical difficulty of enforcing compensation for incidental disservices," marginal private net product exceeds marginal social net product (185). Here, Pigou includes the effects of such things as congestion and destruction of amenity from new factories and from new buildings erected in crowded city centers, the damage to roads from automobiles, the production and sale of alcohol, and the health effects on children from factory labor of women. These activities generate costs to society beyond those incurred by the individuals directly involved, and thereby cause the private net products to exceed the social. The market, then, will tend to overproduce these goods and activities.[11]

---

[11] The emerging recognition that there was something between perfect competition and monopoly – namely, monopolistic competition – led Pigou to suggest further sources of market failure tied to this type of market structure. One of these is advertising, which

Pigou allowed that the divergences between private and social products that arise between contracting parties – as in the case of the principal–agent problems that arise in tenancy situations – may be amenable to resolution by negotiation, but he did not believe that this was possible in situations of third-party effects. However, he said, it is possible for *the state* to step in "to remove the divergence in any field by 'extraordinary encouragements' or 'extraordinary restraints,'" the "most obvious" forms of which are "bounties and taxes" (1932, 192). Thus, one could levy taxes on establishments that serve alcohol, tax gasoline, or impose a car license fee the funds from which can be used to improve roads, tax advertisements, and subsidize scientific research.[12] And in certain cases, "when the interrelations of the various private persons affected are highly complex," bounties and taxes may not be sufficient, and regulations – such as zoning ordinances and other forms of local planning – may be in order (194).

Pigou was convinced that the interactions of large numbers of people would often generate spillovers, and that these external effects invalidated the claims made by certain earlier commentators regarding the beneficial workings of the system of natural liberty. The growth of cities provided a signal illustration of the problems posed:

It is as idle to expect a well-planned town to result from the independent activities of isolated speculators as it would be to expect a satisfactory picture to result if each separate square inch were painted by an independent artist. No "invisible hand" can be relied on to produce a good arrangement of the whole from a combination of separate treatments of the parts. (Pigou 1932, 195)

Because of this, Pigou thought it necessary that "an authority of wider reach" should step in and "tackle the collective problems of beauty, of air and of light," just as had been done for public utilities such as gas and water (195).

While the analysis of externalities had the most significant long-run impact on the literature, it was the third situation of divergence between private and social interests identified by Pigou – the presence of increasing or decreasing returns in production – that was the most

would have no value in a highly competitive system. Because, in his view, advertising often serves merely as an attempt to transfer business from one seller to another, it generates a social net product lower than the private one. A second problem arises because imperfect competition allows for the possibility of fraudulent business practices, which would not be possible in a highly competitive system (1932, 196–203).

[12] Marshall had argued likewise, advocating taxes on those who build houses in highly populated areas to finance the construction of playgrounds.

controversial at the time of his writing. This problem was first probed by Marshall in his elaboration of the idea of consumers' surplus. The issue, of course, is that investments in industries characterized by decreasing returns will raise costs, and thus prices, for all, thereby yielding a social net product that is less than the private one. Conversely, investments in industries that exhibit increasing returns will generate lower costs, and thus prices, for all, meaning that the social net product of such investments exceeds the private one. While Marshall offered a tentative, or provisional, analysis of conditions under which taxes on industries subject to decreasing returns and subsidies to those exhibiting increasing returns could increase national welfare, Pigou's discussion exhibited no such hesitance. In *Wealth and Welfare* (1912, 178–9), Pigou advocated taxes on all industries subject to decreasing returns and subsidies to all industries exhibiting increasing returns, doing so on the grounds that only then could we approximate ideal output in the absence of constant returns. Pigou's discussion on this score was called in for criticism by Marshall, both on certain technical points and because certain things that Marshall considered provisional and qualified were set out in far more concrete terms by Pigou.[13]

The cumulative effect of this discussion was a strong sense that market failure is a rather pervasive problem and that governmental measures are necessary to deal with the situation. As Pigou put it,

In any industry, where there is reason to believe that the free play of self-interest will cause an amount of resources to be invested different from the amount that is required in the best interest of the national dividend, there is a *prima facie* case for public intervention. (1932, 331)

As we shall see later on, this became the mantra for much of the analysis of market failure that was to follow in the coming decades. The question for Pigou, though, was how this *prima facie* theoretical case should work itself out in the realm of economic policy. Here, his *Economics of Welfare* is of comparatively little use, and we must look elsewhere – to his relatively unknown 1935 essay on "State Action and Laisser-Faire," published in the slim volume, *Economics in Practice*.

---

[13] See also Pigou (1932, 213–28) and the discussion of Marshall's notes on Pigou's *Wealth and Welfare* in Bharadwaj (1972). Pigou's work in this vein was, of course, part of the running controversy over the treatment of the problems of increasing and decreasing returns. See, for example, Clapham (1922), Knight (1924), Sraffa (1926), and Young (1928). Several of the articles from this literature are reprinted in Stigler and Boulding (1952).

3. MARKET FAILURE IN PRACTICE

The subject of Pigou's 1935 essay, which is the published text of a lecture given in Cambridge, is "the attitude of economists towards state action" (1935d, 107). Pigou comes right out of the gate with a philosophical argument – not protesting *against* laissez-faire, but stating that it is "unreal and misleading" to form a sharp distinction between state action and laissez-faire:

No defender of so-called laisser-faire desires that the State should do absolutely nothing in matters relevant to economic life. The most ardent believer in the economic harmonies, that are supposed to flow from the unimpeded pursuit by individuals of their private interests, argues that these harmonies will not emerge unless robbery at arms is restrained by law, fraud repressed, and contracts which have been formally accepted enforced. (109)

This, of course, is completely consistent with Adam Smith's discussion in *The Wealth of Nations* (1776), and, as Pigou points out, it is also reflected in the sentiments of Cannan – no friend of the Pigovian-Cambridge tradition – that it tends to be man-made institutions, rather than natural forces, that channel self-interest in beneficial directions.[14] Pigou contends that institutions such as family, property and contract law, prohibition of fraud, and the police are all obvious and almost universally unobjectionable components of the societal structure in the West and help to channel the operation of self-interest to the benefit of society (1935d, 110).

Acceptance of this basic idea changes the entire character of one's thinking about market and state. The "real question," says Pigou, "is not whether the State should act or not, but on what principles, in what degree and over what departments of economic life its action should be carried on." Nor does he find the answers to this question at all obvious: "The issue is not one of yes or no," he said, "but of more or less; of delimiting an uncertain frontier; of weighing, in different departments, conflicting advantages, the balance of which sometimes tips to one side, sometimes to the other" (1935d, 110).

This highly pragmatic sentiment might seem to leave rather little room for the sort of theoretical approach set out in *The Economics of Welfare*. And indeed, given the theoretical nature of that book, it may come as a surprise – at least if one neglects his strong links to Marshall – to note that, in another of these lectures on economics in practice, Pigou called economics "a tradesman among the sciences" (1935a, 2). But Pigou was very

---

[14] See the full quotation from Cannan on p. 45.

much a product of the Cambridge tradition, and so believed that while the elegant systems of equations set out by continental scholars such as Walras and Pareto had a certain "aesthetic appeal," the complexity of the actual economic environment "does not lend itself to triumphs of pure reasoning" (1935a, 3–4). The emphasis, he said, should be on the discovery of "practically useful results," for it is here that economics finds its reason for being – "its promise of fruit rather than ... its promise of light" (1935a, 4–5).

This does not mean, however, that Pigou was willing to write off theorizing or suggest that economists should study only practical problems, as we can see from his strong defense of economic theorizing in the "empty boxes" debate.[15] Pigou cites Clerk Maxwell's work as an important instance of high theory leading to significant practical application – here, in the area of wireless telegraphy. When it comes to finding a proper balance between high theory and more practical analysis, Pigou suggested that economics can learn from the natural sciences, where results sometimes flow from highly practical experiments, but where, in other instances, "Remoter, more fundamental, so to speak more theoretical, investigations sometimes in the end yield the largest harvests" (1935a, 6).

Pigou was well aware, though, that the policy realm introduces a number of complications, the most fundamental of which is that one cannot determine which particular course of action is desirable, without adopting some normative criterion for judging between them (1935b, 132). Many policies are widespread in their effects. "On which human beings," he asks, are the effects to be measured? Do we look at the effects on domestic society? On some subset of society? If the latter, which subset? On the whole world? The answers to questions of this nature, Pigou contends, take us outside the boundaries of economics; they are instead "for the student of Ethics, not for economists" (1935b, 133).

Here, Pigou's perspective, while thoroughly Marshallian in orientation, also supports the controversial position taken by Lionel Robbins in his *Essay on the Nature and Significance of Economic Science* (1932). Robbins contended forcefully that value judgments have no place in economic science, belonging instead to the realm that he labeled "political economy."[16] This line of thinking is much in evidence in Pigou's contention that:

in economics proper the word *ought* has no place. Its business is to study what *tends* to happen, to trace the connection between causes and effects, to analyse the

---

[15] See, e.g., Clapham (1922) and Pigou (1922).
[16] On the relation of Robbins's *Essay* to welfare analysis, see Backhouse (2009) and Backhouse and Nishizawa (Chapter 11).

interplay of conflicting forces. It is a positive science, not a normative science. It is concerned, like physiology, to discover what effects various drugs will produce, not, like medicine, to prescribe what drugs ought to be taken. (1935d, 107)[17]

In both its tendency statement orientation and conscious distancing of economics from normative prescription, Pigou's statement here leaves him at odds with the market failure *cum* government corrective action approach that was to develop from his analysis in *The Economics of Welfare.*

Confining the analysis to the positive side does not render it problem-free, however. In particular Pigou acknowledged that it is very difficult to gauge the effects of many proposals beyond what he called "vague judgments." The problem, he said, is that while economics is very successful at qualitative analysis, it has severe limitations on the quantitative side. The result is that prediction amounts, at best, to "instructed guess-work," although he held out hope that the progress of economics might lead to some advances on this front (1935d, 109).

How does all of this apply to Pigou's discussion of market failure? In attempting to discern the appropriate scope of State action, Pigou argued that the market system leads to two forms of "evils and wastes" (1935d, 113).[18] The first of these arises from the incompetence of individual agents in pursuing their chosen ends. Problems of this nature usually arise from the failure of private agents to properly forecast the market for their products and led, in Pigou's time, to calls for central planning. However, said Pigou, the case for State action (central planning) here comes down to one's willingness to assume that the State can do a better job of forecasting demands than can private enterprise – a proposition that Pigou found rather dubious:

It is easy for a public servant, looking back when he knows the course that demand has taken, to point out the mistakes of those who tried to forecast it. But it is a very different thing for that public servant to make a forecast. The fundamental assumption, on which the whole case for this sort of planning rests, is that public servants will prove specially skilled at this. (114–15)

That Pigou found this assumption "at least a doubtful one" (115) is not surprising in light of his views on the problems with the bureaucratic process, which we will discuss momentarily.

---

[17] As Backhouse (Chapter 6) points out, Hobson held to a rather different view of economic science, which led him to very different welfare conclusions.

[18] A more extensive discussion of Pigou's conception of waste can be found in his essay "Economy and Waste" (1935c).

This issue takes on a somewhat different cast, however, when Pigou turned his attention to the other form of "evils and wastes," where the pursuit of private interests runs counter to the *social* interest. This, said Pigou, justifies state action "in principle" unless one believes that private and social interests are always perfectly compatible. Pigou, of course, rejected the idea of universal compatibility, pointing out that, contrary to what "invisible hand" explanations might imply, institutions are not always structured in such a way as to channel private interests to the best interests of society as a whole (1935d, 115). The theoretical demonstration of this had been one of the major contributions of his *Economics of Welfare*. Nor was this a uniquely Cambridge insight, as Pigou was quick to point out: "the doctrine of the invisible hand evolving social benefit out of private selfishness has never been held by economists – certainly it was not held by Adam Smith – in that absolute and rigid form in which the popular writers conceive it." Rather, he says, "All are agreed that many times the hand falters in its aim" (115).

Pigou broke down the resulting disharmonies into three general categories. The first was disharmonies in production, under which he included instances where firms are able to garner for themselves substantial monopoly power, situations of negative or positive externality, and excessive discounting of the future, the last of which gives rise to problems such as underinvestment and premature depletion of natural resources. The second type of disharmony that he identified is in the distribution of income, where substantial inequalities give rise to social losses.[19] Finally, there is a third manifestation of disharmony in the various problems associated with industrial fluctuations, including in levels of production, consumer demands, and the expansion and contraction of credit (1935d, 116–24). What we have here are, in modern language, allocation failure, distribution failure, and stability failure, respectively – "failures" in the sense that, in each instance, the market fails to generate the best possible result for society.[20] When such market failures arise – that is, when "private self-interest, acting freely, subject only to the ordinary forms of

---

[19] Here, Pigou explicitly invokes the assumption of diminishing marginal utility of income and does so in an almost sarcastic way, noting that, "The ninth course of the plutocrat's dinner, despite the indirect benefit that it may confer on his doctor, yields much less satisfaction on the whole than the milk which the cost of it might have secured for a poor man's child" (121). Pigou also finds this distributional disharmony in the wage bargain, absent employee unions.

[20] Our focus, of course, is allocation failure, although certain aspects of the discussion generalize.

law, does not lead to the best results from a general social point of view" –
there is, says Pigou, "a *prima facie* case for State action" (124).[21]

To this point, the story sounds remarkably like that in *The Economics
of Welfare* and should be familiar to those acquainted with the post-war
neoclassical theory of market failure. But where does the *prima facie*
case actually take Pigou? Specifically, what does this actually imply for
policy? Pigou speaks briefly to this topic in both *Wealth and Welfare*
and *The Economics of Welfare*, noting that "The case ... cannot be
more than a *prima facie* one, until we have considered the qualifications,
which governmental agencies may be expected to possess for intervening advantageously." Here, he gets specifically to the theory-practice distinction, although not characterizing it as such, when he says that "It is
not sufficient to contrast the imperfect adjustments of unfettered private
enterprise with the best adjustment that economists in their studies can
imagine. For we cannot expect that any public authority will attain, or
will even wholeheartedly seek, that ideal" because of information problems faced by, and the pressures brought to bear on, governmental agents
(1912, 247–8; 1932, 331–2). One can hear in this echoes of his predecessors' qualms regarding the ability of government to get things right.

In "State Action and Laisser-Faire," Pigou provides a more elabo-
rate answer, albeit again not the answer one might expect based on the
direction taken by modern Pigovian economics and ascribed to it, and to
Pigou himself, by the critics. The *prima facie* case, Pigou says, "only takes
us a little way"; in deciding on the practical desirability of state action,
"it is not enough to know that a form and degree of it can be conceived,
which, if carried through effectively, would benefit the community." He
had already shown in his *Economics of Welfare* that it was possible to
design such a scheme in theory. When it comes to moving from theory to
practical application, however, things get more complicated:

> We have further to inquire how far, in the particular country in which we are
> interested and the particular time that concerns us, the government is qualified
> to select the right form and degree of State action and to carry it through effec-
> tively. (1935d, 124)

Ascertaining the qualifications of government, in turn, has several
components.

First, the attitude of the citizens toward government action is of great
import, as any actions are more likely to be effectively implemented and

---

[21] Recall that Pigou makes the same argument in his *Economics of Welfare* (1932, 331).
See also p. 49, infra.

carried out if they have substantial public support. Second, there is the issue of the "quality" of the decision-making body that will be determining the form and extent of state action. Pigou says that the quality of the decision-making body will be a function of the intellectual competence of the persons who constitute it, the efficacy of the organization through which their decisions are executed, their personal integrity in the face of bribery and blackmail, their freedom from domination by a privileged class, and their ability to resist the pressure of powerful interests or of uninstructed opinion (1935d, 125).

The basic problem, according to Pigou, is that "Every public official is a potential opportunity for some form of self-interest arrayed against the common interest" (1912, 248), a sentiment strikingly like what one finds in Smith.[22] The financial stakes that accompany many policy proposals are incredibly high and make "Logrolling and lobbying" "powerful forces" that "are certain to be called into play" (1935d, 126). Because of this, politicians are "subject to great pressure from persons who can control votes," a problem that is made all the more difficult by the fact that the lobbying groups are also the sources of politicians' campaign funds (1912, 248). Moreover, the growth of government enterprises generates substantial new bureaucracies and "the employment of tens of thousands of additional public servants," which, in turn, means increased patronage for party leaders (1912, 248). All of this makes the quality of the individuals who make up the governing body of the utmost import for sound policy. Unfortunately, said Pigou, the unseemly aspects of interest-group pressure tend to deter upright people from entering politics, which only serves to further loose the forces of corruption. The results of the political process thus will likely be skewed, in that the efforts of the state are "most likely to be invoked successfully by the strong," regardless of what is actually in society's best interests (1935d, 126). For Pigou, it is these practical concerns of a political nature, rather than "any abstract plea for laisser-faire in matters of trade," that speak most loudly against government interference.

Pigou followed Marshall in believing that, although government in Adam Smith's day was corrupt, inefficient, and capable of achieving little, the 150 years since Smith had seen the rise of "governing authorities ... enormously better equipped for successful action" (1935d, 126). Referencing Marshall's (1907) "Economic Chivalry" essay, Pigou attributed this at least in part to increased levels of education and the "surplus

---

[22] This skepticism about the capabilities of the state is also found in the works by Sidgwick and Marshall. See Backhouse and Medema (2009) for a discussion.

energy" that was made possible by increases in the technology of production, and he praises both the Civil Service for its "high capacity and unquestioned public spirit" and the politicians for their absence of personal corruption (1935d, 126).[23]

Yet, while the quality of the individuals serving on the political front was improving, Pigou was not so naïve as to suggest that governing bodies had reached anything like perfection. In particular, he pointed to four shortcomings that he felt characterized representative assemblies. First, elected officials are chosen for a host of reasons unrelated to economic regulation, and there is thus little reason to expect that they have any particular competence for intervening in industry. Second, the makeup of these assemblies tends to fluctuate a great deal over time, depriving society of the benefits of experience and, with that, what may be more desirable levels of policy continuity. Third, municipal size and appropriate economic size may be vastly different, and thus attempting to set up a public enterprise on the same scale as the municipality may lead to major inefficiencies. Finally, these assemblies are political in nature and thus subject to "injurious forms of electoral pressure" of the types we have mentioned above (1912, 249–50).

While the legislative option was problematic, Pigou argued repeatedly that recent advances in governance structures offer a way around these problems.[24] Specifically, he believed that quasi-governmental entities – he mentions Public Service Boards and Commissions – that are not directly subject to political control offer a means of avoiding some of these problems that was not present in times past. While members of general governmental bodies are elected for a host of reasons often unrelated to the regulation of industry, the specialized boards and commissions offer the opportunity to appoint members whose abilities are well-suited to the regulation of industry. The continuity problem and the influence of electoral whims can be resolved by appointing these individuals for longer terms of service than are standard for elected officials. This would have the further beneficial effect of insulating them from electoral pressures (1932, 333–5; 1935d, 127). Pigou thought that this would increase the likelihood of government interference proving beneficial in any given situation, as compared with former times (1912, 249).

The overarching point, for Pigou, was not that state action is the appropriate response to market failure, but rather that there is no definitive

[23] See also Pigou (1912, 249).
[24] See Pigou (1912, 250; 1932, 333–5; 1935d, 127).

answer that one can give, *a priori*, about the magnitude of the problems associated with state intervention. At times their effects will be "trifling," while at other times they will be "dominant" (1935d, 127). Thus, he said, whether one comes at this from a predisposition toward laissez-faire or toward state action, one is led to a single conclusion:

Inquiring how far the free play of private self-interest makes for social advantage, we find that it frequently fails to do this, but that there are many different forms and many different degrees in its failure. Inquiring how far Government is fitted to take action against these failures, we find that its fitness to do this varies, not only in different places and different times, but also as between interventions directed against different kinds of failure. (127)

The larger lesson that Pigou drew from this is that generalizations are of little or no help in dealing with the difficult issues of economic policy. In particular, he said, "The issue about which popular writers argue – the principle of laisser-faire *versus* the principle of State action – is not an issue at all. There is no principle involved on either side." Instead of appeal to so-called principle, Pigou argued, "Each particular case must be considered on its merits in all the detail of its concrete circumstance" (127–8).

It is interesting to compare Pigou's position here with that of Sidgwick, who, like Pigou (although without the graphical tools), worked out the analytics of market failure and governmental response in a quasi-marginalist framework. Sidgwick concluded that,

the general presumption derived from abstract economic reasoning is not in favour of leaving industry altogether to private enterprise ...; but is on the contrary in favour of supplementing and controlling such enterprise in various ways by the collective action of the community. (1901, 417)

But, he said, abstract deductive analysis cannot provide detailed practical information for policy making: the particular conditions of time and place render sweeping generalizations inappropriate. Sidgwick concludes that, in moving "from abstract principles to their concrete applications ... it seems best to adopt a more empirical treatment" (1901, 418), one that recognizes the potential drawbacks that may be associated with government interference and weighs these against the "evils" that this intervention is designed to remedy. In juxtaposing Pigou's position with these sentiments of Sidgwick, as well as the position of Marshall, we get a clear sense that Pigou's practical approach falls squarely within the larger Cambridge tradition.[25]

[25] This point is also touched on by Daunton (Chapter 4). Sidgwick's position here is reflective of his utilitarian perspective, which Hobson took in a somewhat different direction from that in which Pigou took it. See Backhouse (Chapter 6).

4. CONCLUSION: MARSHALLIAN, BUT NOT NEOCLASSICAL

From whence, then, comes the nearly universal tendency to lump Pigou in with the neoclassical theory of market failure and the economists who promulgated it?[26] One need only scan the pages of *The Economics of Welfare* to see the link. Here, Pigou takes Marshallian economics to the next level, applying the framework to a host of economic problems and deriving the implications that flow logically out of this. The book is an "economics" of welfare that pushed the analytics of his day to the limit. Issues of practice are given almost no place at all in the book – a few pages in a work of many hundreds. It reflects a methodological approach that Sidgwick (1901) labeled the "science" of economics, not his "art" of it. If *The Economics of Welfare* is taken to define Pigou's position *in toto*, then the received view – which we see reflected in, for example, Coase's (1960) challenge – is correct.

The contrast between *The Economics of Welfare* and "State Action and Laisser-Faire," though, could not be more stark. The former shows the *prima facie* case for intervention and from whence it arises; the latter shows how one navigates the waters from the *prima facie* case to reality. "State Action and Laisser-Faire" is the practical application of the insights gained from the theorizing in *Economics of Welfare* and, one could argue, takes us places where economic theory cannot. The essay deals with issues of practice, to the complete exclusion of theory – to the extent, even, of taking a jab at those who wrap themselves in theory with no attention to practical matters. In this sense, the essay is almost the antithesis of *Economics of Welfare*. Writing in "State Action and Laisser-Faire," Pigou argued that

High-sounding generalisations on these matters are irrelevant fireworks. They may have a place in political perorations, but they have none in real life. Accumulation of evidence, the balancing of probabilities, judgment of men, by these alone practical problems in this region can be successfully attacked. (1935d, 128)

In framing the analysis this way, Pigou is working with Sidgwick's *art*, not his science. The essay shows the import of the theory–practice distinction for Pigou himself, and this, in turn, calls into question the accuracy of the "Pigovian" label that was placed on the neoclassical theory of market failures in the middle-third of the 20th century.

---

[26] As evidenced in the ubiquitous references to Pigovian externality theory in the literature, to say nothing of the conflation of Pigou and Pigovian within the Chicago tradition, most notably in Ronald Coase's "The Problem of Social Cost" (1960). On Coase's critique of Pigou, see Aslanbeigui and Medema (1998).

It seems apparent that *The Economics of Welfare* was made to do something that it was neither intended to do nor capable of doing. That it became the foundation for the purely theoretical, nonpractical, neo-classical theory of market failures, then, calls for some attempt at explanation. To say that no one read "State Action and Laisser-Faire," and that everyone simply overlooked or glossed over the practical bits in *The Economics of Welfare*, while perhaps accurate, does not suffice.[27] Larger professional trends certainly have a role to play in the story. The analysis of market failure in *The Economics of Welfare* meshed very nicely with the tools and approach that figured so prominently in the neoclassical ascendancy of the 1940s, 1950s, and 1960s. While Pigou's notion of the national dividend was pushed aside early on in the development of neoclassical welfare economics,[28] his treatment of market failure – via the distinction between private and social net products, in particular – lent itself to the formalization that was at the heart of the neoclassical push to firm up a "scientific" theory describing the role for the state in economic activity. Meanwhile, the quest for determinate, optimal solutions to questions of economic theory and policy in post-war neoclassical theorizing left little room for the practical matters that Pigou dealt with in his essay.

While the theory was to move in an increasingly technical and homogenized direction over the next several decades, Pigou argued that the positive scientific process is facilitated by pluralism, noting that "Divergent methods," such as the historical and mathematical approaches, "are partners not rivals" in building economic understanding (1935a, 22).[29] It is ironic, then, that the very methodological narrowing that Pigou opposes here seems to have factored so prominently into the subsequent interpretation and use of his work.

References

Aslanbeigui, Nahid. 1990. On the Demise of Pigovian Economics. *Southern Economic Journal* 56 (January): 616–27.
   1995. Pigou on Social Cost: Sophistry or Sophistication? Working Paper, Monmouth University.

[27] "State Action and Laisser-Faire" and the book in which it appeared, *Economics in Practice*, are all but unmentioned in the economics literature during the formative era of neoclassical economics, and not at all in any significant work of the period.

[28] See Aslanbeigui (1990) for a discussion of this point.

[29] Again, this is the same position that we see Pigou (1922) taking in the empty boxes debate.

Aslanbeigui, Nahid and Steven G. Mewdema. 1998. Beyond the Dark Clouds: Pigou and Coase on Social Cost. *History of Political Economy* 30 (Winter): 601–25.

Backhouse, Roger E. 2006. Sidgwick, Marshall, and the Cambridge School of Economics. *History of Political Economy* 38 (Spring): 15–44.

   2009. Robbins and Welfare Economics: A Reappraisal. *Journal of the History of Economic Thought* 31 (December): 485–99.

Backhouse, Roger E. and Steven G. Medema. 2009. Market Failure, Government Failure, and the Cambridge School: A New View. Working Paper, University of Birmingham and University of Colorado Denver.

Bator, Francis M. 1958. The Anatomy of Market Failure. *The Quarterly Journal of Economics* 72 (August): 351–79.

Baumol, William J. 1972. On Taxation and the Control of Externalities. *American Economic Review* 62 (June): 307–22.

Bharadwaj, Krishna. 1972. Marshall on Pigou's *Wealth and Welfare. Economica* New Series 39 (February): 32–46.

Buchanan, James M. and W. C. Stubblebine. 1962. Externality. *Economica* 29 (November): 371–84.

Cannan, E. 1913. Review of N. G. Pierson. *Principles of Economics. Economic Review* 23: 331–3.

Clapham, J. H. 1922. Of Empty Economic Boxes. *Economic Journal* 32 (September): 305–14.

Coase, Ronald H. 1960. The Problem of Social Cost. *Journal of Law and Economics* 3 (October): 1–44.

Knight, Frank H. 1924. Some Fallacies in the Interpretation of Social Cost. *Quarterly Journal of Economics* 38: 582–606.

Malthus, T. R. 1798. *An Essay on the Principle of Population*. London: J. Johnson.

Marshall, Alfred. 1907. The Social Possibilities of Economic Chivalry. *Economic Journal* 17 (March): 7–29.

Meade, James. 1952. External Economies and Diseconomies in a Competitive Situation. *Economic Journal* 62 (March): 54–67.

Medema, Steven G. 2003. The Economic Role of Government in the History of Economic Thought. In Jeff Biddle, John B. Davis, and Warren J. Samuels, eds., *The Blackwell Companion to the History of Economic Thought*. Oxford: Blackwell, pp. 428–44.

   2006. Marshallian Welfare Economics and the Welfare Economics of Marshall. In T. Raffaelli, G. Becattini, and M. Dardi, eds., *The Elgar Companion to Alfred Marshall*. Cheltenham: Edward Elgar, pp. 634–47.

   2009. *The Hesitant Hand: Taming Self-Interest in the History of Economic Ideas*. Princeton, NJ: Princeton University Press.

Mishan, E. J. 1971. The Postwar Literature on Externalities: An Interpretive Essay. *Journal of Economic Literature* 9 (March): 1–28.

O'Donnell, Margaret G. 1979. Pigou: An Extension of Sidgwickian Thought. *History of Political Economy* 11: 588–605.

Pigou, A. C. 1912. *Wealth and Welfare*. London: Macmillan.

1922. Empty Economic Boxes: A Reply. *Economic Journal* 32 (December): 458–65.

1928. *A Study in Public Finance*. London: Macmillan.

1932. *The Economics of Welfare*, 4th ed. London: Macmillan.

1935a. An Economist's *Apologia*. In *Economics in Practice: Six Lectures on Current Issues*. London: Macmillan, pp. 1–25.

1935b. The Economics of Restrictions. In *Economics in Practice: Six Lectures on Current Issues*. London: Macmillan, pp. 129–54.

1935c. Economy and Waste. In *Economics in Practice: Six Lectures on Current Issues*. London: Macmillan, pp. 26–51.

1935d. State Action and Laisser-Faire. In *Economics in Practice: Six Lectures on Current Issues*. London: Macmillan, pp. 107–28.

Robbins, Lionel. 1932. *An Essay on the Nature and Significance of Economic Science*. London: Macmillan.

Sidgwick, Henry. 1901. *The Principles of Political Economy*, 3rd ed. London: Macmillan.

Smith, Adam. 1776. *An Inquiry into the Nature and Causes of the Wealth of Nations*. Oxford: Oxford University Press, 1976.

Sraffa, P. 1926. The Laws of Returns under Competitive Conditions. *Economic Journal* 36 (December): 535–50.

Stigler, George J. and Kenneth E. Boulding. 1952. *Readings in Price Theory*. Homewood, IL: Richard D. Irwin for the American Economic Association.

Wellisz, Stanislaw. 1964. On External Diseconomies and the Government-Assisted Invisible Hand. *Economica* 31 (November): 345–62.

Young, A. A. 1928. Increasing Returns and Economic Progress. *Economic Journal* 38 (December): 527–42.

FOUR

Welfare, Taxation and Social Justice

Reflections on Cambridge Economists from Marshall to Keynes

Martin Daunton

I. INTRODUCTION

The emergence of economics as a separate subject (or Tripos, in Cambridge terminology) created intense debate over its relationship with the existing organization of teaching through the 'Moral Sciences' Tripos. John Neville Keynes, the father of John Maynard Keynes, faced considerable mental and emotional anxiety in his attempt to reconcile economic science with ethics and religion. As a young man, he spent much effort attempting to create a philosophy which would unite his nonconformist religion and ethics with political economy. It was very important to him and his friends that economics should involve issues of righteousness and morality. In 1891, his *Scope and Method of Political Economy* attempted to locate economics in relation to ethics, history and other disciplines – an ambition which ultimately left him disillusioned. By this point, the profession of economics might be said to have divided into two streams, represented by the creation of two journals: the *Economic Review* and the *Economic Journal*. Whereas the *Review* saw economics as an ethical science, the *Journal* saw it much more as a positive science – a division that lay behind the debate over the place of economics within Cambridge as part of 'Moral Sciences' or with a separate Tripos. But the divide should not be exaggerated: many of those who supported the separation of economics into a specialist, positive science continued to give economics an ethical dimension – above all John Maynard Keynes. To him, economics continued to be part of the debate over ethics and the conditions for leading a good life (Palfrey 2003; Tribe 2005; Skidelsky 1983, chapter 2).

This chapter focuses on the thinking of Cambridge economists on one element of welfare – taxation, a topic that raises some fundamental issues of an ethical nature. How far should redistribution of income be allowed to proceed on grounds of equity and happiness without destroying economic efficiency and the conditions for the survival of an educated elite? In addressing these issues, I will start with Alfred Marshall and proceed to Arthur Cecil Pigou and John Maynard Keynes.

2. GLADSTONE AND MILL: THE MID-VICTORIAN ORTHODOXY

What were the assumptions on taxation in the third quarter of the nineteenth century, against which the Cambridge economists should be read? The dominant approach to taxation and equity was laid down by Adam Smith, above all in his first maxim:

The subjects of every state ought to contribute towards the support of the government, as nearly as possible, in proportion to their respective abilities; that is, in proportion to the revenue which they respectively enjoy under the protection of the state. The expence of government to the individuals of a great nation, is like the expence of management to the joint tenants of a great estate, who are all obliged to contribute in proportion to their respective interests in the estate. (Smith 1976, Vol. 2, p. 825)

The notion of 'proportionality' was at the heart of mid-Victorian notions of taxation, with the belief that each individual should pay the same proportion of their income to the state for protection and security. The most straightforward way of reading Smith's maxim was to say that a tenant with a quarter interest in an estate would pay a quarter of the costs of management, and someone with a half share would pay half of the costs. By extension, an individual with an income of £200 would pay twice as much to the state as someone with an income of £100. This may be called the benefit or *quid pro quo* approach to taxation, defining the payment of taxes as a contract to cover the benefits received from the state.[1] Indeed, it might even be argued that the poor should pay *more* on the grounds that they were in greater need of protection. This line was adopted by Charles Babbage, the mathematician: he argued that a vendor of apples on the street corner needed the state to protect him from every thieving schoolboy; by contrast, a great merchant firm could shift its capital around the world to minimize risk. Although John Stuart Mill accepted the force of the argument that those who would suffer most from the

---

[1] The benefit approach is outlined in O'Brien 1985, p. 241 and Seligman 1908, chapter 2.

withdrawal of government protection would be those weakest in mind or body, he felt it was overruled by other considerations. As he pointed out, the government was the concern of all and it was wrong to ask in great detail who took more or less: the state was more like joining a club where everyone paid according to his means for the common object.[2]

One important implication of the benefit approach was that the tax system should *not* redistribute income between rich and poor, or even between idle and productive members of society. Such a view was held very firmly by William Gladstone, and it was established as orthodoxy in his budget of 1853 that laid down the main lines of fiscal politics for the next generation. Gladstone believed that both graduated taxes (an increase in the proportion as incomes rose) and differentiated taxes (a higher level of taxation of passive or inactive incomes) were dangerous to social and political stability. Further, graduation and differentiation would discourage saving and investment by reducing the amount of money in the hands of the rich who provided most of the funds for industry. As he pointed out in 1863, graduation was

Generally destructive in its operation to the whole principle of property, to the principle of accumulation, and through that principle, to industry itself, and therefore to the interests of both poor and rich ... it means merely universal war, a universal scramble among all classes, every one endeavouring to relieve himself at the expense of his neighbour, and an end being put to all social peace, and to any common principle on which the burdens of the State can be adjusted. (See note 3)

What applied to graduation was equally applicable to differentiation: an attempt to adjust the tax rate to the type of income might set industry versus land in the same way as graduation would set rich against poor. At most, Gladstone allowed very modest departures from the strict rule of proportion: a tax break for life insurance premiums which would provide security to active risk-takers, and a reduction in the level of income tax on those just above the tax threshold to cover their subsistence needs.[3]

Smith's maxim could also be held to support another approach – ability to pay – by shifting the emphasis to his statement that taxation should be in proportion to 'respective abilities'. In the mid-nineteenth century,

[2] Babbage 1952, p. 49. On Mill, see his evidence in Parliamentary Papers (PP): PP 1852 IX and PP 1861 VII, *Report from the Select Committee on Income and Property Tax*, and Mill 1909, p. 805.

[3] *Parliamentary Debates*, 3rd ser 170, 16 April 1863, cols 224 l-m and 23 April 1863, col. 617–22; Matthew 1979; Zimmeck 1985.

the debate was mainly over the abilities of passive versus active capital. Economists such as John Stuart Mill accepted that income from accumulated capital (land, government bonds) had a higher ability to pay, for it gave a flow of income regardless of health or talent, and left assets at death to support heirs and dependants. Income from trade and professions was liable to risks of illness, old age or economic depression, and left nothing for heirs and dependents. Thus the recipients of 'earned income' needed to save, and had a lower ability to pay. Mill accepted the force of this argument and defined Smith's first maxim as implying 'equality of sacrifice'. This meant a lower rate of tax on incomes from earnings, for the same rate on earned and unearned income 'is to lay a tax on industry and economy, to impose a penalty on people for having worked harder and saved more than their neighbours'. Ideally, Mill believed that taxes should fall on *expenditure*. By this he did not mean an indirect tax on goods but rather that personal savings or retentions in the business should be exempted from tax, so that 'the portion of an income which was saved and converted into capital should be untaxed'. In other words, he felt that tax should ideally fall on the spendable element of income – an approach he admitted to be impracticable. In Mill's view, taxation 'should be made to bear as nearly as possible with the same pressure upon all'. How should this be done? Although he accepted differentiation, he remained uneasy about graduation of taxes on income. He could only admit, like Gladstone, that the 'necessaries of life' should be excluded from taxable income:

The rule of equality and of fair proportion seems to me to be that people should be taxed in an equal ratio on their superfluities; necessaries being untaxed, and surplus paying in all cases an equal percentage. This satisfies entirely the small amount of justice that there is in the theory of a graduated income tax, which appears to me to be otherwise an entirely unjust mode of taxation, and in fact, a graduated robbery. (PP 1861 VII, *Report from the Select Committee on Income and Property Tax*, Q 3540)

Where Mill made an exception was taxation of property at death, for inherited wealth would give some people an advantage in life and might lead to the use of capital by risk-averse *rentiers*.[4]

Although Mill moved some way from the 'benefit' approach towards 'ability', he was still not willing to accept a large measure of redistribution.

---

[4] PP 1852 IX, *Second Report from the Select Committee on the Income and Property Tax*, Qq 5222–69, 5277–5447; PP 1861 VII, *Report from the Select Committee on Income and Property Tax*, Qq 747–50, 1119, 3539–44, 3567, 3578–97, 3708–12, 3757, 3770, 3789; Mill 1909, pp. 219, 228, 804–9.

He was taking a restricted view of the welfare implications of taxation, aiming to create a level playing field between passive and active wealth so that enterprise could flourish. He was not suggesting that the distribution of resources should be changed. Here was the starting point in economic theory and state practice which provides the context for the writings of the Cambridge economists.

3. HENRY SIDGWICK AND ALFRED MARSHALL: CONTINUITY OR RUPTURE?

The analysis of the Cambridge approach must start with Henry Sidgwick, a colleague of John Neville Keynes who was similarly concerned to unite political economy and ethics. As Robert Skidelsky argues, Sidgwick attempted to create a secular philosophy in place of theology, keeping economics as part of ethics. He was a follower of Jeremy Bentham, arguing that the crucial problem was the relationship between rational egoism (pursuit of individual happiness) and rational benevolence (pursuit of universal happiness). The intellectual problem was how to provide a reason for favouring the general good, a desideratum of which Sidgwick was personally convinced. He failed in his attempt to find an answer (Skidelsky 1983, chapter 2).

In his *Principles of Political Economy,* Sidgwick (1887) argued that a more equal distribution of wealth would *prima facie* increase happiness, but that it was necessary to allow for some loss of wealth as a result. Some people would be more idle as a result of receiving more income; the shift from rich to poor would decrease saving and lessen the efficiency of capital; it might lead to higher population growth; and the reallocation of resources from the rich might harm culture. Sidgwick felt that it was impossible to dispense, as Communists proposed, with individualistic stimulus. However, socialism was not open to the same objection, and some progress in that direction by a gradual and judicious extension of government was compatible with sound economic theory. The question was: how far was it safe to go? The pursuit of equality might increase the happiness of the poor – but could also undermine the incentives of the rich, so harming prosperity, and undermining liberty and culture which were preserved by a leisured elite (Sidgwick 1887, chapter 7). As Roger Backhouse has argued, Sidgwick failed to follow through his argument of balancing the gains from equality against the losses from reduced incentives, and he 'simply assumed that the effect of equality on incentives would be so large as to be overwhelming'. Greater equality might be ethically desirable but he was concerned that any limit to the use of taxation in pursuit of this ambition was entirely arbitrary – and he consequently preferred to avoid acting lest the process go too far. He failed to offer any means of balancing utilities to create a social system which his ethics led him to favour, at some point on the continuum between *laissez-faire* and extreme socialism. His approach was therefore not fundamentally different from Mill and Gladstone who feared that the tax system might become the source of class warfare and envy. It made more sense to use taxation as a 'neutral' means of securing revenue for desirable purposes, such as education, than as a tool to change the structure of society (Backhouse 2006, pp. 26–7).

A controversial issue in the history of economics is how far Alfred Marshall attempted to detach scientific economics from the ethics of Sidgwick and John Neville Keynes, while retaining something of Bentham's 'hedonic calculus' of pleasure and pain. Backhouse has recently argued that Marshall owed more to Sidgwick than is usually assumed; what Marshall did provide was a partial solution to Sidgwick's failure to resolve the problem of measuring the gains and losses of utility created by greater equality (ibid., pp. 17, 29, 31–33). In his *Principles*, Marshall stressed the marginal costs of producing another unit of output and the marginal satisfaction to be derived from consuming it. In this approach, an additional pound did not produce the same satisfaction for someone in receipt of an income of £1,000 as for someone in receipt of an income of £100. Equality of sacrifice now had a more complicated meaning, and the marginal revolution led to a shift from the approach of Mill. The aim was to extract the same proportion of happiness or satisfaction that varied according to income: the loss of £10 from an income of £100 might produce the same proportionate loss of happiness as the loss of £50 from an income of £250. Another way of approaching the issue was to calculate the loss of marginal satisfaction on the final *tranche* of income. The final £1 of income for someone earning £100 might produce five times as much satisfaction as the final £1 of income for someone earning £250, so that the tax rate could be five times as high with the same marginal disutility.[5]

How far was Marshall willing to go in raising the tax rate on higher incomes and in rejecting Gladstone's hostility to graduation? Backhouse

---

[5] I do not discuss Marshall's tax/bounty policy on commodities produced under diminishing or increasing returns, or the impact on consumers's surplus, which is considered by Groenewegen (Chapter 2, pp. 25–41).

feels that Marshall still resisted radical change in *Principles*. Although his assessment of marginal satisfaction suggested that equality led to greater happiness, he was still concerned by the 'economic and social perils of collectivism', with the disruption of social organization and loss of incentives. He felt that inventive industrialists 'earned for the world a hundred time or more as much as they earned for themselves', and that attempts to control fortunes made by socially useless speculation were 'futile'. Socialism would require a change in human nature – and if that were not feasible, why not instead create 'economic chivalry' to remove the shortcomings of a society based on private property? Backhouse therefore feels that Marshall did not escape from Sidgwick's dilemma: they shared an ethical preference for equality but worried about the loss of incentives and failed to provide quantitative tools to strike a balance (ibid., pp. 31–3).

However, Marshall *does* appear to have shifted his ground over time. The context for economic discussion was changing at the end of the nineteenth century under the pressure of increased spending on warfare (not least the Boer War) and on welfare. The shift from indirect taxes with the reduction in tariffs meant that more emphasis was placed on direct taxes, and political considerations started to change. The new approach was apparent with the introduction of graduated estate duties in 1894 by William Harcourt. A higher tax on large estates at death could be justified on the same grounds as Mill, as a device to destroy passive accumulations of capital and to stimulate active enterprise. Harcourt was willing to go further and to graduate the income tax. He argued for a new politics of taxation, aiming to reduce tax rates on smaller middle-class incomes and adding a surtax at the top, linked with an attack on landed wealth. By this means, he hoped to appeal to a crucial element of the electorate. Although he was defeated by opposition from the Treasury and Inland Revenue, change came with differentiation of the income tax in 1907 and graduation in 1909. The surtax on large incomes allowed rebates to married men with children and lower levels of tax on modest incomes in order to secure the allegiance of these groups for the Liberal party – not least as an alternative to the Conservative policy of tariff reform (Daunton 2001, pp. 245–55, 321–9, chapter 11; Murray 1980; Emy 1972).

In 1909, opponents of Lloyd George 'people's budget' (which introduced a modest level of graduation into the income tax, as well as attacking landed wealth) turned to Marshall for support. It was not forthcoming. Marshall refused to denounce the budget as socialist, as a device to remove responsibility from individuals and pass it to the state. Instead,

Marshall believed that cautious redistribution from poor to rich would be beneficial. 'For poverty crushes character: and though the earning of great wealth generally strengthens character, the spending of it by those who have not earned it, whether men or women, is not nearly an unmixed good'. Here he was accepting the distinction made by Mill and others between morally uplifting earned income and debilitating unearned income. Spending by the rich tended to lower their character, and he felt that a small check to the growth of their wealth would merely lessen the trend to export capital to other countries that was running at such high levels between 1905 and 1914 (later estimates put it at about 75 percent of total gross domestic fixed capital formation). Indeed, state spending might be beneficial, so long as public bodies did not follow the example of private persons and use it for 'foolish ostentatious expenditure'. 'The notion that the investment of funds in the education of the workers, in sanitation, in providing open air play for all children etc. tends to diminish "capital" is abhorrent to me.' As Marshall pointed out in 1902 to Helen Bosanquet a leading figure in the individualistic, non-interventionist Charity Organisation Society, with which he was long associated:

The high consumption of the rich seems to me excessive and to necessitate in effect a meager life on the part of others ... Is the share of the total price of products which goes to manual labour as large as is compatible with a wholesome and 'free' state of society? Could we by taking thought get the work of our great captains of industry and financiers done with rather less of their present huge gains? (Whitaker 1996b)

The way Marshall posed these questions indicated that the 'context for refutation' had changed, so that the onus rested on opponents of redistribution to indicate that it would harm freedom and efficiency.[6]

In effect, Marshall had moved towards a different assessment of welfare and how to build character. The notion of personal worth and morality remained important to Marshall, as it did to the highly individualistic members of the Charity Organisation Society (COS). The COS argued for 'moral regeneration' as the solution to poverty and the road to prosperity: character could always triumph over adverse conditions, and nothing should be done to weaken self-reliance. The need was to

[6] Marshall's views are in Whitaker 1996a, pp. 231–4, and Pigou 1925, pp. 443–4. They are discussed by Groenewegen 1990, pp. 91–112, Groenewegen 1995, pp. 285–6, 372–5 and Groenewegen 2007, pp. 87–8. The notion of the 'context for refutation' is from Collini 1979, p. 9. Marshall's views on welfare policy are discussed in detail in Groenewegen (Chapter 2, pp. 25–41); see also p. 29 which notes Marshall's view that progressive taxation would enhance the welfare gains of the schemes so financed.

build up and regenerate character to cope with everything that fate could throw at an individual. Marshall was similarly concerned with character, but his approach led to 'moral reform'. In his opinion, participation in a commercial society would lead to responsibility and moral earnestness. He believed that the 'strong individuality of the British race' was best maintained through 'constructive co-operation' by small firms, working together through associations rather than indulging in destructive competition. This did not mean cartels and trusts as in Germany or the United States, for 'broad-based, highly organized freedom of action is characteristically English'. His approach was akin to the new Liberals such as L. T. Hobhouse, who argued that the state should remove impediments to people's ability to look after themselves. Character could only be strengthened if impossible circumstances and structural impediments were removed, and people could then take more responsibility for their own independent, self-reliant lives.[7] In other words, the best way to maintain a free market with all the moral benefits it entailed was to accept a degree of redistribution without going so far that free enterprise was weakened and people became dependent on the state.

Marshall's economics cannot explain the shifts in policy in 1907 and 1909. Insofar as economic ideas, rather than political calculation and financial contingencies, did play a role, the influence came from thinking about rent and socially created wealth in the work of Henry George, Sidney Webb and J. A. Hobson. Their work is not now seen as central to welfare economics, but as Backhouse points out, the subject was more pluralistic in the early twentieth century (Backhouse 2006). Webb and Hobson took George's notion of rent beyond his focus on the unearned increment in land to all forms of socially created wealth, arguing that large fortunes and industrial profits contained a large element that belonged to society as a whole rather than to individuals. They differed in how the unearned element should be defined and appropriated: Webb was more in favour of public ownership and the replacement of the market; Hobson favoured removing the surplus through taxation and preserving private consumption and choice. Their influence on politicians such as Winston Churchill and Lloyd George was apparent, and much more immediate than the writings of Marshall (Ricci 1969–70; Thompson 1994; Daunton 2001, pp. 351–3).

---

[7] For the distinction between 'moral regeneration', 'moral reform' and 'mechanical reform', see Clarke 1978, pp. 5, 14–15, 29; on Marshall, see Daunton 2007, pp. 76–7.

4. PIGOU AND WELFARE ECONOMICS

The first attempt to apply Marshall's marginalism to create a specific welfare economics came from his pupil and successor to the chair of economics at Cambridge, and postdated the major fiscal changes of 1907 and 1909. In *Wealth and Welfare*, A. C. Pigou defined economic welfare as the satisfaction connected with earning and spending the national dividend. His concern was with the creation of the largest possible national dividend, which would be reduced if the marginal net product of resources was unequal between different uses. The question was: how could resources be allocated to ensure the desirable outcome of an equal marginal net product in all uses? The solution was, in part, to control monopolies and to remove impediments to mobility of labour and capital. But another possibility was to transfer resources from the rich to the poor. The result would be an increase in the commodities consumed by the poor, at the expense of those consumed by the rich and by machines. Pigou felt that a loss of income by the rich would leave their efficiency virtually unchanged, whereas an increase in consumption by the poor would produce a higher rate of return – and the same would apply compared with the use of marginal resources in machinery. The condition was that the poor invested in themselves in a competent manner, for otherwise the money would be better left with the rich or invested in machinery. Here was the problem: Pigou felt that the poor could not be trusted and should therefore be under control and direction. As a result, he was moving away from 'moral reform' (the removal of structural impediments to self-reliance) and towards 'mechanical reform' (the subordination of individuals to the state, for the good of society as a whole rather than of individual members). Further, resources would not produce a higher rate of return if transferred to 'defective' or elderly members of society and should be concentrated on two categories: normal men in middle life to cover sickness and unemployment, and above all, the minds and bodies of 'sound' children. Such an approach did not consider the marginal satisfaction of individuals and instead concentrated on their efficiency in contributing to society. This line of argument connected with concerns for Britain's competitiveness and with the debates over 'eugenics' and the character of the British race (Pigou 1912, especially chapter 9).

How far had the economics of Pigou moved away from the ethical approach of Sidgwick? Pigou continued to accept Sidgwick's utilitarianism to a greater extent than Marshall, but he took it in a more radical, redistributive direction. He was concerned with maximizing output or the national dividend: his question was how investment in individuals and income distribution contributed to growth. Although he remained uncertain of the precise outcome, he was less inclined than Sidgwick to abandon the project of measuring the balance of benefits and costs, and wished to take steps to maximize the gains and minimize the losses (Backhouse 2006, p. 38).

The development of Sidgwick's utilitarianism in relation to taxation was not only a theme in Cambridge, for F. Y. Edgeworth used much more sophisticated calculus to produce a more exact utilitarianism. Edgeworth did not study in Cambridge and never held a position there, and the greatest influence on his economic thinking was probably W. S. Jevons. However, he was a friend of both Sidgwick and Marshall, and a colleague of Keynes in editing the *Economic Journal*. His early books, and especially *Mathematical Physics* (1881), were little understood, but he was developing an economical calculus of indifference curves which anticipated Pareto's optimum. He was moving away from what has been defined at the Cambridge approach to welfare economics, with its emphasis on comparing individual utilities. Nevertheless, there were similarities with Sidgwick in his pure theory of taxation of 1897. Edgeworth started from the assumption that taxation should be guided by the utilitarian principle of the greatest happiness which might suggest equality. But he shared the concern of Malthus and Sidgwick that redistribution would harm welfare through population growth and also of Mill that it would undermine liberty and knowledge. Equality was not

consistent with that multiform development of human nature, those manifold unlikenesses, that diversity of tastes and talents, and variety of intellectual points of view, which not only form a great part of the interest of human life, but by bringing intellects into stimulating collision, and presenting to each innumerable notions that he would not have conceived of himself, are the mainspring of mental and moral progression. (Mill 1909, chapter 1, p. 211)

Despite these caveats, he accepted progressive taxation: millionaires had a lower marginal utility on their final tranche of income than taxing money from a larger number of smaller incomes which imposed taxes on those with a higher marginal utility from their final tranche of income. Levelling of incomes would lead to minimum aggregate sacrifice. His aim was not to use taxes to create equality; it was rather to start from what the state needed to collect for its needs. As he explained to the Royal Commission on Local Taxation in 1899, 'the *prima facie* best distribution is that the whole amount should be paid by the wealthiest citizens. The incomes above a certain level should all be reduced to that level; the incomes below that level should be untaxed, the level being determined by the amount which it is required to raise'. Levelling should be moderated by prudence in order to avoid driving money out of the country or 'awakening the predatory instincts of the poor'. The extent of graduation was therefore determined by what the state needed rather than by a precise assessment of indifference curves or utilities. Once the level of taxation had been determined by necessity, Edgeworth's main concern, as expressed in the Royal Commission on Income Tax at the end of the First World War, was to produce a smooth curve of graduation without sharp discontinuities (Daunton 2001, pp. 143–5, 2002, pp. 107–8; Newman 2004).

5. KEYNES AND TAXATION

By contrast, John Maynard Keynes took a different approach, based on G. E. Moore's *Principia Ethica* of 1903 with its concern for leading a good life of friendship and beauty. To an extent, Moore followed Sidgwick's utilitarian approach, arguing that individuals should do those things that will 'cause more good to exist in the Universe than any possible alternative'. This principle retained a link with Bentham's utilitarianism and judged actions by consequences. However, it created the difficulty that the rightness of actions could not be separated from the context or conditions which would shape the actual effects of any action over time. Given the difficulties of working out the probability of the consequences of any act, Moore accordingly fell back on conventional morality in response to the vexed question of how private duty to oneself was to be reconciled with a wider public duty to society. To know how to act requires detailed knowledge of the consequences of all available actions; we cannot have such knowledge and therefore rely on a second-best understanding of what actions are generally better. At this point, Moore moved from a highly sceptical position to a conservative one: the best guide is conventional morality, for society had developed rules that were the best guide to action.

As well as the question of how to act, Moore posed another question: how to define what was 'good' in assessing the consequences of any action. In response to this question, he argued that 'By far the most valuable things, which we know or can know or imagine, are certain states of consciousness, which may be roughly described as the pleasures of human intercourse and the enjoyment of beautiful objects' (Skidelsky

1983). This claim had a formative influence on Keynes and his contemporaries, offering 'the opening of a new heaven on earth' in which nothing mattered except 'timeless, passionate states of contemplation and communion' (ibid.). But Keynes did not use Moore's precept as a justification for mere pursuit of friendship and aestheticism, and he continued to be troubled by the dilemma of reconciling private pleasure and public duty, of deciding on socially desirable conduct.[8]

Hence Keynes's second intellectual interest, in probability. He argued that the best guide to acting on one hypothesis rather than another was the likely outcome, and an assessment of probability was shaped by memory, habits, interests as well as by reason and persuasion. Although Moore and the good life were important, so was the desire to improve society by rational argument and by the careful assessment of what might follow from any course of action. Keynes's *Treatise on Probability* eventually appeared in 1921 and has often been seen as a diversion or even a failure. In reality, his concern for the consequences of action and the limited extent to which they could be known in a world of fundamental uncertainty remained an important feature of his thought. It was more central to his interests than the marginal economics of Marshall: Keynes was as much concerned with time horizons and how to predict the future. The basic approach was explained in an early essay on Edmund Burke, in 1904. 'It is not wise to look too far ahead: our powers of prediction are slight, our command over results infinitesimal. It is therefore the happiness of our own contemporaries that is our main concern; we should be very chary of sacrificing large numbers for the sake of a contingent end' (Skidelsky 1992, p. 62). Uncertainty over the future continued to shape Keynes's economic philosophy between the wars. The pursuit of utopian experiments by Marxists or fascists was misplaced, for how could it be known that the future would be a classless society or an organic community? In any case, totalitarianism and the subordination of the individual removed the circumstances for leading a good life – and he remained loyal to this ambition of the *Principia Ethica* (Skidelsky 1983, pp. 155–7, 183–4, 222–3; Skidelsky 1992, pp. 58–64; Moggridge 1992, ch. 6).

How did Keynes's thinking on taxation and welfare emerge from these two strands of his thought? Essentially, Keynes was consistent in his desire to use economic policy to preserve private property and enterprise

---

[8] The contentious issue of the influence of Moore on Keynes is discussed in Skidelsky 1983, ch. 6 and Moggridge 1992, ch. 5.

as the best conditions for personal and political liberty and the good life. Keynes was not interested in grand schemes of social engineering; his concern was to use the state to restore equilibrium. This ambition was far removed from a desire to create a collectivist society; as he commented at the end of the First World War, 'Nothing can preserve the integrity of contract between individuals, except a discretionary authority in the State to revise what has become intolerable'. In other words, he adhered to the notion of 'moral reform'. Above all, he wished to preserve free enterprise, private property and personal choice. His approach was very clear during the Second World War, when he opposed management of the economy by controls and rationing which would eliminate consumer choice and reduce Britain to a slave state. Indeed, he welcomed Hayek's *Road to Serfdom* as a 'grand book', a timely warning of the dangers of totalitarianism. As Skidelsky shows in his biography of Keynes, Keynes shared the same moral values as Hayek, only differing in the best way to preserve them. In Keynes's view, government action to moderate social problems were more likely to prevent disillusion with liberal values; what Hayek saw as dangerous Keynes welcomed as 'publicness', an idea which connected with his Edwardian search for the good life. These general ethical principles had implications for Keynes's views on taxation which was to be used to restore equilibrium to the economy in order to allow freedom of consumer choice rather than, as increasingly argued by Labour, to plan and control the economy. By using taxation as a macroeconomic device, he could leave microeconomic decisions to individuals.[9]

During the First World War, Reginald McKenna, who succeeded Lloyd George as Chancellor of the Exchequer in 1915–16, argued against a large conscript army in favour of a 'long-haul' policy of funding Britain's allies and supplying munitions. Keynes was close to McKenna, and supplied him with arguments in support of his position. In Keynes's view, if the size of the army were not kept within limits, it would not be possible to maintain it and support the allies; a large army would put too much pressure on the economy and lead to an increase in imports. It followed that McKenna did not wish to increase taxes more than absolutely necessary, both because taxable capacity had been reached and because he expected the war to be long-drawn-out. His policy was based on the 'normal year': permanent taxes, excluding such war-time innovations as the excess profits duty, should only cover interest of loans and a sinking fund, as well as ordinary peace-time expenditure based on the level in 1914. In

---

[9] These comments rely on Skidelsky 1992, p. 160 and 2000, pp. 284–6.

a sense, he was following established practice, since the eighteenth century, that any borrowing should always involve sufficient taxation to pay
interest and provide for a sinking fund – a principle laid down by William
Pitt and pursued throughout the nineteenth century. This approach meant
that British government bonds maintained the confidence of lenders and
held down the cost of borrowing. Later commentators, writing in the
aftermath of the Second World War, remarked that McKenna's approach
was 'one of the strangest principles ever laid down in the history of public
finance' – a claim that misses the long history of his policy and judges him
by the standards of a later period (Peden 2000, p. 92; the criticism is from
Morgan 1952, pp. 92–3). However, it was clear to Keynes that McKenna's
approach would create problems of inflation during the war and leave
serious post-war problems of debt service. Even by earlier standards, as
the Treasury was well aware, McKenna was more reliant on loans than
taxes, so that there was historical precedent for higher taxes. Keynes
went further. Rather than starting from the amount of taxation needed to
pay for loans, would it not make more sense to raise taxes to reduce the
level of demand in the economy in order to limit inflation and post-war
debt? Although Keynes shared McKenna's dislike of a conscript army, on
grounds of personal conscience as well as economics, he was concerned
that the failure to increase taxes or to introduce forced savings was leading to serious problems. In his view, inflation would be more dangerous
for Britain's 'open' economy than for the 'closed' economy of Germany.
The German government could secure goods and labour by expanding
credit, and prices could rise without financial disaster. In Britain, additional spending power would lead to an increase in imports or a fall in
exports, and result in a serious problem in international finance. Keynes
therefore argued for a tax on a basic commodity to remove the excess
spending power of small wage-earners who did not contribute to loans
and were not affected by direct taxation. His proposal was a tax on meat
as part of a policy of transferring excess spending from consumers to
the government. In the event, McKenna's desire for a smaller army was
overruled, but the reliance on loans in preference to taxation continued
(Daunton 2002, pp. 44, 55; Keynes 1971–89, XVI, pp. 117–128).

The consequence was a high cost of debt service after the war that
could easily be portrayed by Labour as a transfer from producers to
parasites or the idle rich. At the end of the war, both Keynes and Pigou
favoured a swift repayment of the debt by means of a once-off levy on
war wealth or on capital, in order to remove the tensions created by huge
transfers to the *rentier* class and to reduce the very high level of income

tax which they both felt was harming enterprise and savings. The policy was adopted by the Labour party in opposition as a way of uniting producers against parasites, an approach which appealed to new Liberals. Keynes realized the political difficulties of introducing a levy which would scare small savers, but he also saw the dangers of other and worse ways of paying off the debt. As he pointed out, businessmen would prefer 'the inequitable and disastrous course of currency depreciation to the scientific deliberation of a levy', and he feared that electors would opt for the easier expedient of using inflation to reduce the real burden of the debt as in Germany and France. However, the idea of a capital levy soon came to trouble the Labour party when it formed its first minority administration in 1924: it could easily be interpreted by the opposition as a socialist menace to property rather than a sensible way of reducing the burden of the war debt. In any case, the net saving from the levy was recalibrated to take account of the reduction in the future yield of the income tax as a result of the impact of the levy on existing wealth. The leadership felt that retreat was expedient, and it bought time by appointing a committee on national debt and taxation chaired by Lord Colwyn which finally reported in 1927. The majority concluded that the levy would produce only a small net saving for a major political upheaval, and that it should be rejected. The minority report, produced by the Labour members, preferred a steeply graduated and differentiated income tax to fall on large unearned incomes, as a pragmatic alternative to the levy (Daunton 2002, ch. 3; Pigou 1920 and 1918; Keynes 1971–89, IV, p. 58 and ch. 2; and XVII, p. 217).[10] It effectively removed the levy from practical politics up to the Second World War.

Both Pigou and Keynes gave evidence to the Colwyn committee, which indicates the development of Cambridge welfare economics. The war had taken government spending to a much higher proportion of national income, and the income tax had reached unprecedented levels. The Colwyn committee was therefore concerned not only with the desirability of a levy compared with other taxes to service and redeem the debt, but was also interested in the general impact of the income tax on production and investment.

Pigou's evidence was somewhat elusive on the impact of a high level of income tax on incentives and enterprise. In his written evidence, he accepted that a general income tax was preferable to taxes on consumption or on particular forms of investment, which would distort

---

[10] The best general account of the debate over the capital levy is Whiting 1987.

decisions. Hence a tax on whisky would be unfair to Irish whisky drinkers compared with English tea drinkers; a tax on income left them both in the same position. He also accepted that the income tax did not enter into prices and therefore did not harm exporters. The question whether the income tax harmed work and enterprise was, he felt, more problematical. It depended on

the functions relating amount of income to amounts of satisfaction yielded by income to representative members of the community. If the scale were so arranged as to impose an equal real sacrifice on the recipients of larger and of smaller incomes, and if everybody understood what was happening, the tax would not affect work or enterprise either way. In view of the fact that (1) the existing British scale is probably graduated more steeply than the principle of equal sacrifice would require and (2) that many people fail to distinguish between money sacrifice and real sacrifice, it is probable that the existing British scale does check work and enterprise to some extent. (*Committee on National Debt and Taxation, I*, p. 41)

The approach of *Wealth and Welfare* seemed to lead to the conclusion that the level of income tax was now too high and that the marginal return to the rich was lower than to the poor. But he retreated from this position in his oral evidence. He saw a tension between distribution (which suggested that it would be best to take most money from the rich) and production (which might be hit and so harm everyone). The problem, he argued, was that it was not known how much satisfaction was derived from successive pounds of income, so that it was not possible to calculate the effect of the income tax on work and enterprise. Somewhat to the frustration of the committee, he refused to commit himself and seemed to back away from his written evidence:

you cannot tell whether it is a discouragement unless you know certain facts about the mathematical function connecting satisfaction with income. You cannot tell, unless you know things about that which you do not know, whether it would be an encouragement or not. (*Committee on National Debt and Taxation, I*, p. 49)

Nevertheless, in later evidence dealing specifically with the capital levy, he returned to his first thoughts, and remarked that 'there is a considerable presumption, though there is no certain proof, that the present high rate of taxation checks work and saving'. Although he no longer favoured a capital levy to reduce the debt, he did still favored its gradual repayment by a sinking fund, much as in the nineteenth century. Pigou's evidence came across as temporizing and evasive, appealing to mathematical precision before retreating into instinct.[11]

---

[11] *Minutes of Evidence taken before the Committee on National Debt and Taxation, Volume I*, pp. 39–58 and *Volume II*, pp. 436–48.

Keynes's evidence, and his later review of the report from the committee, showed how he had moved away from Pigou in a number of respects. Like Pigou, he was now more cautious than at the end of the war about the desirability of a capital levy, though he did not rule it out in all circumstances. Unlike Pigou, he was much less concerned about the damage caused by the high levels of debt and the costs of service; he rejected the use of a sinking fund and saw little reason to be concerned about the burden of income tax on enterprise. The repayment of the national debt was, in his view, a false analogy with the individual's need to escape debt; for the nation it was merely a bookkeeping exercise. As far as the economy as a whole was concerned, repaying debt from taxation was merely a transfer from one form of savings to another which would 'drive the savings into a particular channel instead of letting them find their own outlet'. A rapid repayment of the national debt would return money to 'the class of persons who have least courage and least skill in the utilization of resources': it would go to people with a preference for gilt-edged investments which were not in sufficient supply (*Committee on National Debt and Taxation, I*, pp. 278, 284). This situation would change if the government had its own productive schemes for new roads and so on, which Keynes would like to see happen – but in their absence, there was a danger that the money would seek safe outlets overseas. Consequently, higher taxation to repay the debt was at the expense of industry and individuals who would invest in more productive ways.

Keynes accepted that a problem would arise if the level of income tax was so high that it undermined current effort. In this case, it would make more sense to impose a tax (such as a levy) on accumulated wealth – which he felt had been the case at the end of the war and might potentially be true in the future if spending had to increase for any reason. But Keynes did not see benefit in trying to repay the debt quickly by raising the income tax, given that it merely directed savings into a particular channel that was not necessarily the best use of resources. Further, he did not see any particular evidence that the level of income tax was particularly harmful, given that it had fallen from its oppressive level at the end of the war. Although higher direct taxes might have a detrimental effect by reducing the savings of the rich, even this impact might be mitigated by productive public spending. Otherwise, Keynes saw little indication of any harm from higher direct taxes. There was no sign that income tax was shifted to higher prices for consumers or drove business abroad. The conclusion drawn by the report and accepted by Keynes was that an exceptional measure such as a capital levy was unnecessary, for by comparison it would produce a relatively small yield for considerable administrative effort. 'There is nothing to be done wisely', he remarked, 'except to raise all you can in straightforward direct taxation and the balance from luxuries and drugs in wide, general use'.

Where he disagreed with the committee was in its recommendation for a larger sinking fund to pay off the national debt: in his view, reducing the debt did not make the country better off, for all that was at stake was the distribution of the current national income between individuals. As he pointed out, both capitalists and socialists could support a sinking fund. To the former, a sinking fund – even with heavier taxation – seemed prudent and prevented money being spent on social reforms. A socialist might favour a large fund as a way of reducing transfers to the idle rich and freeing spending in the future for social reform. Both were supported by a general belief that paying off debt must be a good thing. But Keynes was sceptical. Why place burdens on taxpayers in the present, and postpone useful public spending, in order to reduce the national debt when prospective increases in the national income would reduce the real burden on future taxpayers? Such a line of reasoning connected with his advocacy of public works as part of the Liberals' programme for economic recovery. In Keynes's view, the committee was short-sighted in concentrating on the need for a large sinking fund and heavy taxes to reduce the burden of the national debt, when at the very same time it was increasing in real terms by the deflationary policies needed in order to return to gold. As he remarked, more than a third of what was currently owed in war debt was the result of falling prices, so that sinking funds 'are neither here nor there whilst this sort of thing is going on'.[12] The contrast with Pigou is striking: Keynes was less concerned with the level of taxation or burden of the national debt in reducing savings and enterprise, and much more concerned with the type of savings and whether it was productive in either the private or the public sector.

Keynes argued the case for taxation in *How to Pay for the War*. These arguments made during the Second World War were more successful than his arguments before the First World War. Even so, his achievement was limited. Keynes developed a wide-ranging package of measures designed to pay for the Second World War and 'to snatch from the exigency of war

---

[12] Keynes's evidence to the Colwyn committee is reprinted in Keynes 1971–89, XIX, pp. 295–322 and 839–55; see also XIX, pp. 675–95; Daunton 2002, pp. 164–5.

positive social improvements' (Keynes 1940, p. iii). His aim was 'to devise a means of adapting the distributive system of a free community to the limitations of war' (ibid., p. 7), in order to preserve incentives for risk-taking and to offer the maximum choice in spending income. He argued that consumer choice and a relatively free market could be preserved by removing excess spending power and deferring the receipt of some earnings until after the war. This deferred pay or forced savings could be paid to bodies under working-class control, such as friendly societies or trade unions, as 'a big constructive working-class policy' (Daunton 2002, p. 182). In other words, he was continuing the Edwardian strategy of bolstering self-sufficient, autonomous bodies, in order to create self-reliance and liberty. Keynes suggested that support of these bodies could be secured by offering family allowances and a post-war capital levy or annual capital tax to cover the costs of returning the deferred pay. As a result, the debt 'will be widely distributed amongst all those who are foregoing immediate consumption, instead of being mainly concentrated ... in the hands of the capitalist class' (ibid.), so avoiding the animosity against a small group of *rentiers* which threatened political stability at the end of the First World War. Further, the timing of repayment of deferred pay would allow the government to stimulate demand in the event of the onset of depression. Keynes's proposals were designed to create social integration and economic stability within a dynamic free market. Rather than controlling consumption by rationing and planning ('mechanical reform'), he wished to control aggregate spending and then give individuals freedom to determine their own consumption, by their own preferences. By such means, they could decide for themselves what the 'good life' entailed. He argued that his scheme would have greater political and popular appeal than 'tinkering' with the income tax. 'What the public require is a sense that imagination has been used, that a novel fiscal instrument has been forged, that social justice has been preserved, that a basis for further social improvement has been laid' (Keynes 1971–89, vol. 22, p. 273).

The scheme was only partially implemented. Although taxes provided a much larger part of war finance than in the First World War and a modest scheme of deferred pay was introduced, neither the Trades Union Congress nor the finance departments of the state were convinced. The unions saw the scheme as a hidden form of taxation: the forced savings were not really savings at all, for there was no interest, no date for repayment, and no right to transfer. The Treasury and Inland Revenue understandably preferred a simple scheme of direct taxation, but also misunderstood the intentions of Keynes. One official feared that the scheme meant that the state would 'assume control of the individual to the point of making him save when the state thinks he ought to save and trying to make him spend when the state thinks he ought to spend. I regard that as a totalitarian interference with human liberty'. He misunderstood the intention, which was to limit the role of planning and control over people's choices of consumption by rationing, heavy taxation of certain goods and direct controls over their supply. As Keynes said at the start of the war, planning should be kept within limits, for there was a 'profound connection between personal and political liberty and the rights to private property and private enterprise'.[13]

Keynes believed that a successful economy was a precondition for a liberal political system and personal freedom which underlay the good life. How did he stand on the issue that so troubled Sidgwick – the extent to which an ethically desirable pursuit of equality would harm incentives and lead to socialism? Keynes did not believe in the pursuit of equality beyond a certain stage, for he accepted that a cultured elite was necessary for a civilized society. He also accepted that personal profits were desirable for the maintenance of a prosperous economy based on private property. His concern was less with redistribution to create equality as an end in itself than to restore the equilibrium of the economy, by giving income to people with a higher marginal propensity to consume.

Of course, he was far from believing that individuals should be allowed to suffer severe hardships in pursuit of economic growth. He was disinclined to argue for severe structural changes to the economy in pursuit of growth and improvements in welfare in the long term. Rather, he took the existing institutional system as given. The point applies in particular to wages and international monetary policy. The fundamental assumption running through Keynes's approach to the reconciliation of international with domestic prosperity (so important in terms of the return to gold in 1925 and in his wartime schemes for the post-war financial system) was that economies were 'sticky' and not fluid, so that costs were very difficult to adjust. Keynes did not provide any consistent or convincing explanation of this 'stickiness' but it was crucial to his belief

---

[13] Keynes 1940, pp. iii, 7, 10–11; The National Archives, T171/355, 'Note by the Board of Inland Revenue on the proposal to treat part of an income tax payment as a deferred credit available to the taxpayer at the end of the war', G. B. Canny, 6 Jan. 1941; IR64/100, 'Revised proposals for a war surcharge', J. M. Keynes, 5 Jan. 1941; T171/372, C. J. Gregg to R.V.N. Hopkins, 9 July 1945. For a recent assessment of the scheme, see Toye 1999; Skidelsky 2000, p. 39; Moggridge 1992, ch. 24.

that monetary policy should be adjusted to domestic stability and prosperity. He did not think about structural change, or ways in which wages
and costs could be made less sticky. The 'stickiness' of costs was taken as
given rather than as something to be understood and tackled head on. His
approach was most clearly expressed in *The Economic Consequences of
Mr Churchill,* where he attacked the decision of 1925 to return to the
gold standard at an overvalued exchange rate. Keynes argued that the
economy was 'sticky' rather than fluid so that costs could not be readily
adjusted, and he assumed that the exchange rate should adjust to domestic
costs and prosperity, rather than the other way around. As he remarked,
the idea of 'automatic adjustments' was 'an essential emblem and idol of
those who sit in the top tier of the machine'. Why should workers accept
that their wages should be automatically adjusted downwards? Keynes
preferred to adjust the international exchange rate to domestic costs. He
was temperamentally hostile to structural changes, fearing that the costs
would be high and not worth the pain of transition. As he saw it, the
problem was instability rather than any deep structural defect. The solution was to avoid policy mistakes and to navigate around problems, concentrating on monetary policy and macro-economic management, with
little attempt to understand the internal operations of industry and its
competitive position. The problem with Keynes's approach, so it seemed
to his critics, was that he allowed instabilities to be removed by demand
management, while doing nothing to encourage efficiency and improved
productivity (Daunton 2007a, pp. 22–9; Keynes 1971–89, XIX, pp. 218,
224, 233–4; Skidelsky 1992, p. 205).[14]

Keynes did not himself develop his ideas on taxation during
the war, for he was more concerned with negotiating the post-war
international economic order and seeking financial assistance from
the United States. His ideas were developed by James Meade, an
Oxford-educated economist who had joined the 'Cambridge circus'
in 1930–31 and was now working alongside Keynes in the government service as a member of Economic Section. His most important contribution was a proposal on trade policy to complement
Keynes's currency plan, but he also extended Keynes's proposal for
deferred pay to profits in order to balance the economy after the
war. Although Meade argued in favour of a capital levy as a way of
paying off the war debt, this view no longer received the same degree
of support as after the First World War. Not only was the level of

---

[14] On criticisms of Keynes and demand management, see Clarke 1990, pp. 191–3.

debt considerably lower as a result of taxation; the interest rate was also low, so that the cost of servicing the debt was reduced. Instead, Meade turned to a differential profits tax or an annual capital tax as a way of adjusting the economy. At times of inflationary pressure, taxation could be increased on distributed profits in order to encourage retentions; at times of deflation, reserves should be taxed at a higher rate in order to encourage and preserve incentives by retaining profits for later distribution. In other words, it was a form of 'deferred pay' applied to income from capital. Meade claimed that such a policy would both control inflation and preserve incentives by retaining profits for later distribution. Such an approach did not imply ideological aversion to profits and distributions, and argued only for a variation over the cycle in order to maintain stability. Like Keynes in *How to Pay for the War*, Meade also argued for an annual capital tax, on the grounds that an individual's tax liability was more accurately assessed by measuring both the ownership of capital and the flow of income. This point was to become ever more relevant after the war, when economists such as John Hicks realized that high levels of income tax could be avoided by taking untaxed capital gains on the increased value of shares.[15]

For Meade, as for Keynes, the main role of fiscal policy was to stabilize the economy over the cycle and to preserve free enterprise. However, the Treasury and Inland Revenue were sceptical, fearing too great an involvement in the internal affairs of industry. Their attitude was clear: discrimination in the level of profits tax over the cycle or according to the use of reserves 'would mean, in effect, that the government would take over the running of industry' and that state control over savings and spending amounted to a 'totalitarian interference with human liberty' (Daunton 2002, p. 203). As in the case of Keynes's scheme of deferred pay, these fears misunderstood Meade's intention of using taxation as an alternative to direct controls, by influencing

---

[15] On the capital levy, see The National Archives, T230/94, 'The postwar treatment of the national debt: the capital levy'; 'The postwar treatment of the national debt: the fiscal problem set by the debt'; 'The postwar treatment of the national debt: debt repayment and unemployment policy'. See also T230/95, 'The capital levy'. The issue is discussed in Daunton 2002, pp. 186–90. For Meade's proposal on profits taxation, see The National Archives, T171/391, B(47)9 'Stabilisation and the taxation of company profits' and B(47)13, 'Differential taxation of undistributed profits'. Much of this material is reproduced in Meade (1988). See also Meade's Cabinet Office Diary (Meade 1990). On capital gains, see Hicks 1947.

demand and investment to create stability in a free market. Unlike many members of the Labour party, he believed that much industry should remain in private hands and that prices should be used to allocate goods and resources.[16]

Keynes differed from the policies adopted by Labour after the war. Not only did Labour rely very heavily on direct controls on the supply side of the economy, the government also raised tax rates on large incomes and on large fortunes left at death, in conscious pursuit of equality on grounds of ethics and efficiency. The government also turned to differential taxation of profits in the budget of 1947, imposing a higher rate on distributed profits and a lower rate on retentions within the firm. Investment was, so it was assumed, more efficient and rational if undertaken by large-scale concerns run by managers, whether in the public sector or the private market, rather than by private individuals in search of gain. The concerns of Sidgwick and his successors were no longer central to policy, which stressed instead the socially created, unearned nature of so much wealth – a triumph of the views of rent proposed by Webb and Hobson which were in many ways as influential in welfare economics as Marshall and Pigou. To most of the Labour party, large profits or income were not earned by the merits of the individual, but expropriated from society which had established the circumstances for value to be created. Furthermore, higher taxation of dividends would control inflation and secure the assent of unions to voluntary wage restraint. It would move from an external capital market controlled by financiers to an internal market controlled by salaried managers. Despite initial support for the proposal in 1943, Keynes had serious reservations by 1946, for he felt that retained profits would not benefit the economy: the problem was rather how to encourage *higher* distributions. He feared that shareholders who were liable to high levels of income tax preferred to retain profits in order to avoid the tax and to take the benefit in higher share values. Managers also wished to retain money in order to provide a margin to cover their inefficiency. A higher level of distributions would encourage the external capital market and stimulate efficiency (Daunton 2002, pp. 198, 203–4). But hostility to distribution of profits dominated the Labour party, and the Treasury was more concerned with issues of compliance and legitimacy than sophisticated analysis of the welfare implications of the tax system and redistribution.

---

[16] For the Treasury's concerns, see Daunton 2002, pp. 203–4.

6. CONCLUSION

The influence of Cambridge economics on policy formation up to 1945 was strictly limited. The intellectual justification for the shift to differentiation and graduation of the income tax came less from the marginal revolution of Marshall and the welfare economics of Pigou than from more unorthodox views of rent and socially earned income which had a greater impact on new Liberals and Labour. Neither is it likely that ideas of any complexion were the major driving force for change, which depended much more on pragmatic considerations. The Treasury and Inland Revenue were willing to increase the income tax in order to meet the need for revenue, and opposed the capital levy or a shift to indirect taxes on the grounds of administrative convenience and practicality. Keynes remarked in 1927 that the Inland Revenue was 'one of the best run and most useful institutions in the country, a remarkable creation of the British genius for administration' (Keynes, 1971–89, XIX p. 675). Above all, they were concerned with the compliance of the taxpayers and the ease of collection of taxes. Politicians were concerned with electoral considerations, so the new Liberals were willing to turn to graduated and differentiated income tax as a preferred alternative to the Conservatives' option of tariff reform. For their part, the Conservative governments between the wars maintained higher levels of taxation by shifting its incidence from married men with families on middling incomes who formed their crucial electoral constituency. Cambridge welfare economics might provide justification for the shift from a flat-rate, undifferentiated income tax to a graduated and differentiated system, and offered convincing arguments why higher taxes and redistribution might not be economically harmful. However, justification is not the same as causation.

References

Babbage, C. 1852. *Thoughts on the Principles of Taxation with Reference to a Property Tax and Its Exceptions*. 3rd ed. London: J. Murray.

Backhouse, R. E. 2006. Sidgwick, Marshall, and the Cambridge School of Economics. *History of Political Economy* 38(1): 15–44.

Clarke, P. 1978. *Liberals and Social Democrats*. Cambridge: Cambridge University Press.

1990. The Treasury's Analytical Model of the British Economy between the Wars. In M. O. Furner and B. Supple (eds.), *The State and Economic Knowledge: The American and British Experiences*. Cambridge: Cambridge University Press.

Collini, S. 1979. *Liberalism and Sociology: L. T. Hobhouse and Political Argument in England.* Cambridge: Cambridge University Press.

Daunton, M. 2001. *Trusting Leviathan: The Politics of Taxation in Britain, 1799–1914.* Cambridge: Cambridge University Press.

2002. *Just Taxes: The Politics of Taxation in Britain, 1914–1979.* Cambridge: Cambridge University Press.

2007a. Britain and Globalization Since 1850: II, The Rise of Insular Capitalism, 1914–1939. *Transactions of the Royal Historical Society* 17: 22–29.

2007b. *Wealth and Welfare: An Economic and Social History of Britain, 1851–1951.* Oxford: Oxford University Press.

Emy, H. V. 1972. The Impact of Financial Policy on English Party Politics before 1914. *Historical Journal* 15: 103–31.

Groenewegen, P. D. 1990. Marshall on Taxation. In R. McWilliams Tullberg (ed.), *Alfred Marshall in Retrospect.* Aldershot: Edward Elgar, pp. 91–112.

1995. *A Soaring Eagle: Alfred Marshall, 1842–1924.* Aldershot: Edward Elgar.

2007. *Alfred Marshall: Economist, 1842–1924.* Basingstoke: Palgrave Macmillan.

Hicks, J. R. 1947. The Empty Economy. *Lloyds Bank Review* ns 5: 1–13.

Keynes, J. M. 1940. *How to Pay for the War.* London: Macmillan.

1971–89. *The Collected Writings of John Maynard Keynes.* London: Macmillan.

Matthew, H. C. G. 1979. Disraeli, Gladstone and the Politics of Mid-Victorian Budgets. *Historical Journal* 22: 615–43.

Meade, J. E. 1988. *The Collected Papers of James Meade.* Vol. 2: *Value, distribution and growth* and 1990, Vol. 4: *The Cabinet Office Diary, 1944–1946.* Ed. S. Howson. London: Allen and Unwin.

Mill, J. S. 1909. *Principles of Political Economy.* Ed. W. J. Ashley, London: Longmans Green.

Moggridge, D. 1992. *Maynard Keynes: An Economist's Biography.* London: Routledge.

Moore, G. E. 2004. *Principia Ethica.* Reprinted Mineola, NY: Dover Publications.

Morgan, E. V. 1952. *Studies in British Financial Policy. 1914–1925.* London: Macmillan.

Murray, B. K. 1980. *The People's Budget, 1909/10: Lloyd George and Liberal Politics.* Oxford: Clarendon Press.

Newman, P. 2004. Francis Ysidro Edgeworth, 1845–1926. In H. C. G. Matthew and B. Harrison, (eds.), *Oxford Dictionary of National Biography.* Vol. 17, 716–18.

O'Brien, D. P. 1985. *The Classical Economists.* Oxford: Oxford University Press.

Palfrey, D. 2003. *The Moral Sciences Tripos at Cambridge University, 1848–1860.* PhD thesis, University of Cambridge.

Parlimentary Papers (PP): PP 1852 IX and PP 1861 VII, *Report from the Select Committee on Income and Property Tax.*

Peden, G. C. 2000. *The Treasury and British Public Policy, 1906–1959.* Oxford: Oxford University Press.

Pigou, A. C. 1912. *Wealth and Welfare.* London: Macmillan.

1918. A special levy to discharge war debt. *Economic Journal* 28: 135–156.

1920. *A Capital Levy and a Levy on War Wealth.* Oxford: Oxford University Press.

ed. 1925. *Memorials of Alfred Marshall.* London: Macmillan.

Ricci, D. M. 1969–70. Fabian Socialism: A Theory of Rent as Exploitation. *Journal of British Studies* 9: 105–21.

Seligman, E. R. A. 1908. *Progressive Taxation in Theory and Practice.* 2nd ed. Princeton: Princeton University Press.

Sidgwick, H. 1887. *Principles of Political Economy.* 2nd ed. London: Macmillan.

Skidelsky, R. 1983. *John Maynard Keynes, I: Hopes Betrayed, 1883–1920.* London: Macmillan.

1992. *John Maynard Keynes, II: The Economist as Saviour, 1920–37.* London: Macmillan.

2000. *John Maynard Keynes, III: Fighting for Britain.* London: Macmillan.

Smith, A. 1976. *An Inquiry into the Nature and Causes of the Wealth of Nations.* Eds. R. H. Campbell, A. S. Skinner and W. B. Todd, 2 vols. Oxford: Clarendon Press.

Thompson, N. 1994. Hobson and the Fabians: Two Roads to Socialism in the 1920s. *History of Political Economy* 26: 203–20.

Toye, R. 1999. Keynes, the Labour Movement and How to Pay for the War. *Twentieth Century British History* 10: 255–81.

Tribe, K. 2005. Political Economy and the Science of Economics in Victorian Britain. In M. Daunton (ed.), *The Organisation of Knowledge in Victorian Britain.* Oxford: Clarendon Press, pp. 115–37.

Whitaker, J. K., ed. 1996a. *The Correspondence of Alfred Marshall, Economist, vol. III: Towards the Close, 1903–1924.* Cambridge: Cambridge University Press.

1996b. *The Correspondence of Alfred Marshall, Volume II: Economist at the Summit, 1891–1902.* Cambridge: Cambridge University Press.

Whiting, R. C. 1987. The Labour Party, Capitalism and the National Debt, 1918–24. In P. J. Waller (ed.), *Politics and Social Change in Modern Britain: Essays Presented to A. F. Thompson.* Brighton: Harvester.

Zimmeck, M. 1985. Gladstone Holds his Own: The Orgins of Income Tax Relief for Life Insurance Purposes. *Bulletin of the Institute of Historical Research* 58: 167–88.

PART TWO

OXFORD ETHICS AND THE PROBLEM OF WELFARE

FIVE

The Oxford Approach to the Philosophical Foundations of the Welfare State

Yuichi Shionoya

I. INTRODUCTION

Thinking about welfare and the welfare state has been reflected, among others, in three branches of intellectual activity: economics, ethics, and ideology. While economics and ethics are academic disciplines, ideology is practical and sometimes opaque thought in political and social movements that occasionally results in legislation. Issues of welfare or well-being demand a wide range of intellectual approaches, although they are often mingled together in economic, political, and social thought. For this reason, historical studies of welfare thought and policy should at least cover these three areas and investigate their interrelationship in a historical context.

Debates on welfare issues have a longer history than the rise of so-called welfare economics and the welfare state in the twentieth century might suggest. The welfare thought specifically coined as "welfare economics" in the 1920s and the "welfare state" in the 1940s in Britain had been in circulation under different labels before these designations arose. The late nineteenth and early twentieth centuries in Britain and Germany provided an intellectual scene in which the total configurations of economics, ethics, and ideology in the context of welfare first showed systematic patterns. This period corresponds to Schumpeter's periodization "from 1870 to 1914" in the history of economics (Schumpeter 1954). Although the main topic of this period must no doubt be the establishment and development of neoclassical economics by the Marginal Revolution, Schumpeter did not fail to characterize an aspect of economics during this period as the "*Sozialpolitik* and the Historical Method."

The relationship between the *Sozialpolitik* and historicism was a distinctively German doctrine, and the crucial factor connecting the two was ethics. Gustav von Schmoller, the leader of the younger German Historical School, whose academic career covered the entire period in question, formulated a research program of the School as a "historical and ethical approach" (Shionoya 2005a, chapter 2). For Schmoller, the ethical claim as a guide to the historical research should ultimately serve as the basis of the *Sozialpolitik* applied to the discussion and solution of the social issues of the day. Hence, I have argued elsewhere that Schmoller's approach to economics is better characterized as a "historical, ethical, and realistic approach," meaning that his "historical and ethical economics" remained neither a description of history nor a prescription of morality, but aimed at a practical solution to social reform (Shionoya 2006).

In this chapter, discussing the British scene, I distinguish two approaches to the welfare state or social policy in the period 1870 to 1914 when British laissez-faire liberalism was over and the collectivist ideas were spreading. I call these the Cambridge approach and the Oxford approach. The distinction depends on different specifications of economics, ethics, and ideology in each approach. The Cambridge approach was based on neoclassical economics and utilitarian ethics and substantiated by Henry Sidgwick, Alfred Marshall, and Arthur Cecil Pigou. Its policy prescriptions include remedies for market failures, poverty, and inequality of distribution. Pigou's welfare economics succeeded in systematizing the Cambridge approach, but the approach remained largely extraneous both to the mainstream of value-free economics and to practical thinking about social policy (Harris 1992, p. 141). Nevertheless, within a narrow circle of theory-oriented academia, excessive attention has been given to the Cambridge approach as if it were the dominant and exclusive approach to welfare thinking, perhaps because of Marshall's established authority.

From the history-oriented standpoint in economics, however, arises the claim that the Oxford approach was based on historical economics and T. H. Green's Idealist philosophy, both of which flourished at Oxford during the period, and actually contributed to the ideology of the new liberalism. This chapter focuses on the Oxford approach which represented the "*Sozialpolitik* and the Historical Method" in Britain. I use the term "Oxford approach" to distinguish the tripartite set of the welfare thinking during the period from the concept of the new liberalism, which has primarily denoted ideology.

Contemporary moral philosophy has entailed dual confrontations between right and good, on the one hand, and between right and virtue, on the other. The first debate between liberals and utilitarians was brought to an issue by John Rawls's priority rule of right over good. The second confrontation between liberals and communitarians has proved to be not only an argument based on narrow conceptions of liberty and community, but also an argument at cross-purposes (Shionoya 2004). Recent studies on the new liberalism contend that the new liberals had transformed liberalism by ridding it of its self-centered, narrow individualism through the cultivation of virtue, community, and civic solidarity and achieved the coordination of liberty and community (Simhony and Weinstein 2001, pp. 1–25). Hence, an examination of the Oxford approach will contribute not only to the historical interpretation of the new liberalism but also to the contemporary understanding of welfare and the welfare state.

In what follows, I begin with a brief look at the research field concerned, which is replete with scholarship of high quality by political historians (Section 2). Then I present a philosophical view on the welfare state and social security based on a coherent system of ethics, and emphasize the primary importance of virtue ethics (perfectionism) in interpreting the notions of welfare or well-being (Section 3). Then I revert to the Oxford Idealist, moral and political philosopher T. H. Green, who expounded the philosophy of perfectionism most extensively in opposition to utilitarianism. His moral and political theory will be examined from the contemporary perspective after Rawls (Section 4). Based on an understanding of Green's perfectionism, I discuss its influences on the Oxford historical economics stimulated by Arnold Toynbee and on the new liberalism represented by J. A. Hobson and L. T. Hobhouse to identify the Oxford paradigm with the components of economics, ethics, and ideology (Section 5). To complement the main argument, I speculate about a precursory role of John Ruskin in the formation of the Oxford approach (Section 6). The paper concludes with a summary of the Oxford approach in comparison with the Cambridge approach (Section 7).

2. CONFLICTING VIEWS ON GREEN: HISTORICAL VERSUS RATIONAL RECONSTRUCTION

I begin with a short reference to the current conflicting views on Green. The term new liberalism refers narrowly to the reform program of the

British Liberal Party in the period 1906–14.[1] This program is often interpreted as the first major step on the way to the welfare state in Britain,
though this interpretation has been at issue in scholarship. It is generally
agreed that the basic tenets of liberalism were fundamentally reformu-
lated in a crucial and decisive manner during this period (Freeden 1978,
p. 1). New liberalism in a broader sense refers to changes in philosophical, economic, and social thought at the end of the nineteenth century in
Britain. With regard to the role of Green, however, the dominant view
seems to have been a negative appraisal of his role as the advocate of the
new liberalism. This assessment challenged the early textbook version
that credited British Idealism, Green in particular, with major responsibility for the transformation of liberalism. Thus, Peter Clarke remarks:

It is certainly a mistake to hail him [Green] as a collectivist or an architect of the
welfare state. In his lecture on "Liberal Legislation and Freedom of Contract"
(1881) Green did not go beyond an advocacy of a moderate reform of the land
laws and – with much more fervour – legislative restriction of the sale of drink.
(Clarke 1978, p. 15)

Clarke later repeats the same idea in a more general form in his authoritative history of Britain:

The posthumous influence of the Hegelian philosopher T. H. Green, dead for a
quarter of a century by 1906, has been too freely invoked in understanding the
outlook of the Edwardian Liberal Party. Plainly not all New Liberals were philosophers, still less neo-Hegelians; and Green's politics of moral regeneration
did not envisage anything like a welfare state. (Clarke 1996, p. 44)

Michael Freeden, in his work on Liberal social reform, provides a more
detailed analysis:

At the very most, Idealism must be regarded as one element amidst a general
progressive movement in ideology, philosophy, economics, science, and practical politics. Had Green not existed, liberalism would still have become collectivist and favourably oriented to progressive reform. ... Owing to the historically
"accidental" fact that Idealism dominated for a while the training ground of
England's intellectual and political elite – Oxford – it came to assume an importance disproportionate to what it would normally have received in the English
climate of ideas. ... Oxford provided the *emotional* atmosphere and motivation
to study social problems and undertake social work rather than the intellectual
justification and framework for social reform. ... Rather than Idealism giving

---

[1] In the welfare reform of 1906–14, old age pensions, insurance against ill-health and
unemployment, school meals, and medical services for children were introduced.
Minimum wages were fixed in certain industries, and some attempt was made to alter
the distribution of income and wealth (Hay 1975, p. 11).

birth to a new version of liberalism, it was liberalism that was able to assimilate certain aspects of Idealism into its mainstream and thus bestow new meaning upon Idealist tenets. (Freeden 1978, pp. 17–18)

Behind these appraisals lie echoes of Melvin Richter's classic work of intellectual history based on the sociology of knowledge. Richter even argued as early as the 1960s the similarity of Green with the Manchester School, and Green's religious purpose of replacing Evangelicalism with a metaphysical system oriented to the union of faith and reason (Richter 1964). From this perspective, the view that Green belonged to the old liberalism might save him from the accusation of collectivism.

It seems dangerous to take the Richter-Clarke-Freeden approach as it stands; it will be helpful to remember its methodological features. First, their appraisals were derived from investigations of Green's practical reform proposals as expressed in his political lectures and activities, neglecting his ethical theory. Second, the assessment most often concerned the absence of the impact of his philosophy on specific British legislation rather than on the thought of new liberalism in a broader sense. Third, the standard of evaluation consisted of the dichotomy of individualism versus collectivism, that staple of nineteenth-century analysis. In this context, a prejudice of any British historians who abhor German Idealism lest "the Rhine flows into the Thames" might permeate historical and theoretical research. British analytical philosophers including Bertrand Russell and G. E. Moore may have influenced the unfavorable evaluation of Idealists.

There are, on the other hand, affirmative views on Green's place in the history of social policy; in the last two decades, in fact, there has been a growing interest in reconsidering Green's role in subsequent developments of moral and political philosophy (Brink 2003, Carter 2003, Wempe 2004, Leighton 2004). Moreover, there has been an apparent resurgence of a proper concern with the British Idealism in general (Nicholson 1990, Boucher and Vincent 2000). For instance, Peter Weiler derives a positive appraisal of Green, although he admits that the new liberals were more serious than Green about the widespread poverty caused by the capitalist system:

His [Green's] moral concerns influenced a whole generation of social reformers, and more important, he provided one basis for the main Liberal justification of the welfare state. His redefinition of freedom and of society permitted the state action to assure all men of the possibility of a decent life. This idea of the state as a positive force was shared by the new Liberals. But their proposals were more than an extension of Green's. (Weiler 1982, p. 40)

Jose Harris recently reviewed the intellectual background of the transformation of welfare provision between the 1870s and the 1940s in
Britain. She concludes:

I have no desire to suggest that idealism or any other form of theory offers the
sole key to the twentieth-century transformation of the British state. But the
predominance of idealism – with its emphasis on corporate identity, individual altruism, ethical imperatives and active citizen-participation – meshed and
interacted with the mundane working of social policy in Britain during the first
half of the twentieth century at many different levels. (Harris 1992, p. 137)

I shall examine the possibility that Green's moral philosophy offered a
theoretical foundation of the welfare state, influencing various branches
of welfare thinking. This attempt does not necessarily contradict the
Richter-Clarke-Freeden approach, which is confined to the historical
research rather than the theoretical or systematic one. Here we see two
different approaches to Green: a historical reconstruction and a rational
reconstruction. Even though Green's influences on the theory and practice of the new liberalism and on the subsequent formation of the welfare
state turned out to be limited in a historical context, it can still be argued
that his conception of positive freedom based on the ethics of virtue provides the notion of the welfare state with an essential groundwork. I inter-
pret Green's contribution to the welfare state on the ground of its rational
reconstruction, with reference to our ethical conceptual framework, and
maintain that he anticipated the distinct notion of positive welfare policy.

3. THE PERFECTIONIST CONCEPTION OF THE
WELFARE STATE

The welfare state is conceived as consisting of the three grand systems of
capitalism, democracy, and social security. As far as the scope of the welfare state is concerned, this conception is consonant with the formulation
by T. H. Marshall of the historical developments of citizenship: the welfare state has advanced through three stages of citizenship: "civil rights"
for individual freedom developed in the eighteenth century; "political
rights" for individual participation in public decision-making, in the nineteenth century; and "social rights" for economic welfare and security, in
the twentieth century (Marshall 1964 [1950]). The outcome of these developments was what Marshall termed "Democratic-Welfare-Capitalism,"
and what I call the welfare state. The skeleton of the welfare state is that
the two institutional constraints of democracy and social security have
been imposed on the workings of a capitalist market system.

Social security is a public scheme for the allocation of economic resources to meet "basic human needs," which are to be satisfied to achieve the full status of citizenship. Basic human needs are those elements that human beings require to function normally in the individual and social perspectives. Social security has two objectives by the use of a public scheme. First, it provides a public "safety net" to cope with risk when individuals cannot satisfy their own basic needs. Second, it further creates a "springboard" to ensure those individuals economic and social opportunities to achieve autonomy, to develop their capacities, and to help them realize self-fulfilment through the satisfaction of their basic needs. The former is negative welfare policy; the latter is positive welfare policy.

Here I will briefly analyze the moral nature of the welfare state in the light of a broad system of moral philosophy, drawing on my previous work (Shionoya 2005b). In view of the richness of the intellectual composite of welfare thinking, we need a sufficiently broader frame of reference than a naïve dichotomy like "intervention versus laissez-faire." From the examination of major approaches from Aristotle to the present in moral philosophy, we find three different objects of moral evaluation: (a) the act or behavior of individuals, (b) the being or character of individuals, and (c) the rule or institution. Corresponding to these three objects, there are three distinct approaches (utilitarian, Aristotelian, and Kantian) with an exclusive emphasis on one of three basic value terms: (a) good, (b) virtue, and (c) right, respectively. Their theoretical structures are naturally different in addressing different subject matters. The basic and abstract value terms of *good, virtue,* and *right* are transformed into the operational value terms of *efficiency, excellence,* and *justice,* so that they can be linked to a wider knowledge of moral and social theories.

We need coordination of ethical systems consisting of three branches, which are characterized by a set of specified objects of moral evaluation, basic value terms, and operational value terms: (a) "act-good-efficiency," (b) "being-virtue-excellence," and (c) "rule-right- justice." We conceive that human welfare is served by the matrix values of (a), (b), and (c), not by a scalar value of, say, happiness or utility. The ordering of priority is right over virtue and good, and virtue over good.

As the task of social security consists of satisfying basic needs, it is reasonable to presume that its first moral basis is the ideal of virtue ethics for the existential or ontological aspect of human beings. Basic needs should be understood not as the minimum conditions of biological subsistence but those of human excellence, improvement, perfection, and self-realization. The ideal of excellence or perfection, supported by the satisfaction of basic needs, demands a life of human flourishing for all individuals through the development of capabilities in the context of association with others and social practice.

Traditionally the safety-net function of social security has been emphasized as a measure against risk in social life. This idea is best explained by the contractarian theory of justice, such as the difference principles of John Rawls (1971). His principles of justice, prescribing equal basic liberties, fair equality of opportunities, a scheme of social insurance for self-respect, and resultant differences in economic and social status, articulate the tripartite structure of the welfare state in terms of capitalism, democracy, and social security. Justice ethics is the second moral basis of social security; it is concerned with the rule or institutional aspect of society.

The third moral rationale of social security is derived from the defect of the insurance market for the collective management of risk. Even if basic needs are likely to be unmet, the device of insurance as a measure against risk is available in the market. Insurance mitigates the consequences of uncertainty through cooperation among the insured. But there is asymmetry of information between policyholders and suppliers of insurance in the insurance market, resulting in adverse selection, a case of market failure. Improvement of efficiency by preventing market failure is the third reason for a mandatory social insurance system; the standard of efficiency is concerned with the evaluation of the act aspect of human beings, which is motivated by rational self-interest.

To summarize, the moral foundations of social security as a non-market system are excellence, justice, and efficiency. The welfare state is not simply a technical device to effect a redistribution of income and a guarantee of minimum material conditions but is designed as a moral community to cultivate the human capabilities of its members. Michael Freeden, based on his historical inquiries of welfare ideologies, derives three categories of the rationale behind welfare policy: the socialization of virtue, the collectivization of risk, and the identification of need (Freeden 2003, pp. 12–20). In my view, these mixed ideologies can be restructured as a conjugation of the "safety-net" function for a pooling of risk and the "springboard" function for realization of virtue on the common basis of human need. Put differently, social policy is conceived in terms of negative and positive welfare measures, both based on the conception of human need, whose fulfillment or non-fulfillment is conducive to human flourishing (virtue) as well as human vulnerability (risk).

The relevance of perfectionism to today's welfare thinking, I suggest, will be explained with reference to the idea of positive welfare in "the Third Way" politics of the British New Labour (Giddens 1998), Amartya Sen's (1985) capability approach to economic ethics, and the notion of a common good in communitarianism (Etzioni 1996). I find, however, no reference whatever to Green's system of moral philosophy in the current literature.

4. PERFECTIONISM AND LIBERALISM IN GREEN

Green was the most notable of the leading members of the British Idealists, which included F. H. Bradley, Bernard Bosanquet, David Ritchie, Henry Jones, R. G. Collingwood, and Michael Oakeshott. Green's moral theory is a theory of the good as human perfection. Although he uses the concept of the good as perfection, his theory is typically classified as the ethics of virtue in our scheme. The perfection is taken to be the ultimate end of rational conduct and is otherwise described as the realization, development, or completion of human faculties or capabilities.

He begins his *Prolegomena to Ethics* (1997b [1883]) with an attack on the empiricist epistemology of Locke and Hume and develops a transcendental discussion acknowledging the source of knowledge to be the prior framework set by the mind of the subjects. Criticizing naturalistic strands in ethics from the Idealist standpoint, Green rejects hedonistic utilitarianism, which regards desire and pleasure as the sole motives for action, and argues that moral agents deliberate about their desires and regulate their action according to their deliberations; there can be no experience of the external world such as "felt desire" antecedent to the conscious subject.

Green derives self-realization or human perfection as the demands of moral agents, which also include concern for the good of others. He claims that full self-realization can take place only when reciprocal relations hold between moral agents. Thus, self-realization or perfection means the conception of good in terms of the proper exercise of various essential or important human capacities and leads to the concept of a common good in a community in which each person cares about others for their own sakes. Self-realization is achieved in interpersonal association with the universal membership, whose aims and goals are established as a common good. The common good does not refer to particular entities which individuals commonly desire, such as Rawls's primary goods, but rather to the common pursuit of self-realization by the members of a given society. Avital Simhony rightly suggests three senses of "common" in Green's common good: self-realization is "mutual" good (as opposed to separate or private), "universal" good (opposed to particular or exclusive), and "distributive" good (opposed to collective or aggregative) (Simhony 2001, pp. 72–3).

Hence the notion of self-realization as the common good involves reconciling individuality and sociability in contradistinction to the notion of self-centered and independent individuals pursuing private interests in a competitive society. For Green, sociability is an individual ethical attribute rather than social constraints imposed on individuals by an organic community (Freeden 1996, p. 184). This viewpoint characterizes Green's view on the relationship between individual and society.

An important point with regard to Green's attitude toward utilitarianism is not whether the ultimate end for a human being should be identified with pleasure or self-realization, but whether the self should be considered as fleeting and unstable feeling or enduring and abiding existence through time. To use my own terms of person as "stock" and "flow," Green's basic thesis is that except for the self as a "stock" of character rather than a "flow" of feeling, one cannot conceive of a virtuous life based on learning by doing, which is further specified as the virtues of wisdom, fortitude, self-control, justice, and so on (Shionoya 2005b, pp. 19, 58–9, 82–3).

Green does not dispense with the concept of desire because the objects necessary for a fulfillment of capabilities are to be desired deliberatively. The concept of desire warrants Green's moral theory being explored by economic reasoning. It follows that Green's ethics will replace the utilitarian economics of efficient resource allocation and open up the way to an economic discourse on virtuous utilization of resources, on which the perfectionist conception of the welfare state should depend.

It is the task of political philosophy for Green to conceive institutions as intermediary devices for securing the interaction between self-realization and the common good. In political philosophy Green extends his central idea of moral philosophy, namely self-realization, into the political sphere by arguing what the state should do; he introduces the concept of freedom as a way for the object of human flourishing to be practically realized through institutions. He identifies true freedom with self-realization. For Green, self-realization – true freedom – requires positive economic, social, and cultural conditions as well as the absence of compulsion or restraint by others.

We do not mean merely freedom from restraint or compulsion. We do not mean merely freedom to do as we like irrespectively of what it is that we like. We do not mean a freedom that can be enjoyed by one man or one set of men at the cost of a loss of freedom to others. When we speak of freedom as something to be so highly prized, we mean a positive power or capacity of doing or enjoying something worth doing or enjoying, and that, too, something that we do or enjoy in common with others. We mean by it a power which each man exercises through the help or security given him by his fellow-men, and which he in turn helps to secure for them. (Green 1997a [1881], pp. 370–1)

This is what Isaiah Berlin attacked, calling it "a classic statement of positive liberty" in his celebrated essay on two concepts of liberty (Berlin 1969, p. xlix). There are three important points about Green's conception of freedom. Green claims, first, not negative freedom but positive freedom; second, not freedom to do anything one wants but something morally worthy; and third, freedom not for the good of atomistic individuals but for the self-realization of individuals as a common good pursued by all members of society. Thus, he wants to revise the traditional, restrictive conception of liberalism and justify the state intervention by the notions of the common good and of positive freedom. But he is against holism, a view that there are any social entities such as nations or classes that exist over and above the individuals who comprise them. As he says:

Our ultimate standard of worth is an ideal of *personal* worth. All other values are relative to value for, of, or in a person. To speak of any progress or improvement or development of a nation or society or mankind, except as relative to some greater worth of persons, is to use words without meaning. (Green 1997b [1883], p. 193)

The state, for Green, is a means to achieve the moral goal of the perfection of personality and depends for this purpose on the harmonious maintenance of rights for all citizens. Another important concept of political philosophy, along with the concept of freedom, namely rights, is also defined in terms of the common good. Green denies that individuals could have rights independently of their social relations.

The following passage shows the conceptual unity of social institutions, the common good, and self-realization:

The institutions by which man is moralized, by which he comes to do what he sees that he must, as distinct from what he would like, express a conception of a common good; ... through them that conception takes form and reality; ... it is in turn through its presence in the individual that they have a constraining power over him, a power which is not that of mere fear, still less a physical compulsion, but which leads him to do what he is not inclined to because there is a law that he should. (Green 1997c [1886], pp. 429–30)

Green's vision of perfection is not a static ultimate state in which the moral ideal is realized but a process of moral progress as the German

Idealists conceived. "We have no knowledge of the perfection of man as the unconditional good," but "our life is directed to its attainment" (Green 1997b [1883], p. 206). Green's perfectionism, interpreted as the evolutionary process of interaction between morality and institutions, provides a basis for developing a historical-ethical approach to the economy and society by historical economists, the new liberals, and Hobhouse's evolutionary sociology in particular.

It is illuminating to label Green's moral philosophy as "liberal perfectionism" and his political philosophy as "perfectionist liberalism" (Hinton 2001). Unlike the contemporary communitarians who claim, in opposition to Rawls, that the common good precedes right (justice) or that a sense of identity precedes reason, I assert that Green's moral and political philosophy can be made consistent with Rawls's theory of justice. Because for Green, virtue is the common good defined, as we have seen in a universal context, his key notions such as perfection, freedom, justice, and rights are all conceptualized on the basis of an equal consideration to all citizens and of reciprocity between them. As Rex Martin emphasizes, for Green, rights are justified by a mutual benefit for each citizen, which underlies social recognition of rights (Martin 2001, pp. 57–9).

However, there is a difference between Rawls and Green with regard to the relationship between their theories and institutional designs. While Rawls's two principles of justice are to be embodied in institutions, Green's perfectionist principles are left to the voluntary act of free and equal citizens and to the evolutionary process of their interaction under the virtue-promoting institutional conditions. The voluntary nature of perfectionism is clear from his following argument:

Our modern legislation then with reference to labour, and education, and health, involving as it does manifold interference with freedom of contract, is justified on the ground that it is the business of the state, not indeed directly to promote moral goodness, for that, from the very nature of moral goodness, it cannot do, but to maintain the conditions without which a free exercise of the human faculties is impossible. (Green 1997a [1881], p. 374)

The institutions Green advocated for legislation on labor, education, and health are to be designed as the conditions for the perfection of all individuals as the common good, whereas the Rawlsian institutions are the conditions of procedural justice permitting people to pursue their plural conceptions of good without differentiating the nature of good.

There is currently a great deal of old-fashioned criticism of perfectionism and positive freedom for committing paternalistic interference in the lives of citizens and for violating value neutrality in the life-styles of liberal societies. Committing paternalism and violating neutrality, the critics argue, are likely to lead to the danger of totalitarianism and dictatorship. What Green really meant, however, lies between the two poles: collectivism and the old liberalism.

5. THE NEW LIBERALISM, BRITISH HISTORICISM, AND SOCIAL POLICY

The economic and political basis of the new liberalism was developed, in particular, by the two Oxford graduates Hobson and Hobhouse. The core of the new liberalism is described by Peter Weiler:

> The essential contribution of the new Liberals to the Liberal tradition was their reevaluation of the state, a reevaluation which was in turn based on a redefinition of society. The old Liberals thought of society as simply an aggregate of individuals. ... In contrast to this view, the new Liberals, drawing on Victorian sociology and philosophic idealism, thought of society as an organism, a unity of political, social, and *economic* forces. ... Man could not live apart from society; indeed he could only be truly free within society. With this new view of man and society as a basis, the new Liberals had arrived at Green's idea of positive freedom. ... The significant application of these ideas, however, was not in the political sphere but in the *economic*. ... Since each man's freedom to develop his capacities was the keystone of political Liberalism as defined by Mill, it was clear that the *economic* system must be changed, if this liberal ideal of freedom was to be retained. But traditional Liberal *economic* policy offered no remedies for this situation. It was this policy, therefore, that the new Liberals proposed to revise. (Weiler 1982, p. 17, emphasis added)

Instead of closely perusing Hobson and Hobhouse, I quote this summary remark to suggest the thread of reasoning running from Green to the new liberals. Although the new liberals depended on Green's concept of positive freedom, they did not content themselves with the scope of his moral and political thought but tried to work on economic system and policy. However, they are distinguished from the subsequent social democratic thinkers in that they placed more emphasis on the transformation of society by the construction of a moral community (Clarke 1978, p. 5). It is in this context that the new liberalism got another stimulus from the British historical economics, which was also a product of Green's moral inspiration, as well as from an early moralistic critique of economics by John Ruskin, whom we discuss below.

Alon Kadish's remarkable study of the group of Oxford economists during the 1880s and the 1890s reveals that their economic research, historical economics in particular, was:

part and parcel of a wider *Weltanschauung* in which the general principles of
Green's Idealism, accepted more or less unquestioningly, were applied, with a
combination of additional influences ... to academic work and, in the form of a
political and social ideology, to practical issues. (Kadish 1982, p. 42)

Kadish adds that this influence was due not only to the logical content
of these ideas but also to the personal inspiration of certain Oxford
dons, whose outstanding example was Arnold Toynbee. I shall examine
how a historical approach and an ethical viewpoint were combined in
Toynbee's study of the Industrial Revolution, which became a powerful
spur to historical economists at Oxford, such as W. J. Ashley, L. L. Price,
and W. A. S. Hewins.

Toynbee begins his lectures on the Industrial Revolution with the
relationship between theoretical and historical approaches to economics, which was the subject matter of the *Methodenstreit* in Austria and
Germany. His lectures were given from October 1881 to May 1882 at
Oxford just before the *Methodenstreit* broke out between Carl Menger
and Gustav von Schmoller in 1883–84. While the *Methodenstreit* was
rooted in the misunderstanding and intolerance of both parties, Toynbee
recognized the need to coordinate the two approaches. Criticizing Cliffe
Leslie, an early advocate of historicism in Britain, who condemned the
theoretical method as radically false, Toynbee had realized the practical
importance of combining the two approaches even without a methodology that would serve to resolve the conflict between theory and history.

Toynbee characterizes the basic assumptions of theoretical (Ricardian) economics as self-love and competition; in other words, the
neglect of the instinct of benevolence and the demise of the concept of
institution:

Thus the economists, firstly, regard only one part of man's nature, and treat him
simply as a money-making animal; secondly, they disregard the influence of cus-
tom, and only take account of competition. (Toynbee 1920, p. 3)

He considers two practical purposes of using history against theory. First,
the historical method investigates the stages of economic development in a
given country and compares them with those in other countries to discover
laws of universal application. Through these investigations the historical
method will reveal how economic laws are relative, although theoretical
economists are likely to speak as if their laws were always universal on a
deductive basis. Second, the historical method uncovers in history those
problems which are overlooked by theoretical economists due to their basic
assumptions. Historical economists pursue facts, standing on a vivid sense

of the problems of their own time. Toynbee calls this approach "a principle of selection" rather than "a principle of perversion" (ibid., p. 6) The principal problem he selects in the *Lectures* is the growing poverty of the working classes, which he thinks should be alleviated by institutional measures.

Between these two purposes, Toynbee, with his too-short life, in fact did not embark on constructing a general economic theory by means of historical comparisons but was engaged in using history as a guide to moral questions. The scenario of his lectures on the Industrial Revolution is to present an alternative interpretation of economic development which cannot be envisaged by the laissez-faire economics built on the assumptions of self-interest and unrestricted market competition. As he describes his basic insight of research, "[t]he essence of the Industrial Revolution is the substitution of competition for the mediaeval regulations which had previously controlled the production and distribution of wealth" (ibid., p. 64). The historical method applied to the Industrial Revolution, he argues, illuminates the particular need of institutional measures to cope with the reality of growing poverty and conflicting interests between the classes because "the proper limits of Government interference are relative to the nature of each particular state and the stage of its civilization" (ibid., p. 6).

Toynbee concludes:

The effects of the Industrial Revolution prove that free competition may produce wealth without producing well-being. We all know the horrors that ensued in England before it was restrained by legislation and combination. (ibid., p. 73)

[T]he whole meaning of civilization is interference with this brute struggle. We intend to modify the violence of the fight, and to prevent the weak being trampled under the foot. (ibid., p. 66)

Alfred Milner, one of Toynbee's closest Balliol friends, wrote in his reminiscence: "For the sake of religion he [Toynbee] had become a social reformer; for the sake of social reform he became an economist" (Milner 1920, p. xxi). This passage well summarizes how the Oxford set of welfare ideas consisting of ethics, economics, and ideology was coherently embodied in Toynbee himself. Toynbee's influence, sometimes called "magnetic," on his contemporaries also depended on his moral, religious, and social activities through various civic-reform associations, which were originally inspired by Green. To work on the urgent social problems throughout the late 1870s and early 1880s, Oxford economists concentrated on economic history in a policy-oriented manner without spending too much time on theory (Kadish 1993, p. 68). Toynbee focused on the moral regeneration of society, implemented both by the cooperation of capital and labor and by the intervention of the state through social reform. His program of social reform was limited to old age pensions, housing for artisans, and regulations of working conditions (Koot 1987, p. 88).

To complete the Oxford paradigm it is necessary to discuss, though briefly, the two leading proponents of the new liberalism: Hobhouse and Hobson. The new liberals went far beyond Green's moral and political doctrine in that they paid explicit attention to the economic conditions in which maladies such as unemployment and poverty had deprived people of freedom. It was recognized that there existed another big institutional scheme beside the government and community (i.e., the capitalist industrial system). Although Hobhouse was critical of Green's metaphysical basis of positive freedom, he was greatly influenced by Green's moral and political philosophy. He accepted Green's thesis of self-realization and dressed it up in the terminology of evolutionary theory (Collini 1979). Hobhouse's goal was a harmonious and organic society in which the development of the potentiality of all members is realized via the progressive organization of conditions of life (Hobhouse 1911). He argued that for this goal to be reached, the economic system should be controlled by the state, including regulation of competition and redistribution of wealth.

The economics aspect of the Oxford approach was brought to fruition in Hobson's welfare economics. Apparently, Hobson tried to develop in terms of economics Ruskin's thesis that "there is no wealth but life," but this would not have contradicted Green's thesis of self-realization. He acknowledged that Green's lecture on "Liberal Legislation and Freedom of Contract" represented the aim of the new liberalism (Hobson 1938, p. 52).

Hobson's concept of organic welfare, a desirable standard of welfare, depends on his view of society as an organic society (Hobson 1914). Organic welfare, which corresponds to Green's common good, is not a sum of separate individual goods but connected to the structure of output. For Hobson, the approach to income distribution was crucial for reforming the maldistribution of income and oversaving, both of which were considered as causes of economic depression, unemployment, and poverty. The organic view of society led him to the recognition that social cooperation must produce a surplus value greater than the aggregate of separate individual activities. His division of income into costs and surplus (each defined in terms of objective and subjective), instead of wages, interest, and rent, seems to be instrumental in combining Green's self-realization with the virtuous utilization of economic resources. It is insightful to conclude that the theory of "organic surplus value" is the key to Hobson's economic philosophy (Allett 1981). While costs consist of the minimum necessary to sustain various productive agents, market competition prevents some from attaining a minimum income and allows others to obtain a surplus. The surplus or "unearned increment" is the source necessary for self-realization of the individuals and should belong to the public as a whole, but actually goes to waste through the market. The standard of social well-being, Hobson argues, is realized by the natural evolution of an organic society.

The thought of the new liberals looks more or less uniform on the moral and political dimension because they shared Green's thesis of self-realization. However, the economist Hobson gives it a richer and more complex form: (1) criticism of classical economics for the distinction between facts and values; (2) rejection of hedonistic utilitarianism as the basis of economics from the viewpoint of self-realization; (3) refutation of Pigouvian identification of national income with economic welfare; (4) the conception of organic well-being, oriented to the higher quality of life, which gives a guiding principle of human valuation; (5) conception of plural values of virtue in the evaluation of human conduct, with due places for physical, intellectual, and moral satisfaction, instead of a utilitarian single value of pleasure; (6) evaluation of work and consumption in terms of Schumpeterian creation and imitation; and (7) the process of historical evolution, as the subject matter of economics, caused by moral progress and social experience. These diverse claims constitute important aspects of the attempts to apply Green's moral vision to economics and would be compared to the monolithic approach of Cambridge welfare economics.

6. RUSKIN AND THE OXFORD APPROACH

In constructing the concept of the Oxford approach to welfare, we cannot neglect the role of John Ruskin. Insofar as we have examined the Oxford paradigm with reference to the moral philosopher Green, the historical economist Toynbee, and the new liberal Hobson, it will be natural to trace the influences of Ruskin on these three thinkers. Ruskin's career at Oxford fully overlapped the careers of the three.

Of the three, Hobson was the most influenced by Ruskin, whose ideas were essential to the shaping of Hobson's economics. Hobson was not conscious of any direct influences from Green, except for the general moral atmosphere of Oxford. While Hobson's career as a heretic to orthodox economics started with a theory of over-saving, his lifetime pursuit of humanistic and ethical economics showed the inheritance of the economic and social thought of Ruskin. After his writings on art ensured his fame, Ruskin turned to "wrathful and dilettantic criticism of the sins of capitalism" (Schumpeter 1954, p. 411). Although orthodox economists paid no attention to Ruskin's criticism of economics, Hobson took it seriously; he not only wrote a systematic treatise on Ruskin's social thought but also tried to develop his own welfare economics based on Ruskin's vision (Hobson 1898). The central theme of Ruskin's vision was the conception of wealth as life:

> There is no wealth but life. Life, including all its powers of love, of joy, and of admiration. That country is the richest which nourishes the greatest number of noble and happy human beings; that man is richest who, having perfected the functions of his own life to the utmost, has also the widest helpful influence, both personal, and by means of his possessions, over the lives of others. ... The maximum of life can only be reached by the maximum of virtue. (Ruskin 1997 [1860], p. 222)

Following Ruskin's proposal of substituting the human standard of welfare and vitality for the money standard of wealth and value, Hobson reached the conclusion that:

> The true "value" of a thing is neither the price paid for it nor the amount of present satisfaction it yields to the consumer, but the intrinsic service it is capable of yielding by its right use. Of commercial goods, or any other class of goods, those which have a capacity of satisfying wholesome human wants are "wealth," those which pander to some base or injurious desire of man are not wealth, but "illth," availing, as they do, not for life but for death. Thus he [Ruskin] posits as the starting-point of Political Economy a standard of life not based upon present subjective valuations of "consumers," but upon eternal and immutable principles of health and disease, justice and injustice. A man or a nation is wealthy in proportion as he or it is enabled to satisfy those needs of nature which are healthy, and thus to realize true capacities of manhood. (Hobson 1898, p. 79)

Hobson held that the standard for evaluating cost, utility, and value must be qualitative, not quantitative, reflecting plural human values (Hobson 1938, chs. 14 and 16). We can probably understand their notion of human standard by referring to the contemporary concept of basic human needs, which could be scrutinized in terms of virtuous utilization of resources from the viewpoint of virtue ethics (Shionoya 2005b, p. 118–30).

Toynbee was an admirer of Ruskin. As an undergraduate, Toynbee joined Ruskin's unrealistic project of road digging at Oxford, designed for the purposes of physical training and public service (Kadish 1986, pp. 32–6). Ruskin offered an emotional criticism of industrialization without forging necessary tools, which should replace utilitarian philosophy and laissez-faire economics. Toynbee's interest in economics was certainly stimulated by Ruskin's condemnations of capitalist economy and laissez-faire economics. Contrary to Ruskin's nostalgia for a bygone social system, Toynbee entertained an optimistic belief in progress and regarded self-help of individual as the driving forces of progress. Contrary to Ruskin's insistence on paternalistic intervention of the state, Toynbee held that government and civic action was required to support and encourage self-help (ibid., pp. 36–8). With respect to an understanding of the moral aspect of society, Green's influence on Toynbee through religious conviction was crucial.

Following Ruskin's vision, Hobson and Toynbee actually developed different types of economics – Hobson's theoretical-ethical economics and Toynbee's historical-ethical economics – but Green's moral philosophy must have been a mediating role, if seen from the viewpoint of system construction of the Oxford approach.

It is strange that in the literature on Ruskin and Green, as far as I know, there is no description of their relationship beyond the following:

Thereafter [the late 1860s] no one at Oxford, with the possible exception of Ruskin, rivaled him [Green] in his power to stir men from their inherited allegiances and make them aware of how much remained to be done by way of reform. (Richter 1964, p. 293)

Both Ruskin and Green were sometimes counted in the succession of preachers, half a dozen in number, produced by nineteenth-century Oxford (ibid., p. 137). Even if they were vehement preachers, there was a definite difference. The Oxford tradition, whose intellectual direction was issued by Ruskin's stirring rhetoric, was provided with ethical substance by Green. Furthermore, although Green's virtue ethics or perfectionism was developed independently of Ruskin's preaching, its content was an ethical formulation of Ruskin's humanized conceptions of wealth and value. Based on Ruskin's rhetoric and Green's ethics, Toynbee's historical-ethical economics and Hobson's theoretical-ethical economics constituted an indispensable scaffolding of economics for the Oxford approach and led to the social and political movements of the new liberalism.

In view of the long history of welfare thinking, which is as long as the history of economics, it is the remarkable distinction of Hla Myint that he proposed a broader concept of welfare economics at the ethical level in addition to welfare economics at the physical level (classical economics) and at the subjective level (neoclassical economics); he located in the new camp Carlyle, Ruskin, and Morris, who objected to orthodox economics on emotional, aesthetic, and humanitarian grounds (Myint 1948, pp. 199–228). The Oxford approach formulated in this paper, as distinct from the Cambridge approach, amounts to building and legitimizing what Myint called welfare economics at the ethical level.

7. CONCLUSIONS

Economics in Cambridge at the period in question was basically neoclassical despite a difference between Marshall and Pigou: the Marshallian partial surplus analysis and the Pigouvian general equilibrium analysis (ibid., pp. 173–98). In principle, welfare judgments were based on the sophisticated analysis of a departure from optimum production and exchange. Welfare economics formulated by Pigou was based on the explicit assumption of viewing economic welfare and national income as coordinate, and the ethical foundation was to a large extent a utilitarian theory of good with ad hoc reasoning on distributive justice. Cambridge economics and ethics had no theoretical contact with the new liberal reform. Ideological commitment to the new liberalism among the Cambridge economists, if any, would have remained a matter of personal belief. There was a critical moment when Cambridge economics might have had connection with the new liberal reform: immediately after the deaths of Green and Toynbee, Marshall at Bristol was invited by chance to Balliol (1883–84), the stronghold of the Oxford approach, but he could not learn much from their disciplines (Groenewegen 1995, pp. 294–5).

In contrast, the Oxford approach entailed a mixture of success and failure. The structure of the Oxford approach in terms of economics, ethics, and ideology was consistently nonutilitarian. Oxford ethics had a low reputation by the standard of the British empirical philosophy; however, its perfectionist ethics, critical of traditional utilitarianism and concerned about quality, not quantity, of utility deriving not only from consumption but also from production, had greater influences on popular ideology through the moral preaching of Green and Toynbee. Although Oxford economics was underdeveloped by the standard of analytical economic theory, it had a distinct historical perspective, which could accommodate abstract moral philosophy to social practice and stimulate statistical inquiries of poverty as the realistic basis of social policy.

Granted that the new liberalism was a mixture of complex ideas, its proposals of social reform were not mere ideologies of emotion, inspiration, and enthusiasm, but reforms supported by the theoretical backbone of perfectionist ethics and historical economics. Both perfectionist ethics and historical economics had been transplanted from Germany and thus were received unfavorably in Britain, so that their flourishing seemed to remain a provincial affair. Nevertheless, the Oxford approach, as a package, succeeded in nourishing the genuine German seeds of welfare thinking into the growth of the new liberalism on the British soil.

It is well known that Alfred Marshall at his inaugural lecture (1885) at Cambridge, after his short stay at Oxford, seriously wished Cambridge to send out into the world an increasing number of those who, "with cool heads but warm hearts," are "willing to give some at least of their best powers to grappling with the social suffering around them" (Marshall 1925, p. 174). He might have been recollecting the moral climate at Oxford. This mission was far better performed at Oxford by Green and his pupils. One observer remarked:

The school of Green sent out into public life a stream of ex-pupils who carried with them the conviction that philosophy, and in particular the philosophy they had learnt at Oxford, was an important thing, and that their vocation was to put it into practice. ... Through this effect on the minds of its pupils, the philosophy of Green's school might be found, from 1880 to about 1910, penetrating and fertilizing every part of the national life. (Collingwood 1970, pp. 15–17, cited in Carter 2003, p. 14)

References

Allett, J. 1981. *New Liberalism: The Political Economy of J. A. Hobson.* Toronto: University of Toronto Press.

Berlin, I. 1969. *Four Essays on Liberty.* Oxford: Oxford University Press.

Boucher, D. and A. Vincent, eds. 2000. *British Idealism and Political Theory.* Edinburgh: Edinburgh University Press.

Brink, D. O. 2003. *Perfectionism and the Common Good: Themes in the Philosophy of T. H. Green.* Oxford: Clarendon Press.

Carter, M. 2003 *T. H. Green and the Development of Ethical Socialism.* Exeter: Imprint Academic.

Clarke, P. 1978. *Liberals and Social Democrats.* Cambridge: Cambridge University Press.

1996. *Hope and Glory: Britain 1900–1990.* London: Penguin Books.

Collingwood, R. G. 1970. *Autobiography.* Oxford: Clarendon Press.

Collini, S. 1979. *Liberalism and Sociology: L. T. Hobhouse and Political Argument in England 1880–1914.* Cambridge: Cambridge University Press.

Etzioni, A. 1996. *The New Golden Rule: Community and Morality in a Democratic Society.* New York: Basic Books.

Freeden, M. 1978. *The New Liberalism: An Ideology of Social Reform.* Oxford: Clarendon Press.

1996. *Ideologies and Political Theory: A Conceptual Approach.* Oxford: Clarendon Press.

2003. The Coming of the Welfare State. In *The Cambridge History of Twentieth-Century Political Thought*, eds. T. Ball and R. Bellamy. Cambridge: Cambridge University Press.

Giddens, A. 1998. *The Third Way: The Renewal of Social Democracy.* Cambridge: Polity Press.

Green, T. H. 1997a [1881]. Lecture on Liberal Legislation and Freedom of Contract. In *Collected Works of T. H. Green*, vol. 3, ed. P. Nicholson. Bristol: Thoemmes Press.

 1997b [1883]. Prolegomena to Ethics. In *Collected Works of T. H. Green*, vol. 4, ed. P. Nicholson. Bristol: Thoemmes Press.

 1997c [1886]. Lectures on the Principles of Political Obligation. In *Collected Works of T. H. Green*, vol. 2, ed. P. Nicholson. Bristol: Thoemmes Press.

Groenewegen, P. D. 1995. *A Soaring Eagle: Alfred Marshall 1842–1924*. Aldershot: Edward Elgar.

Harris, J. 1992. Political Thought and the Welfare State 1870–1940: An Intellectual Framework for British Social Policy. *Past and Present* 135(1): 116–41.

Hay, J. R. 1975. *The Origins of the Liberal Welfare Reforms 1906–1914*. London: Macmillan.

Hinton, T. 2001. The Perfectionist Liberalism of T. H. Green. *Social Theory and Practice* 27(3): 473–99.

Hobhouse, L. T. 1911. *Liberalism*. London: Thornton Butterworth.

Hobson, J. A. 1898. *John Ruskin Social Reformer*. London: James Nisbet.

 1914. *Work and Wealth: A Human Valuation*. London: Macmillan.

 1938. *Confessions of an Economic Heretic*. London: Allen & Unwin.

Kadish, A. 1982. *The Oxford Economists in the Late Nineteenth Century*. Oxford: Clarendon Press.

 1986. *Apostle Arnold: The Life and Death of Arnold Toynbee 1852–1883*. Durham: Duke University Press.

 1993. Oxford Economics in the Later Nineteenth Century. In *The Market for Political Economy: The Advent of Economics in British University Culture, 1850–1905*, eds. A. Kadish and K. Tribe. London: Routledge.

Koot, G. M. 1987. *English Historical Economics, 1870–1926: The Rise of Economic History and Neomercantilism*. Cambridge: Cambridge University Press.

Leighton, D. P. 2004. *The Greenian Moment: T. H. Green, Religion and Political Argument in Victorian Britain*. Exeter: Imprint Academic.

Marshall, A. 1925. The Present Position of Economics. In *Memorials of Alfred Marshall*, ed. A. C. Pigou. London: Macmillan.

Marshall, T. H. 1964 [1950]. Citizenship and Social Class. In *Class, Citizenship and Social Development*. New York: Doubleday.

Martin, R. 2001. T. H. Green on Individual Rights and the Common Good. In *The New Liberalism: Reconciling Liberty and Community*, eds. A. Simhony and D. Weinstein. Cambridge: Cambridge University Press.

Milner, Lord. 1920. Reminiscence. In A. Toynbee, *Lectures on the Industrial Revolution of the Eighteenth Century in England*. London: Longmans, Green, & Co.

Myint, H. 1948. *Theories of Welfare Economics*. London: Longmans.

Nicholson, P. P. 1990. *The Political Philosophy of the British Idealists: Selected Studies*. Cambridge: Cambridge University Press.

Rawls, J. 1971. *A Theory of Justice*. Cambridge, MA: Harvard University Press.

Richter, M. 1964. *The Politics of Conscience: T. H. Green and His Age.* London: Weidenfeld & Nicholson.

Ruskin, J. 1997 [1860]. Unto This Last. In *Unto This Last and Other Writings.* London: Penguin Books.

Schumpeter, J. A. 1954. *History of Economic Analysis.* New York: Oxford University Press.

Sen, A. 1985. *Commodities and Capabilities.* Amsterdam: North-Holland.

Shionoya, Y. 2004. A Reconciliation of the Liberal and Communitarian Debate in the Light of the *Methodenstreit.* In *The Invisible Hand and the Common Good,* ed. B. Hodgson. Berlin: Springer.

2005a. *The Soul of the German Historical School: Methodological Essays on Schmoller, Weber, and Schumpeter.* New York: Springer.

2005b. *Economy and Morality: The Philosophy of the Welfare State.* Cheltenham: Edward Elgar.

2006. Schmoller and Modern Economic Sociology. *Schmollers Jahrbuch,* 126(2): 177–95.

Simhony, A. 2001. T. H. Green's Complex Common Good: Between Liberalism and Communitarianism. In *The New Liberalism: Reconciling Liberty and Community,* eds. A. Simhony and D. Weinstein. Cambridge: Cambridge University Press.

Simhony, A., and D. Weinstein, eds. 2001. *The New Liberalism: Reconciling Liberty and Community.* Cambridge: Cambridge University Press.

Toynbee, A. 1920. *Lectures on the Industrial Revolution of the Eighteenth Century in England.* London: Longmans, Green, & Co.

Weiler, P. 1982. *The New Liberalism: Liberal Social Theory in Great Britain 1889–1914.* New York: Garland Publishing.

Wempe, B. 2004. *T. H. Green's Theory of Positive Freedom: From Metaphysics to Political Theory.* Exeter: Imprint Academic.

SIX

J. A. Hobson as a Welfare Economist

Roger E. Backhouse

I. INTRODUCTION

John Atkinson Hobson is renowned as an economic heretic. As a result of the remarks made by Keynes in his *General Theory* (1973 [1936]: 364–71) Hobson's heresy is generally associated with underconsumption. It can legitimately be argued that this permeates his work, from his first book, written with A. F. Mummery (1992 [1889]) to his writing on unemployment in the 1930s, taking in his analyses of industrial capitalism and imperialism along the way. Furthermore, in his autobiography, *Confessions of an Economic Heretic* (1938) Hobson presents underconsumption as the heresy that led to his systematic exclusion from academia.[1] However, the *Confessions* also presents a different view. Underconsumption is 'an early heresy' – 'the first open step in my heretical career' (1938: 30). His 'most destructive heresy' (1938: 168), on the other hand, was that bargaining power was unequal between buyers and sellers, meaning that 'whether under monopoly or so-called competitive conditions, markets are intrinsically unfair modes of distribution'.

Distribution by needs is not even approximately achieved by the ordinary higgling in a so-called competitive market. Everywhere, inequality of bargaining conditions, based on differences of needs, is represented in different amounts of gain. (Hobson and Mummery 1992 [1889]: 191–2)

---

[1] Hobson 1938: 30–1, 83–4; cf. Kadish (1990) who questions this account.

This chapter is an extensively revised version of a paper first prepared for a workshop at Hitotsubashi University in 2005. I am grateful to Peter Cain, Tamotsu Nishizawa and Donald Winch for their frequent and helpful advice. The chapter also reflects ongoing conversations with Steven Medema on welfare economics.

The reason why more attention had been paid to underconsumption than to this critique of markets was that the former was 'a quarrel within the range of quantitative economic science' (Hobson and Mummery 1992 [1889]: 164); the latter was ignored because it was too radical.

However, both of these heresies rested on a third – his view of welfare as nonquantitative and not capable of being measured in terms of money. This was the fundamental heresy being, so he believed, an integral part of the 'organic' view of society on which his entire social thought rested. In the *Confessions*, after recounting his early heresy, he continued:

The two main lines of this departure lie in the development of a 'humanistic' interpretation of the processes of production and consumption, and in the revolt against the accepted theory of *laissez-faire* as a security for the welfare of the community regarded as a productive and consumptive whole. (Hobson 1938: 8)

He then reiterated this theme in his final chapter, summarizing 'humanist economics'. On the way, he repeatedly attacked the pretensions of economics to be an exact science and even to be a science at all. Hobson was, as Wesley Clair Mitchell (1969) rightly classified him in his lectures, first and foremost a welfare economist.

Hobson's welfare economics was not taken seriously in Cambridge. Marshall, in 1900, in a letter to E. R. A. Seligman, declined an invitation to review Hobson's *The Economics of Distribution* (1900)[2] writing that he had no time to read Hobson: 'Hobson is shrewd: but his overwhelming haste is so vexatious to a slow worker' (Whitaker 1996 II: 279).[3] A year later he made a similar remark to R. T. Ely: 'There is an immense deal that is most fascinating about him; & he is certainly very able. But he is in a hurry & so he disappoints me whenever the only good work is slow work' (Whitaker 1996 II: 335). Marshall felt that Hobson had misunderstood him on marginal productivity and on consumers' surplus. In his *Principles*, Marshall (1949: 339) described him as 'apt to underrate the difficulty of the problems which he discusses'; he was, however, worth taking seriously on the 'realistic and social sides of economics'. Marshall did read *Work and Wealth*, and on one point agreed with his

---

[2] Cf. Whitaker 1996 II: 413.
[3] Clarke (1978: 133) points out that Hobson had sent Marshall comments on his *Principles* and Marshall had reciprocated by commenting on *The Social Problem* (1901). Marshall knew Hobson well enough to give him a copy of the fourth edition of his *Principles* (Whitaker 1996 II: 338).

criticism of Pigou for relying too much on static methods, though overall he felt that Hobson's criticisms of Pigou were unjustified (Bharadwaj
1972: 32–3). The instances where Pigou cites Hobson in *Wealth and
Welfare* and *The Economics of Welfare* are consistent with Marshall's
view. In the former, he cites him five times, four of which involve historical facts. In the latter, the only reference (which remained through all
four editions) was on evidence that inventions might cause unemployment. He remained completely silent on the challenge Hobson had made
to his welfare economics.

Outside Cambridge, on the other hand, Hobson was taken more seriously. His colleagues in the Workers Education Association, Henry Clay
and R. H. Tawney, expressed similar ideas about welfare.[4] Hobson was
also more widely respected in the United States.[5] Ely, in replying to the
letter mentioned above, told Marshall that, though he personally feared
that Marshall's judgment was correct, it was widely felt in the United
States that 'the English economists have not done justice to Hobson'
(Whitaker 1996 II: 336). The economist that Wesley Clair Mitchell
(1969)[6] chose as representative of welfare economics was Hobson, not
Pigou. Walton Hamilton (1919a, b) listed Hobson alongside Pigou, Smart,
Cannan, Tawney and Clay as students of welfare. Paul Homan (1927:
776, 789–90; cf 1928) considered Hobson a more creative economist
than Pigou.

Though Pigou ignored Hobson's welfare economics, Hobson paid significant attention to Pigou. Though not numerous (by modern standards
Hobson cited few other economists) his books contain citations of Pigou
at crucial points, and Cain (1992: v) is right to claim that *Work and Wealth*
can be considered a radical response to Pigou's *Wealth and Welfare*. Not
only was Hobson explicit in his criticism and rejection of marginalist economics but he remained a critic of Pigou. In *Wealth and Life*, though there
were few citations of Pigou, he pointed out that Pigou's methods offered
no basis for normative conclusions (Hobson 1929: 126–8). Comparison
helps place both types of welfare economics in perspective.[7]

---

[4] The ideas of Hobson, Clay and Tawney are discussed in relation to their religious commitments (or lack of them) in Backhouse (2008).
[5] See Rutherford (2007). Rutherford (1994), Edgell and Tilman (1994) and Neale and
Mayhew (1994) also discuss Hobson's U.S. connections but pay little attention to his
welfare economics.
[6] This publishes notes on Mitchell's lectures, delivered as early as the 1918.
[7] The following reappraisal can be compared with Medema's reappraisal of Pigou in
Chapter 3.

2. THE CONTEXT OF HOBSON'S WELFARE ECONOMICS

Hobson came, as he put it, 'from the middle stratum of the middle class of a middle-sized industrial town of the Midlands', predisposing him towards 'a complacent acceptance of the social order' (Hobson 1938: 15). He went to Oxford, and though he gives no indication of being converted to idealism in the way that many of his contemporaries were, he nonetheless acknowledged the influence of his years there.[8]

I think that my mind received from these years of study a disposition and a valuation that were of immense service in liberating me from the easy acceptance of the current ideas and feelings of an age rightly designated as materialistic and narrowly utilitarian. Something more than that I received from the atmosphere of an Oxford in which Jowett, T. H. Green, and Mark Pattison were leading figures, though my only personal contact, not a close one, was with Pattison, in his declining years. (Hobson 1938: 26)

The precise nature of the 'something more' is not elucidated.

Hobson (1929: x–xv) attached particular importance to the 1880s. In this decade, events conspired to break up what he called the complacency of the mid–Victorian era: agriculture collapsed, people moved into cities and the problem of slums became prominent. Critics of industrialism, from Carlyle to Ruskin and F. D. Maurice were, for the first time, taken seriously. Poverty came to be seen as 'a social disease, demanding social treatment and capable of remedy' (1929: xi). This 'spirit of moral revolt, the appeal to justice and humanity' (1929: xiii) also influenced academic economists, the most important of whom was Marshall who wrote that 'ethical forces are among those of which the economist has to take account' (1929: xiv). However, though Marshall acknowledged ethics, it was incidental to his theory.

In other words, what condemnations of the hardships and injustices of current industrialism appear in the authoritative economics of this period were not incorporated in the structure of the economic theory, but were of the nature of *obiter dicta* or qualifying reflections. (Hobson 1929: xiv)

Whether or not Hobson was right about the 1880s,[9] it is significant that Hobson later chose to see it this way: his own work involved taking insights, seen by Marshall and his contemporaries, and incorporating them into the body of economic theory in a way that they had failed to do.[10]

---

[8] Oxford idealism is discussed in detail in Chapter 5 by Shionoya.

[9] For one discussion, see Stedman Jones (1884).

[10] This is consistent with the view, stressed by Donald Winch (2009), that Hobson failed to recognise the extent of his debt to Marshall.

Though Hobson (1938: 38) claimed that his main ideas had come earlier, in his *Evolution of Modern Capitalism* (1894), a book he had written because the Fabian, William Clarke, was unable to fulfil his obligation to write it, the main impetus to his writing on the 'humanization of economic science and art' came from an invitation from Charles Mallet to write what became *John Ruskin: Social Reformer* (1898). Whereas he had previously been repelled by certain aspects of Ruskin's work, he now began to see the logic of his position. Central to this was seeing terms such as *wealth*, *value* and *profit* in their proper relation to life, instead of being interpreted so as to serve a business mentality. These ideas were developed in lectures to the Christian Social Union, and published in Stanton Coit's *Ethical World*, a Saturday penny paper started in 1898, to which Ramsey MacDonald was also a significant contributor, before being more fully written up as *The Social Problem* (1901).[11] In this, perhaps the first full statement of Hobson's position, it is clear that the economic cannot be separated from the political and social.

Of more direct significance was Hobson's involvement with ethical societies.[12] After a spell in the London Ethical Society and the Charity Organisation Society, alongside the idealist philosophers J. H. Muirhead and Bernard Bosanquet, in 1897 he joined his Oxford friend, and Fabian, Graham Wallas at the South Place Ethical Society, whose pastor, Stanton Coit, had moved it in a more socialist direction (Clarke 1978: 53–4). He became active in politics, through his journalism and his contacts with prominent Liberals and Fabians.[13] *The Industrial System* (1909) had the luck to appear just a fortnight after Lloyd George's so-called people's budget. This book, subtitled 'An inquiry into earned and unearned income', built on ideas about rent as a surplus that Hobson had been developing since the 1890s, adding the novel distinction between the 'productive' and the 'unproductive' surplus. The former included any payments necessary to induce growth. The latter served no useful function: rather it served to increase saving, contributing to problems of underconsumption and imperialism. The *Nation*, a New Liberal weekly with which Hobson was associated, wrote of this book as 'a theoretical exposition of the principles of democratic finance at the very

---

[11] On the *Ethical World*, see MacKillop (1986: 147–61).

[12] See Backhouse (2008). See also Hobson (1938: 49–58); Clarke (1978: 51–4).

[13] It was, of course, at this time that Hobson took up, through his reporting of the Boer War, the theme of imperialism to which much attention has been paid (see Cain 2002).

moment at which Mr Lloyd George has been administering a practical demonstration' (29 May 1909, quoted in Clarke 1978: 115).[14]

Thus when Pigou's *Wealth and Welfare* was published in 1912, though Hobson had not published a major work on welfare economics per se, he had written extensively on the ethical principles surrounding welfare, on the problem of income distribution, and had been actively involved in the political debates surrounding the Liberal government's moves towards what eventually became the welfare state.

3. THE NEW UTILITARIANISM AND SOCIAL REFORM

In *The Social Problem*, Hobson called for a 'new utilitarianism':

This science and art of social utility is clearly sundered from the old utilitarianism which was individualistic and hedonist in its standard, and purely quantitative in its method or calculus. (Hobson 1901: v–vi)

It differed from the old utilitarianism in viewing problems from the perspective of society as a whole, in adopting ethical judgments broader than hedonism, and in allowing that activities might differ in quality as well as in quantity. Though an analysis of society, involving sociology and politics, the book was formulated as a critique of political economy, whether in its older or newer form. Hobson was, in a sense, retrieving utilitarianism from what it had suffered in the hands of economists.

[O]ur setting must be in the full sense of the work, 'utilitarian'. The premature abandonment of the utilitarian setting by many thinkers, through pique arising from the narrow and degrading interpretation given to the term, has not been justified. ... The particular vices of some special form of utilitarianism, the insistence that desirability was entirely to be measured by quantity and never by quality, the stress upon physical enjoyment, and the short range of measurement, which were somewhat incorrectly attributed to Bentham's system, are not inherent in utilitarianism, and need not deter us from using its convenient language. (Hobson 1901: 4–5)

He could hardly have made it clearer that his intention was to rehabilitate utilitarianism.

In seeking an ancestor for his broader view of the social question, Hobson goes back briefly to Adam Smith whose concept of the wealth of nations was 'large and liberal', encompassing not just goods

---

[14] In Chapter 8 Toye points out that, whilst Hobson and fellow New Liberals may have influenced politicians, the evidence is circumstantial. He contrasts this with the evidence that members of the government were reading H. G. Wells at this time.

but 'knowledge, freedom, health, and character' (Hobson 1901: 21). Smith was also inspired by social justice, Hobson linking him with Thomas Paine and William Godwin.[15] Laissez-faire was a policy to provide freedom for labourers, not the policy of 'despotism and degradation' that it became at the hands of the subsequent generation of 'mill-owners, financiers, and their intellectual henchmen' (Hobson 1901: 22). Smith's broad conception of freedom was narrowed by the generation of utilitarians that seized control over political economy soon afterwards.

What went wrong within political economy, Hobson claimed, was that wealth came to be associated with marketable wealth and with material goods: with the getting of wealth at the expense of using it (Hobson 1901: 26). The only well-developed part of economics concerned the production of material goods. Economists paid attention to other motives, including moral and religious ones, but such qualifications to the notion that men were driven by greed and idleness were 'purely parenthetic, ... not built into the body of the science' (Hobson 1901: 37). His targets were Cairnes, for whom moral and religious motivations amounted to frictions, Sidgwick, who excluded culture, and Marshall who excluded 'moral wealth' on the grounds that it could be considered wealth only by poetic licence (Hobson 1901: 36–7). The error, represented by Marshall, was considering the getting and spending of wealth to define a 'fairly homogeneous group' of activities (Hobson 1901: 52). Marshall, in practice, understood 'the ordinary business of life' very narrowly, as merely the getting and spending of money (Hobson 1901: 20). These claims, to which Hobson objected on Ruskinian grounds, were later developed extensively in *Work and Wealth*.

Another theme that became important in his later work was his attack on the pretensions of economics to be a science. A reason why economists were dumb concerning the social question was that they believed economics to be a science and that they were not 'practitioners', able to offer remedies for problems such as unemployment or poverty (Hobson 1901: 18). In the hands of economists from Smith to Mill and Jevons, on the other hand, 'the science grew out of the art' (ibid.) Historical research and theorizing about method were important, but it was also necessary to diagnose remedies. Another reason was that the important problems faced by society were not purely economic, and hence not amenable to analysis by 'economic science' alone. For example, to

---

[15] Rothschild (2001) has recently emphasized this side of Smith.

adjudicate on the merits of the 'Eight Hours' Question', it was necessary to consider not just the strictly economic effects, but also the effects on workers' leisure. Similarly, free trade should be judged, not just by its effects on material consumption, but in relation to 'the total effects – hygienic, intellectual, and moral – arising from town and factory life ... in organic relation to the direct gains of increased industrial wealth' (Hobson 1901: 20).

Confronting the Cambridge economists, especially John Neville Keynes, directly, Hobson denied that positive and normative questions could be separated: 'If a "fact" has moral import, ... that moral import is part of the nature of the fact, and the fact cannot be fully known as fact without taking it into consideration' (Hobson 1901: 66–7). The study of positive facts alone amounted to a policy of 'moral emasculation' (ibid.). It was defended on the grounds that it was necessary to study one thing at a time, but Hobson found this unacceptable, for organisms (including society) had to be seen as a whole. Such an attitude was a symptom of a more general intellectual over-specialization, where researchers became like the earthworm:

The most minute specialist in the animal kingdom is, perhaps, the earthworm, which devotes its life to passing sedulously through its body tiny fragments of the little patch of earth in which it lies. To this process it has sacrificed every other function, and yet it knows less about the earth even than the mole, and much less than the rabbit. So with the intellectual earthworm. (Hobson 1901: 232)

Such a strategy was, even from the point of view of acquiring knowledge, generally a failure.

Consistent with this view, Hobson did not refrain from addressing possible solutions. All but the last of the points so far mentioned come from Book I of *The Social Problem*, entitled 'The science of social progress'. This was followed by Book II, almost three times as long, on 'The art of social progress'. Here he engaged with questions of social philosophy: individualism and socialism, private property and distribution according to need. The existence of this part of his book is, for the present argument, more important than its content. Suffice it to say that Hobson was systematically critical of individualist solutions, even where they were proposed by socialists. Thus he described as fatuous the attempts of Carlyle, Ruskin and Christian Socialists to achieve reform through voluntary actions by employers (Hobson 1901: 136). More fundamentally, wealth was created by society, not simply by the individual.

4. LIFE, WORK AND WEALTH

Hobson defined the purpose of *Work and Wealth* as being to complete the task identified by John Ruskin: 'to determine what are in reality useful or life-giving things, and by what degrees and kind of labor they are attainable and distributable' (*Munera Pulveris*, quoted in Hobson 1914: 10). He interpreted this as developing a human standard of value by which the welfare of society could be established. Society was, he claimed, an organic whole and had to be analyzed as such. 'Organic welfare' was a measure of welfare that took account of society as an organic structure, the value of whose parts depended on their role in the whole. Hobson interpreted it as meaning that 'every act of production or consumption' had to be valued 'with regard to its aggregate effect upon the life and character of the agent' (1914: 14). At its most general, it was no more than 'a synonym for good life' (1914: 12) and had very little content. The notion acquired content as Hobson applied it to the process of production and consumption of wealth.

Hobson used his concept of organic welfare to develop a critique of what he called 'current economic science'[16] which had three defects (1914: 9): an exaggerated stress on production, a standard of value that bore no consistent relation to human welfare and a mechanical conception of the economic system caused by valuing human actions according to their relation to the production of non-human wealth. More specifically, economic science assumed that production involved human costs (associated with labour and the supply of capital) and that consumption merely yielded utilities: the utilities associated with production and the costs associated with consumption were neglected. The reason for this was that economists had developed their theories of production in great detail but had completely neglected the study of consumption: analysis stopped, Hobson claimed, once goods passed over to the household, there being a serious lack of research on the family (1914: 110). To work out the human value of national income it was necessary to look backwards to the processes in which goods were produced and forwards to the processes in which they were consumed. His more detailed summary of this (1914: 35) merits being considered in detail.

Or the several stages of interpretation may be expressed as follows. [1] A given money income must first be resolved into the concrete goods which it expresses: [2] those goods must then be resolved into the various efforts of

---

[16] The significance of the word 'science' will be discussed later.

production and satisfactions of consumption, estimated according to the current ideas and desires of the individuals who experience them: [3] these current individual estimates of the desirable must be adjusted by reference to an ideal standard of the socially desirable. The extent of this latter process of adjustment will, of course, depend upon how far the actual current ideas and feelings of individuals are kept in essential harmony with the true standard of social well-being by the natural evolution of an organic society.

The first stage in this argument was to consider individual goods. The reason for this is, the second step in his argument, that Hobson believed that valuation in terms of money bore little relation to human valuation. He analyzed this in two stages: looking backwards to factor supply and forwards to consumption.

Using the conventional classification, Hobson divided the costs of production into the returns to land, capital and labour, dividing the last of these into ability and common labour. Rents, the return to land, had to be paid in a system of private property but corresponded to no human cost. There might be a private cost to using land, but the 'organic cost' was zero. More controversially, he applied the same argument to that part of the capital stock resulting from 'the automatic saving of the rich' (1914: 98). The rich had so much that no human cost was involved in their investing part of their incomes. Hobson argued that this was particularly true for what Milton Friedman later called transitory income. For the working class, on the other hand, saving involved very high human costs: it might be at the expense of consumption that was badly needed to sustain living standards for the poor. In between came the middle classes: some of their saving entailed no human cost that required compensation by payment of interest. Other saving by the middle classes did involve human cost.

Hobson's analysis of the human cost of labour owes a clear debt to Ruskin, for he takes as his starting point the work of the artist, for whom work has no net human cost: the work is rewarding in itself (provided the artist has enough to support himself). As art becomes commercialized, control is lost and human costs rise. Similarly, science could be creative and be of direct value to the scientist. At the other end of the scale was repetitive manual labour, exemplified by machine minding (1914: 61):

To feed the same machinery with the same quantity of the same material at the same pace, so as to turn out an endless number of precisely similar articles, is the absolute antithesis of art.

Repetition and routine could be of value, sparing people the effort of creative thought, but on the whole such work was costly (1914: 83). Work was also costly when liberty and spontaneity were suppressed, as in the case of domestic service: if a servant performed the same task as a housewife, the human cost was higher because it involved doing someone else's bidding (1914: 85). As was to be expected, middle class occupations came in between these two poles, though closer to that of the artist: the professional man, like the artist or the scientist, was constantly doing new things. The result was that Hobson considered manual labour to have the highest human cost and professional labour much less – a reversal of the ranking suggested by their relative wage rates.

At the other end of the process, Hobson argued that consumption required the development of tastes and above all knowledge. Where consumption was necessary to survival, the process of consumption was simple, but when living standards rise, people are faced with 'ever larger and more numerous elements which carry little or no "survival value", [and] the possibilities of error and of disutility appear to multiply' (1914: 117). Echoing Veblen, whose *Theory of the Leisure Class* (1899) he cited with approval, he argued that having business organized for profit led to consumption that was harmful, to the degradation of many consumption goods and to the stimulation or suppression of wants according to the interests of business rather than the interests of consumers (1914: 112). Many wants were 'artificial' (1914: 118). Conventions might help guide expenditure where the value of different activities was uncertain. Interestingly, given Hobson's largely middle class perspective, he argued that there could be value in certain activities that economists frequently dismissed as wasteful working class spending, such as high spending on public holidays, on drink and on funerals (1914: 127).

Hobson went on to deduce the optimal distribution of wealth:

Now the Human Law of Distribution, in its application to industry, aims ... to distribute Wealth, in relation to its production on the one hand and its consumption on the other, so as to secure the minimum of Human Costs and the maximum of Human Utility. (1914: 163–4)

People's common humanity meant that, in such a distribution, every adult should have a minimum standard of life, adjusted for their specific needs (1914: 168). There would be some inequality but much less than currently existed. Though he did not accept that people were identical, he believed that rents of ability were largely the result of 'artificial restrictions in opportunity of education and of competition, which have no natural basis' (1914: 166). Equality of opportunity and 'approximate' equalization of income would destroy these (1914: 169).

These ideas on welfare were reiterated and expanded in *Wealth and Life* (1929). There, he criticized orthodox economists, not for analysing a selfish, gain-seeking 'economic man', but for failing to acknowledge that this is what they were doing (1929: 454–5). Such work, proceeding 'by a process of abstraction and assumptions which are a serviceable falsification, or simplification, of the subject-matter submitted to this scientific treatment' was a legitimate part of the scientific division of labour.

In all the deductive framework of an economic science, it is right frankly to adopt, in the 'as if' spirit, a simplification of man, in his capacity of producer-consumer and buyer-seller. ... [However,] In the objective studies, upon a statistical basis, to which economics is more and more addicting itself, the consideration of non-economic motives and activities are necessarily brought up for purposes of interpretation and, so far as is admissible, of quantitative estimation. (Hobson 1929: 455)

There was, however, a critical note in that he argued that when economists found, as they would, that other motives were operating, they would 'regard these as "friction" interfering with the purely economic conduct'. He then proceeded, in a passage the first sentence of which is reminiscent of Mitchell (1925), though there is no evidence for such a link, to claim:

The new knowledge, acquired by observation and experiment in the field of industrial psychology, is laying a solid foundation to an inductive political economy, and is sapping the distrust with which the practical business man formerly regarded the counsels and prophesies of the theoretical economists. Much of this knowledge, the accurate records of close study of economic behaviour, may also be regarded as an approach towards a more humanist interpretation of economic processes, in so far as it re-inserts in the economic plan many of the factors eliminated in the earlier search for the laws and principles of a deductive science. (Hobson 1929: 455)

However, such a 'behaviourist' economics cannot of itself pronounce on welfare, which involves qualitative valuation:

The economic treatment will remain essentially quantitative, the humanist treatment qualitative. The former will seek to answer the question, 'How many men can live with the highest average standard of economic life upon this area?' The latter will ask, 'What population will yield the best results in terms of human personality as expressed in due satisfaction of all physical and spiritual needs?' (Hobson 1929: 456)

The success of the economic art would lie in making itself redundant.

5. HOBSON AND THE UTILITARIAN TRADITION

On the face of it, despite the calls for a 'new utilitarianism' discussed above, it is hard to think of Hobson as a utilitarian. His emphasis on society as an organism, his great reliance on evolutionary arguments and his complete rejection of the marginalism that underlies the utilitarian calculus would seem to place him far outside the utilitarian tradition. However, despite rejection of marginalism, much of Hobson's case was couched in utilitarian terms. His talk of minimizing human costs and maximizing human utility bore a close resemblance to the utilitarian minimization of pain and maximization of pleasure.[17] To speak of the costs associated with consumption and the utility associated with labour is entirely consistent with utilitarianism, of which it could be seen as an extension.

The main difference between Hobson and the utilitarians would appear to be that utilitarianism involves measuring welfare through the summation of individuals' utilities, whereas Hobson argued for a different standard of welfare: what he called 'organic welfare'. To obtain this, as the quotation on page 12 shows, he had to go beyond individuals' valuations of their own consumption to social valuations. As he recognized, this involved making ethical judgments. This was something that earlier utilitarians had been quite prepared to do. Mill (1969: 211) had written that 'some *kinds* of pleasure are more desirable and more valuable than others'. He sought to justify this by arguing that it reflected the judgment of those capable of experiencing both higher and lower pleasures (implying a hierarchy in which inferior people could not experience the same range of pleasures as superior with people). It was clearly an ethical judgment, not least because it involved one person evaluating the pleasure experienced by another. Though Bentham did not differentiate utilities in this way, he was nonetheless prepared to make moral judgments about what did and did not increase or decrease pleasure or pain. Mitchell (1969 II: 505–6) reached the same conclusion.

He [Hobson] does not talk about pleasures and pains, but about sacrifices and utilities. To all intents and purposes his terms mean to this generation [circa 1918] what Bentham's terms pleasure and pain meant to the generation that was flourishing between, say, 1800 and 1833. ... Hobson is in many respects far more akin spiritually to Bentham than to any other writer previously discussed, not simply in his procedure, his methods of thought, but in his fundamental interest.

---

[17] Hamilton (1915: 582) went so far as to refer to Hobson's 'hedonism'.

It is also worth noting that Hobson (1898: 85) argued that his hero, Ruskin, though in no sense a hedonist, might 'not inaptly be classed as a utilitarian'.

A further Utilitarian element in Hobson's work is that, although it was full of evolutionary arguments, he defended his ethical judgments in terms that could have been taken straight from Sidgwick's *Methods of Ethics* (1874): an appeal to common sense. In the final chapter of *Work and Wealth*, Hobson (1914: 320) pointed out that his 'human valuation of industry involved at the outset the arbitrary assumption of a standard of value'. This made sense only if there could be wide agreement on such a standard. His argument was, though people disagreed about how to define abstract terms such as 'human welfare', there would be widespread agreement on practical issues.

The truth of our standard and the validity of our calculus are established by this working test [consensus on practical issues]. It is not wonderful[18] that this should be so, for the nature and circumstances of mankind have so much in common, and the processses of civilisation are so powerfully assimilating them, as to furnish a continually increasing community of experience and feeling. It is, of course, this fund of 'common sense' that constitutes the true criterion [of welfare]. (Hobson 1914: 321)

Hobson went on to ask whether 'common sense' could be adequate, pointing out that it had to be read as 'enlightened common sense', which he implies should be that of 'the many' rather than 'the few'. He acknowledged that there were limits beyond which scientific analysis could not be taken. However, it bears repetition that appealing to common sense in this way was precisely the method of Sidgwick. It is also worth pointing out that several of his remarks on the standard of consumption and the generation of 'artificial wants', though no doubt owing as much to Veblen, resonate with Marshall's (1949: 575ff.) discussion of standards of comfort and standards of life.

In contrast, the Cambridge economists accepted only a limited form of utilitarianism. They used marginal analysis and made the assumptions necessary to adopt an aggregative approach, differentiating their approach from the tradition represented by Pareto and Robbins (see Blaug 1997). However, they tried to distance themselves from utilitarianism. According to Raffaelli (2003), Marshall had abandoned utilitarianism as an ethical philosophy as early as 1870. He sought to turn economics into an engine of economic analysis based on a minimum

---

[18] In the sense of 'surprising'.

of assumptions, in which ethical judgements did not intrude.[19] Pigou's welfare economics arguably returned to the earlier Mill-Sidgwick approach, but using the analytic apparatus worked out by Marshall (see O'Donnell 1979: 588). However, mindful that utilitarianism could be seen as hedonism – discredited by G. E. Moore – he was careful to use the term satisfaction rather than utility, thereby seeking to distance himself from imposing ethical judgements.

There is another sense in which Pigou moved away from utilitarianism. As Sidgwick (1901: 81–5) had recognized, utilitarianism led directly to the conclusion that welfare (where goods are valued at their average utilities) would not necessarily be proportional to wealth (where they are valued at marginal utilities). Pigou took up this theme when, at the start of *Wealth and Welfare* (1912: 5), he provided a list of reasons why economic welfare (which took account of satisfactions) was not the same as total welfare (which depended on cognitions, emotions and desires as well as satisfactions) and discussed the importance of feeling, character and conditions of work on welfare. Yet he went on to deny their importance when he argued that the failure of 'economic welfare' to measure 'total welfare' was 'of but slight importance' (Pigou 1912: 4), thereby negating one of the direct consequences of utilitarianism.[20] This was grounded on a subjective, seemingly unsubstantiated judgment of probability (Pigou 1912: 11).

Similarly, Pigou found many reasons to shy away from the radical implication that utilitarianism implied that incomes should be equalized. He relied on the purely negative argument that there was no reason to suppose that increases in the national dividend would not be associated with increases in the earnings of labour and hence with rises in economic welfare (1912: 95). Furthermore, artificial raising of wages (by unions or government) might harm the national dividend (Pigou 1912: 243). In both cases, Pigou is using unsubstantiated quantitative judgements to disregard a theoretical implication of utilitarianism. The best route to redistribution was voluntary transfers, a very conservative conclusion (Pigou 1912: 358–65). One might conclude from this that Pigou was using utilitarianism as little more than a framework within which to pursue the 'scientific' and ostensibly ethically neutral economics of Marshall.

Hobson, in contrast, emphasised the divergences between wealth and welfare that Pigou acknowledged but disregarded. Where Sidgwick, Marshall and arguably Pigou, stepped back from radical programs of

---

[19] See Backhouse (2006). Of course, to say this is not to claim he was successful.
[20] After Chapter 1, such factors were neglected (see Levin 1956: 128).

redistribution, Hobson firmly embraced the radical cause, providing it with a theoretical basis grounded in his new utilitarianism.

6. HOBSON AND PIGOU ON 'SCIENTIFIC ECONOMICS'

Perhaps the greatest difference between Pigou and Hobson was their attitude towards being scientific. They shared the belief that science involved quantification, but from that starting point they moved in different directions. On the opening page of *Wealth and Welfare*, Pigou (1912: 3) defined economic welfare as 'those parts of the community's net income that enter easily into relation with the measuring rod of money'. It was because economic welfare was measurable that it could be the subject of scientific analysis. He was explicit in excluding other factors:

Economic welfare, however, does not contain all welfare arising in this connection [the earning and spending of the national dividend]. Various good and bad qualities indirectly associated with income-getting and income-spending are excluded from it. It does not include the whole psychic return, which emerges when the objective services constituting the national dividend have passed through the factory of the body; it includes only the psychic return of *satisfaction*. Thus economic welfare is, as it were, a part of welfare. (Pigou 1914: 3–4; emphasis in original)

This statement provides a wonderfully concise statement of Hobson's critique of orthodox economics. However, whereas Hobson explored precisely these psychic returns, arguing that they meant organic welfare was very different from national income, Pigou went on to minimize the significance of gaps between welfare and that which could be measured in terms of money.

Hobson did not explicitly challenge these boundaries of 'economic science' but went beyond them. The result was that he presented his work as an attack on science. He wrote,

the mechanical method of marginalism lies in its insistence upon applying a quantitative method of interpretation to the most qualitative portion of the subject matter ... Indeed, it is for this reason that economic science, though able to supply relevant and important evidence, can never solve conclusively any social-economic problem, even in that field of action where her authority is most strongly asserted. (Hobson 1914: 344–5)

This implied that it was not just Pigou's economics, but economic science itself that was limited. Hobson made it clear that he associated science with quantification: it was impossible to base 'safe mechanical rules' to guide policy on 'measured facts', which were 'soft and ineffective tools' (Hobson 1914: 323).

Some contemporaries accepted this boundary of 'economic science'. Macgreggor (1914: 560), in reviewing *Work and Wealth*, claimed that in some chapters Hobson aimed at a 'scientific treatment' while in others he 'lets himself go on broader questions'. Hobson's reasoning was described as 'sociological and partly economic'. He concluded that (perhaps safely for a Cambridge economist writing in the *Economic Journal*) the book was 'a great contribution to sociology, taking economics as its point of departure' (Macgreggor 1914: 563). In contrast, John Maurice Clark (1914: 177) more perceptively noted that though Hobson's book was presented as an attack on science, it should be appraised as a work of social science. Similarly, Mitchell (1969: 514) claimed that Hobson was 'trying to make a social science of welfare'. Despite Hobson's remarks about 'economic science', he believed that his analysis was scientific and of practical value (Mitchell 1969: 518). Mitchell himself claimed that Hobson's analysis of welfare was just as scientific, in the sense of developing a 'non-numerical but quantitative analysis' as Edgeworth, Marshall or Wieser.[21]

As for Hobson's concept of 'organic welfare', one might argue that, even though it may have been based on a discredited concept of organicism (Handman 1915: 314), such terminology was inessential and that in principle there was little difference between this and Pigou's 'social' costs and benefits. Though he did not express it this way, he was arguing that production had costs that were not reflected in market transactions, implying, as did Pigou's distinction between private and social costs, that market prices did not reflect the marginal costs and benefits that were appropriate to judgements about welfare. In short, Hobson, had he been inclined to do so, could have expressed himself in language that would have been less likely to place him at odds with Pigou. Later on (Hobson 1926: 469ff.), he did try to do this, expressing his critique in hedonistic terms, criticizing Pigou and Edwin Cannan for not being consistent in their hedonism.

However, this would not have eliminated the differences with Pigou, for these lay not only in beliefs about the appropriate domain of inquiry and the language and methods appropriate for analysing it, but also in purely economic assumptions. He denied that goods were perfectly divisible, that capital and labour could move freely from one employment to another, and that conditions were static (Hobson 1914: 170–4;

[21] Mitchell (1969: 508–20) provides the best available discussion of whether Hobson's ideas on welfare can be considered 'scientific'.

c.f. 1925).[22] Such assumptions were made solely in order to permit mathematical analysis, but because Hobson did not wish to use mathematics, he could reject them as inappropriate.[23] It is also clear from earlier discussions that he did not take preferences as given and that he believed that economic agents had different levels of bargaining power. Perhaps more interesting, he wrote of consumption as an almost Hayekian discovery process. Where consumers were purchasing goods necessary for their survival, rationality might prevail, but beyond that point they had to discover what they wanted (Hobson 1914: 113–20). Marginalism was misleading because, at the margin, expenditures must be random as consumers experiment with goods to find out what they want.

7. CONCLUSIONS

As Green had turned idealism, a conservative philosophy in the hands of Hegel, into a radical, liberal doctrine, so Hobson turned Ruskin's critique of political economy into a doctrine with radical implications, verging on socialism. His influence on policy is unclear, but these ideas certainly circulated in radical circles – associated with the Liberal Party before 1914 and the Labour Party after 1918 – out of which the welfare state emerged. In seeking to ground estimations of welfare on widely shared value judgements (or, at least, on ones believed to be widely shared) he was following in a well-established 19th century tradition. That placed him at odds with the intellectual outlook, represented most clearly in economics with Robbins's *Essay*, and exemplified in philosophy by logical positivism, which sought to dispense with metaphysics. To oppose the scientific pretensions of economics was, quite apart from any looseness in his own arguments, to swim against the tide. For Hobson (1929:128), Pigou and Robbins were on the same side in adopting a narrow view of science:

Supporters of Pigou contend that, if we introduce distinctively ethical criteria, we and ourselves in a region not merely outside measurable facts, but outside agreed facts. This is clearly put by Mr. Lionel Robbins [1927: 176]. 'It is not because we believe that our science is exact that we wish to exclude ethics from

---

[22] Such criticisms of marginalism surfaced again and again in his work, notably Hobson (1900, 1901, 1925).

[23] Of Marshall, he wrote that his 'hankerings after humanity continually break the rigour of his mathematical proclivities' (Hobson 1901: 58; cf. Clarke 1978: 133). Mathematical analysis constrained what could be said, excluding much of the human dimension of economic activity.

our analysis, but because we wish to confine our investigations to a subject about which positive statement of any kind is conceivable.'

Hobson saw Robbins as a supporter of Pigou, not despite the views on economic science for which he is famous, but *because of* those views. If note is taken of Robbins's (1927: 175–6) remark that 'there is more to be said for utilitarianism as a necessary fiction of pragmatic politics than he [Hawtrey] is willing to allow', the gap between him and Pigou appears even narrower.[24] It is thus not surprising that in 1935, as Medema (Chapter 3: 42–61) observes, that Pigou could endorse Robbins's remark that ethics lie outside economic science.

Comparison with Hobson also serves to distance Pigou and Cambridge welfare economics from utilitarianism.[25] They were utilitarian in that they made interpersonal comparisons, but they shied away from the most distinctive implications of utilitarianism: the ideas that wealth and welfare might diverge and that redistribution from rich to poor had a tendency to raise welfare. Pigou understood both points but he was extremely cautious in drawing conclusions from them.[26] In contrast, these ideas were central to Hobson's welfare economics. Thus, despite his immense debt to Ruskin, his biology-inspired organicism and his rejection of marginalism, Hobson was arguably more of a utilitarian than Pigou. Furthermore, in many ways Hobson was more in the tradition of the early utilitarians: he was an active, politically engaged reformer whose ideas were rooted in what he believed to be commonly shared human values. Perhaps Hobson played a role, combining economic analysis with political involvement, closer to that of Mill because he never became a professional academic economist, but the contrast still holds.

It is probably significant that the main supporters of Hobson's welfare economics were associated with American institutionalism, a movement that, by the 1940s, came to be seen as out of touch with prevailing conceptions of what it meant to be scientific. With the waning of institutionalism, economists such as J. M. Clark and Hamilton were seen as less central figures than they appeared to be at the time. Mitchell's reputation has remained, but he has come to be seen as a

---

[24] Robbins also echoed this view of the practical necessity of utilitarianism long after his *Essay*.

[25] Levin (1956: 127) has also pointed out that whereas Mill and Marshall saw human character as important in itself, Pigou was concerned with how population quality would affect output.

[26] See the discussion of his views on taxation in Chapter 4 by Daunton.

number cruncher rather than as an economist whose views on economic theory need to be taken seriously. This has made it easier for historians to dismiss Hobson as a marginal figure, focusing on his underconsumptionism and his theory of imperialism (where the stature of Keynes and Lenin means his ideas are harder to neglect) and to forget the welfare economics that, according to his own confession, constituted his most destructive heresy.

References

Backhouse, R. E. 2006. Sidgwick, Marshall and the Cambridge School of Economics. *History of Political Economy* 38(1): 15–44.

2008. Faith, Morality and Welfare: The 'English School of Welfare Economics'. *History of Political Economy* 40 (Annual Supplement): 212–36.

Bharadwaj, K. 1972. Marshall on Pigou's Wealth and Welfare. *Economica* 39: 32–46.

Blaug, M. 1997. *Economic Theory in Retrospect*, 5th edition. Cambridge: Cambridge University Press.

Cain, P. J. 1992. Introduction. In *Work and Wealth*, by J. A. Hobson, v–xiv. Bristol: Thoemmes Press.

2002. *Hobson and Imperialism: Radicalism, New Liberalism and Finance 1887–1938*. Oxford: Oxford University Press.

Clark, J. M. 1914. Review of Work and Wealth by J. A. Hobson. *Quarterly Journal of Economics* 29(1): 177–80.

Clarke, P. 1978. *Liberals and Social Democrats*. Cambridge: Cambridge University Press.

Edgell, S., and R. Tilman. 1994. John Hobson: Admirer and Critic of Thorstein Veblen. In *J. A. Hobson after Fifty Years*, ed. J. Pheby, 211–24. London: Macmillan.

Hamilton, W. H. 1915. Economic Theory and 'Social Reform'. *Journal of Political Economy* 23(6): 562–84.

1919a. An Appraisal of Clay's Economics. *Journal of Political Economy* 27(4): 300–9.

1919b. The Institutional Approach to Economic Theory. *American Economic Review* 9: 309–18.

Handman, M. S. 1915. Review of Work and Wealth by J.A. Hobson. *American Economic Review* 5: 314–15.

Hobson, J. A. 1894. *The Evolution of Modern Capitalism*. London: Walter Scott.

1898. *John Ruskin: Social Reformer*. London: James Nisbet. Reprinted in Hobson 1992.

1900. *The Economics of Distribution*. London: Macmillan.

1901. *The Social Problem*. London: Nisbet.

1909. *The Industrial System: An Inquiry into Earned and Unearned Income*. London: Longman.

1914. *Work and Wealth*. London: Macmillan. Reprinted Bristol: Thoemmes Press, 1992.

1925. Neo-classical Economics in Britain. *Political Science Quarterly* 40(3): 337–83. Reprinted in Hobson 1992.

1926. Economic Art and Human Welfare. *Journal of Philosophical Studies* 1:467–80. Reprinted in Hobson 1992.

1929. *Wealth and Life*. London: Macmillan.

1938. *Confessions of an Economic Heretic*. London: George Allen and Unwin.

1992. *Writings on Distribution and Welfare*. Bristol: Thoemmes Press.

Hobson, J. A., and Mummery, A. F. 1992 [1889]. *The Physiology of Industry*. London: Routledge/Thoemmes Press.

Homan, P. T. 1927. The Impasse in Economic Theory. *Journal of Political Economy* 35(6): 776–803.

1928. *Contemporary Economic Thought*. New York: Harper.

Kadish, A. 1990. Rewriting the Confessions: Hobson and the Extension Movement. In *Reappraising J. A. Hobson: Humanism and Welfare*, ed. M. Freeden, 137–66. London: Routledge.

Keynes, J. M. 1973 [1936]. *The General Theory of Employment, Interest and Money. The Collected Writings of John Maynard Keynes*, volume VII. London Macmillan.

Levin, H. J. 1956. Standards of Welfare in Economic Thought. *Quarterly Journal of Economics* 70(1): 117–38.

Macgreggor, D. H. 1914. Review of Work and Wealth by J. A. Hobson. *Economic Journal* 24: 560–63.

MacKillop, I. D. 1986. *British Ethical Societies*. Cambridge University Press: Cambridge.

Marshall, A. 1949. *Principles of Economics*. London: Macmillan.

Mill, J. S. 1969. Utilitarianism. In *Essays on Ethics, Religion and Society (The Collected Works of John Stuart Mill)*, volume 10, ed. J. M. Robson. Toronto: University of Toronto Press.

Mitchell, W. C. 1925. Quantitative Analysis in Economic Theory. *American Economic Review* 15(1): 1–12.

1969. *Types of Economic Theory: From Mercantilism to Institutionalism*. New York: Augustus Kelley.

Neale, W. C., and A. Mayhew. 1994. Hobson, Veblen and American Institutionalism. In *J. A. Hobson after Fifty Years*, ed. J. Pheby, 225–37. London: Macmillan.

O'Donnell, M. G. 1979. Pigou: An Extension of Sidgwickian Thought. *History of Political Economy* 11(4): 588–605.

Pigou, A. C. 1912. *Wealth and Welfare*. London: Macmillan.

1920. *The Economics of Welfare*. London: Macmillan.

1932. *The Economics of Welfare*. 4th ed. London: Macmillan. Reprinted 1946.

Raffaelli, T. 2003. *Marshall's Evolutionary Economics*. London: Routledge.

Robbins, L. C. 1927. Mr. Hawtrey on the Scope of Economics. *Economica* 20: 172–8.

1935. *An Essay on the Nature and Significance of Economic Science*. 2nd ed. London: Macmillan.

2001. *Economic Sentiments*. Cambridge, MA: Harvard University Press.

Rothschild, E. 2001. *Economic Sentiments: Adam Smith, Condorcet and the Enlightenment*. Cambridge, MA: Harvard University Press.

Rutherford, M. 1994. J. A. Hobson and American Institutionalism: Under-Consumptionism and Technological Change. In *J. A. Hobson after Fifty Years*, ed. J. Pheby, 188–210. London: Macmillan.

2007. American Institutionalism and Its English Connections. *European Journal of the History of Economic Thought* 14(2): 291–323.

Sidgwick, H. 1874. *The Methods of Ethics*. London: Macmillan.

1883. *Principles of Political Economy*. London: Macmillan.

1901. *Principles of Political Economy*, 3rd edition. London: Macmillan.

Stedman Jones, G. 1884. *Outcast London*. New York: Pantheon Books.

Veblen, T. B. 1899. *The Theory of the Leisure Class*. New York: Macmillan.

Whitaker, J. K. 1996. *The Correspondence of Alfred Marshall, Economist*. 3 vols. Cambridge: Cambridge University Press.

Winch, D. 2009. *Wealth and Life: Essays on the Intellectual History of Political Economy in Britain, 1848–1914*. Cambridge: Cambridge University Press.

SEVEN

The Ethico-Historical Approach Abroad

The Case of Fukuda

Tamotsu Nishizawa

I. INTERNATIONAL DIFFUSION OF ETHICO-HISTORICAL THINKING

It was around 1870 that a new interest in social reform, a new spirit of 'historicism', and a new activity in the field of economic 'theory' began to assert themselves (Schumpeter 1954, 753). This was the context – that of 'revolutions' and heated discussions – out of which the neoclassical economics was formed, and in which economics was to be professionalized and institutionalized particularly by Alfred Marshall and the Cambridge economists in Britain. This was also the time when the German historical school, or the ethico-historical school, was developed and disseminated internationally, and economic sociology, institutional economics, arose out of the ethico-historicism and the social reform movement. Like neoclassical economics, this spread internationally and became much stronger in the backward countries or the latecomer countries such as Germany, America, and Japan. Welfare economics has usually been discussed in the context of scientific neoclassical economics and utilitarianism in Cambridge, not in the context of the ethico-historical approach for social reform. In contrast, this chapter places the welfare economic studies against the background of the ethico-historical thinking in the age of social reform, which in Britain largely emanated from the Oxford idealism of T. H. Green, John Ruskin, and Arnold Toynbee, as discussed by Shionoya (in Chapter 5).

Schumpeter argued that one economics from 1870 to 1914 was the '*Sozialpolitik* and the historical method' (Schumpeter 1954, Part IV, Ch. 4). This seems to have been an international phenomenon: there was an international dimension of ethico-historical thinking. The link between the *Sozialpolitik* and historicism was clearly German in origin, and the crucial factor connecting the two was not so much history as ethics. The ethical claim, leading the historical research of the school, served as the basis of the *Sozialpolitik*. The research programme of the German historical school was explicitly formulated by Gustav Schmoller as a 'historico-ethical' approach to economics; his historical and ethical economics became an applied science addressing practical solutions for social reform in Germany (Shionoya 2006, 179).

Schumpeter discussed the English historical school as an offshoot of the German historical school and compared the British new liberal social reform, the British version of the *Sozialpolitik*, with the better-developed German social policy. He attended Sidney Webb's lectures at the London School of Economics (LSE) in 1906 or 1907 and wrote that 'he [Webb] must have presented in that course just about what a German *Kathedersozialist* would have done' (Schumpeter 1954, 833).[1] W. A. S. Hewins, an Oxford economist and the first director of the LSE, wrote to Sidney Webb that 'in Germany you and Mrs. Webb are held in the highest estimation of all English writers on economics. … Schmoller is very keen about the School, … I think the transference of the "centre of force" in economics from Germany to London is by no means impossible' (22 September 1898, Passfield Papers 10/2/i/82, LSE Archives).

As Hutchison (1978, chapter 4) has shown, a major turning point both in economic policy and theory in Britain occurred roughly at the same time as the foundation of the *Verein für Sozialpolitik* (in 1872). J. S. Mill's recantation of the wages fund theory, J. M. Ludlow's studies on the progress of the working classes, and Lujo Brentano's studies on trade unions in England, all happened in this same period. Also at this time, the young Marshall felt with increasing urgency that economic studies were important for human well-being, as revealed in his 'Lectures to Women' (1873), focusing on workers' welfare, and in 'The Future of the Working Classes' (1873). These developments accelerated the fall of the English classical school and the rise of the English historical school, a change influenced by a series of Oxford-trained economists: W. J. Ashley, W. A. S. Hewins, and Edwin Cannan, inspired by Arnold Toynbee; R. H. Tawney and the English social policy school led by the Webbs; and new liberal social reformers like J. A. Hobson

---

[1] The Webbs lent the support of their great influence on a large section of opinion to methodological views akin to those of the German historical school (Schumpeter 1954, 824).

and L. T. Hobhouse, who had been influenced by the Oxford idealism. This group had a strong connection with the LSE and have been called the 'LSE institutionalists' (Boulding 1957, 3) and the 'English school of welfare economics' (Hamilton 1919, 318).

The roots of the American institutionalist movement, with its interest in empirical investigation and applied policy analysis, also went back to the impact of the German historical school in America in the 1880s and 1890s, and to the progressive reform movement in the same period (Rutherford 2007). The Japanese Society of Social Policy, strongly influenced by the German historical school, started in 1896. The German historical (ethico-historical) school; the English historical school; the Oxford economists; the English social policy school, largely based on the Oxford approach of idealism by Green and Ruskin; the American institutionalists; and the Japanese Society for Social Policy were not isolated phenomena but were part of a worldwide intellectual movement.

This chapter approaches this international movement, crucial to an understanding of welfare economics in Britain in this period, through a study of the Japanese economist Tokuzo Fukuda (1874–1930). He studied in Munich, where he co-authored with his teacher Brentano, a book entitled *Labour Economics* (*Rodo Keizairon*) in 1899 in Japanese. This was the inauguration of his welfare economic studies, which was to culminate in his final work *Welfare Economic Studies* (*Kosei Keizai Kenkyu*) in 1930. As will be shown, though Fukuda studied the orthodox Cambridge welfare economics of Marshall and Pigou, it was particularly from Hobson that Fukuda learned much about the ethical and humanist approach to welfare economics. Fukuda had been inspired by Hobson's *The Industrial System: An Inquiry into Earned and Unearned Income* (1909) and *Work and Wealth: A Human Valuation* (1914), as well as Pigou's *Wealth and Welfare* (1912) and Cannan's *Wealth* (1914). When Fukuda wrote, 'I can't stop being happy', after reading Hobson's *Wealth and Life: A Study in Values* (newly published in 1929) and Cannan's *A Review of Economic Theory* (1929), he expressed his belief that their works were moving in the same direction as his own final work [i.e., *Welfare Economic Studies* (Fukuda 1930, 2)]. In fact, he wanted to meet Hobson in London when he visited there in 1925; unfortunately Hobson was ill, but the then director of the LSE, Beveridge, introduced Fuduka to Cannan and other LSE economists. Fukuda met Mrs. Hobson by the courtesy of F. W. Hirst (Fukuda 1930, 2–3).

It was Hobson's welfare economics (not Pigou's) that was taken most seriously, not only in the United States (see Hamilton 1915, Rutherford 2007, and Chapter 6 by Backhouse) but also in Japan. Moreover in China, there was published in 1934 a book entitled *A Study of Hobson's Welfare Economics*; its author was William Tien-Chen Liu, professor of economics at Fu Jen University of Peiping and sometime fellow of Northwestern University, where he probably got his Ph.D. Japanese pioneering economist, Fukuda became more sympathetic towards the idealist, ethico-historical approach of the Oxford economists.

2. FUKUDA'S *WELFARE ECONOMIC STUDIES* IN ITS HISTORICAL SETTING

Tokuzo Fukuda, who taught at Tokyo Higher Commercial School (then Tokyo University of Commerce, now Hitotsubashi University) and Keio Gijuku (now Keio University) published his 800-page *Welfare Economic Studies* (*Kosei Keizai Kenkyu*) only two months before he died in 1930. Fukuda pursued welfare economic studies from his maiden work with Brentano (1899) to the end of his life, culminating in this posthumous work. (As Fukuda says in the preface to *Labour Economics*, he had had his ideas of social welfare as based on the 'relationship between labour conditions and labour productivity' since his student days at the Higher Commercial School in Tokyo in the 1890s.) This chapter approaches welfare economics in its formative age through Fukuda's welfare economic studies. Fukuda, one of the greatest pioneers of modern economic science in Japan, was very active in the Japanese Society for Social Policy. Fukuda also learned extensively from the English economists, notably Marshall, whose *Principles of Economics* he urged his student (K. Otsuka) to translate into Japanese.

Fukuda's economic studies, as seen from his *Collected Works on Economics* (*Keizaigaku Zenshu*) (6 vols. 1925–27), which was dedicated to his beloved teacher Brentano on his eightieth birthday, covered a very wide range of areas, but his most important studies were probably the political economy of welfare (i.e., welfare economics and social policy which were related and blended in his studies). In his *Welfare Economic Studies,* Fukuda commented on the state of economic studies in Japan: 'It is said that economics has reached a deadlock. Often we hear voices proclaiming the ruin of the German historical school or the bankruptcy of the marginal utility theory. Among my fellow scholars, not a few have cast their eyes towards the quickly taken escape routes of Marxism, or

especially historical materialism'. Other people called for and rushed
to accept new principles, such as institutional economics in America,
new liberalism in Britain, Schumpeterianism, Spann's universalism, and
Max Weber's 'ideal type'. Fukuda could pay no heed to any of these, nor
hold out greater expectations for the mathematical approach of Walras,
Edgeworth, or Pareto. Therefore, he declared that 'the only course left
to me is to move forward on the thorny trail of welfare economics forged
by our teachers Hobson, Pigou, and Cannan' (Fukuda 1930, 3–6).

After World War I, during the years of the Taisho democracy movement, the Russian Revolution, and the Rice Riots, Marxism began to
flourish among the Japanese intellectuals, quickly replacing the German
historical school. The birth of the Economics Faculties at the Imperial
Universities in Tokyo and Kyoto in 1919 and the inauguration of Tokyo
University of Commerce in 1920 occurred at about the same time. The
newly created Economics Faculty at Tokyo became the centre of Marxian
economists. But a number of economists were expelled from their posts by
the Maintenance of the Public Order Act. Hajime Kawakami, with whom
Fukuda had long argued productively, was forced to leave Kyoto in 1928.
K. Otsuka, who translated Marshall's *Principles* into Japanese, became
deeply involved in Marxian studies, and shared responsibility for the parallel (or competitive) lectures on the principles of economics with Fukuda
(Otsuka on Marxian economics; Fukuda on modern, or neoclassical
economics) at Tokyo University of Commerce, was arrested in 1933. The
young Shigeto Tsuru, who died in 2006, was politically active at the high
school in Nagoya, arrested, and struck off the school. He then went to
America to study under Schumpeter at Harvard in its golden age. Tsuru, who
was inspired by Ruskin and loved the phrase 'no wealth but life', criticized
the 'national income' concept (the calculated figure of national income)
or the measuring rod of money, and wrote 'In Place of GNP' (Tsuru 1943,
1971). Fukuda's welfare economic studies had been put forward against
these backgrounds, and he sought for an alternative to Marxism or socialism, trying to construct a theoretical foundation of the new social policy for
welfare struggle instead of class struggle, or the welfare state.

Fukuda shared the traditional Japanese notion of 'economy' as
'administering the nation and relieving the suffering people', as it says
in Confucianism. The Japanese Society for Social Policy, led by Noboru
Kanai, shared these ideas too, and they saw economics as interwoven with
moral and political issues, and embodying the duty of the government
to demonstrate concern for the social welfare of its subjects. Fukuda
praised the best-selling book *Tale of Poverty* (*Binbo Monogatari*, 1917)

by Kawakami, who was shocked by the poverty in East London while he stayed there in 1914. He quoted a lot from Charles Booth and used Rowntree's poverty line, praising Lloyd George's social reform around 1910. But Fukuda criticized Kawakami and argued that the roots of the social problem lay not in material poverty itself: what mattered was not material wealth or property but human life – the life of human beings and the humanity of labour. Fukuda was very sympathetic towards John Ruskin and William Morris, in particular, Ruskin's claim that 'there is no wealth but life'. Kawakami was also attracted to Ruskin and wrote on *Unto This Last* in 1917–18, and one of Kawakami's students became enthusiastic about Ruskin's writings and founded the Ruskin Society in Japan, while one of Fukuda's students, N. Okuma, wrote *Ruskin and Morris as Social Thinkers* (*Shakaishisoka toshiteno Ruskin to Morris*) in 1927 before going on to develop life economics and family economics.

3. FUKUDA, BRENTANO, AND MARSHALL: BACKGROUND

Fukuda wrote, as a student in the 1890s, 'I often wished that I could attend just once a lecture by [Wilhelm] Roscher'. As a young promising scholar, Fukuda was sent by the government for three years of study of commercial science in Germany, and he arrived in Leipzig on 5 May 1897. By that time, Roscher had passed away, so he studied instead with Karl Bücher, and then transferred to Munich in the autumn, where he became a student of Brentano, who had once succeeded Roscher at Leipzig. Fukuda submitted his dissertation, which was revised and published as 'Die gesellschaftliche und wirtschaftliche Entwicklung in Japan' ('Social and Economic Development of Japan') in 1900, the year after Fukuda and Brentano co-authored *Labour Economics*. This book included a translation of Brentano's, *Über das Verhältniss von Arbeitslohn und Arbeitszeit zur Arbeitsleistung* (*On the Relations of Labour Wages and Working Hours to Labour-Efficiency*) (1876; 2nd ed., 1893) preceded by Fukuda's very long and substantial introduction. Its purpose was to introduce to Japan the ideas of Brentano on recent labour questions, especially regarding the relationship between working hours, workers' wages, and their productive capability, and to investigate whether Brentano's theory could be applied to the Japanese case (Fukuda 1925–27, V: Preface 19–20).[2]

---

[2] See Nishizawa 2007, Ch. 4 Section 3. Future references to Fukuda's *Collected Works on Economics* [Fukuda (1925–27)] will be indicated by volume number and pages.

Fukuda had submitted to his school the Report of Final Year Study Trip, a substantial field research and analysis of silk textile industries in 1894. In Part I, Fukuda discussed production, exchange, consumption, and distribution, referring to Marshall; and concluded the section on 'Industrial Association' that 'the improvement of people's morality in the country induces to the progress of productive capability of its country', referring to Sidgwick's *Principles of Political Economy* (1883, Bk. 3, Ch. 9 on 'private morality') and Marshall's *Principles of Economics* (1961, Bk. 1, Ch.1). He stressed the improvement of the morality of the workers by means of education and training; but he appealed not to the government but to the morality of the entrepreneur (Fukuda 1894, 68–9). Fukuda then intended to draw a paper out of this report, but it was not formed and he kept the ideas to himself. Probably in Munich he drafted a note 'Studien zur Geschichte [der] Lage des Seidengewebes-industrie' ('Studies on the History of Conditions of the Silk-weaving Industry') to show and discuss with Brentano. Fukuda had thought over the workers' welfare based on labour conditions and their productivity; and he got what he wanted and sought after when he read Brentano's writing, *Über das Verhältniss von Arbeitslohn und Arbeitszeit zur Arbeitsleistung*, which 'dispelled almost all his doubts and questions for years' (see Nishizawa 2007, 521–2).

According to 'Memoire' by Fukuda's close friend Seki, during Fukuda's postgraduate course at the Higher Commercial School in 1895–96, he said, 'my close reading of [Wilhelm] Roscher's volumes on economics led me to develop an interest in the German historical school economics'. But Seki also stated that in the summer of 1895, when both were teaching at Kobe Commercial School, 'Professor Marshall's *Principles of Economics* [or *Elements of Economics of Industry*] was your [Fukuda's] favorite book'. It is not very clear how far Fukuda and Seki read Marshall's work in the early 1890s, but in 'Notes on Readings', which Seki is believed to have written in January 1893, there appears a note of 35 pages entitled 'Some notes on Marshall's *Principles of Economics* [or *Elements of Economics of Industry*]: discusses mutual benefit-ism, discusses "co-operation"' (see ibid. 522–3).

Seki wrote this note about the same time that T. Inoue (at Tokyo Senmon School, now Waseda University) began to translate Marshall's *Elements of Economics of Industry*. Inoue's translation, first published in July 1896, soon became a best-seller; it went into its eighth printing in 1899 and into a revised, eleventh printing in 1902. Inoue presented copies of the third and fourth printing to Marshall via J. Soeda, who studied under Marshall in 1885–86, for which Marshall thanked him cordially in his letters of 9 April 1897 and 17 September 1897. Curiously, the introduction to this translation was a translation of Marshall's Preface to *Principles of Economics* (Inoue 1899). In the reading list of the first year students at Waseda in 1893, there was a translation of Adolph Wagner's review of Marshall's *Principles of Economics* (in the *Quarterly Journal of Economics*, April 1891) (see Nishizawa 2007, 523).

Marshall's *Economics of Industry* had been translated by K. Takahashi (published in 1886), who later became the celebrated minister of finance and called 'Keynes of Japan'. In fact Noboru Kanai, a founder and central figure of the Japanese Society for Social Policy, who graduated Tokyo University in 1885, also tried to translate Marshall's *Economics of Industry* before he left for Germany in 1886 but seemed not to have finished. Kanai, who met Marshall in Conrad's seminar at Halle, moved to London in 1889 and stayed at Toynbee Hall for a while and met Marshall again there. Kanai investigated the conditions of workers' life in the East End of London. He highly praised Arnold Toynbee, who, as a great historical economist, had been of quite the same principles as the German historical school and had renovated the economic thinking a great deal. Toynbee was identified with the social reformers and enormously influential to the succeeding generations. Kanai was also influenced by Marshall, and at Tokyo he taught economic principles following Marshall, though he was not so much impressed by Marshall's *Principles of Economics*, Volume I, just published, and expected much more from Volume II (Kawai 1939, 46, 60; Kanai 1891, 230–3).

4. *LABOUR ECONOMICS* BY BRENTANO AND FUKUDA

Fukuda stressed the importance of labour among the agents of production. He argued that the productive powers of labour would be affected by the health and strength of its population, labour capability, high or low wages, and short or long working hours. Then he made a case for the theoretical studies on the relation of labour conditions to productive powers, asserting that bad or good labour conditions would affect not only labour capability but also labour incentives. He also argued that technology would affect labour efficiency. Quoting from *Eight Hours for Work* by John Rae (1894), he argued that other productive agents like raw materials and machines were going to be made uniform across the countries but that it would be difficult for labour to be made uniform in the same way. It would be the country which had strong and wise workers with high productive capability that would gain the victory in the world market (Fukuda, V: 2304–8, 2313–15).

Brentano had been doing empirical research on British labour questions to provide a comparative analysis with Germany. He went to England in 1868 with Ernst Engel of the Prussian Statistical Office to do empirical and historical work on labour questions; then he was pressed to write the essay on the history of guild. Engel had thought of an 'industrial partnership' to calm down the social tension in Berlin. Engel's 'industrial partnership', involving profit-sharing, directed Brentano's attention to the social reform movement in England (Sheehan 1966, 16–17). With the help of J. M. Ludlow, a Christian socialist who also inspired Marshall, Brentano published *On the History and Development of Gilds, and the Origin of Trade-Unions* in 1870 and *Die Arbeitergilden der Gegenwart* (Present-Day Trade Unions) (2 vols., 1871–72).[3] In 1871, the Trade Union legislation, on which the subsequent rise to power of the unions was founded in England, was passed. 'A major turning-point in economic policy' in Britain occurred around 1870. 'The long re- or e-volution in the economic role of government ... may be dated from somewhere about 1870', roughly at the same time as the turning point in economic theory in Britain (Hutchison 1978, 94–5). In Germany the *Verein für Sozialpolitik* was founded in 1872. It was about the same time that Marshall started to inquire into the labour questions; he gave 'Lectures to Women', whose subtitle was 'Some Economic Questions Directly Connected with the Welfare of the Labourer' in 1873, and his initial inquiry resulted in *The Future of the English Working Classes* in the same year. The question was then 'whether progress may not go on steadily if slowly, till the official distinction between working man and gentleman has passed away'; Marshall there pressed 'a moralizing capitalism'. 'What was common to both Marshall and T. H. Green was the stress upon a moralized capitalism through which the highest potentialities of mankind were to be developed. ... Both Marshall and Green saw history not only as a transition from status to contract, but also as a transition from self-interest to self-sacrifice and altruism' (Stedman Jones 1971, 7). In this aspect Marshall separated himself from those contemporaries, chiefly Jevons, Sidgwick, and Edgeworth, who preserved a closer

---

[3] Some 80 letters from Ludlow to Brentano from 1868 to 1908 are kept in 'Nachlass Lujo Brentano' at Koblenz Bundesarchiv. Brentano's book *On the History and Development of Gilds, and the Origin of Trade-Unions* is dedicated to Ludlow. Marshall often used *History of the Progress of the Working Classes* by Ludlow and Lloyd Jones (1867) in his 'Lectures to Women'.

relationship between economics and utilitarianism (Collini, Winch, and Burrow 1983, 318). Marshall professed himself in sympathy with the aims of socialism and spoke without explanation or qualification of the 'evils of inequality'; also he was 'the first theorist to prove theoretically that laissez-faire … did not assure a maximum of welfare to society as a whole. … On the whole, the economic professions of all countries were politically supporters of the countertendencies to liberalism rather than of the still dominating liberal ones. In this sense, we can say that the alliance between economics and liberalism – and, with exceptions, between economics and utilitarianism – was broken' (Schumpeter 1954, 765–6).

Brentano believed that, to become as prosperous as Britain, Germany would need to raise wages and shorten working hours; thus he sought to show that high wages and short working hours were linked to high labour efficiency. For Brentano, the most important issue in the age of social reform then taking place was the creation of trade unions and labour laws to protect the economic interests of workers. He emphasized fostering improvements from the bottom up through labour unions and expounded his social liberalism and production-oriented social policy theories in his *Die Arbeitergilden der Gegenwart*. Beginning by mastering the available information on British trade unions, he found that wages in Britain were twice as high as in Germany, and Britain's working hours were nine compared with Germany's eleven. He argued that Germany's labour efficiency came nowhere near to matching Britain's because its working hours were extremely long and its wages half those of Britain. For those who intended to make the country prosperous and strong, the studies on the relationship between wages and working hours and productive powers were 'the alpha and omega of social reform'. Following Brentano, Fukuda concluded that the social reform which meant to lead and enhance the culture of the massive working classes should also have the powers to bring about the political and economic '*machtstellung*' of the country (Fukuda, V: 2359–60, 2466).

5. MARSHALL AND FUKUDA: WELFARE ECONOMIC STUDIES

Fukuda's lectures on economics just after returning to Japan were largely based on the notes of his teacher Brentano's lectures. Then Fukuda was engaged in drawing up the 'Principles of Economics' and published *Principles of National Political Economy* (*Kokumin keizai genron*) in 1903, which revealed in its conception the strong influence of the German historical school and which he thought a 'failure' as a publication. In August 1904, Fukuda was suddenly ordered to take a leave of absence from Tokyo Higher Commercial School because of a conflict with its president. In October 1905, he began lecturing at Keio Gijuku, where he used Marshall's *Principles of Economics* as his text-book. From then until March 1918, he compiled commentaries on the first four books of *Principles* for his lectures and published them as *Lectures on Economics* (*Keizaigaku Kougi*) in three volumes (1907–9), which went very well, and was revised and enlarged, and finally became volume one of his *Collected Works*.

In 1905, when Fukuda started to lecture at Keio Gijuku, the German translation of Marshall's *Principles* came out with Brentano's introduction. Brentano's introduction was translated and included in the first Japanese translation of the *Principles* by Otsuka. Fukuda attached a 'revisor's supplementary introduction' to Otsuka's translation, where he stated that Marshall's *Principles* were 'the pinnacle of contemporary economics, as my mentor Brentano wrote in his introduction to the German translated edition, so there was no need to attempt to add anything further'.[4]

Fukuda began his *Lectures on Economics* with the first passage from Marshall's *Principles*. 'Economics is a study of mankind in the ordinary business of life; it examines that part of individual and social action which is most closely connected with the attainment and with the use of the material requisites of well-being' (Marshall 1961, 1). Marshall thought that the destruction of the poor was their poverty and the study of the causes of poverty was the study of the causes of the degradation of a large part of mankind. The problems of poverty and ignorance cannot be totally eradicated from human society by economics alone but 'the greater part of the facts and reasoning necessary to resolve these problems are encompassed within the sphere of economic research, and my greatest interest in this field of study lies therein' (Marshall 1961, 4).

Fukuda probably saw 'the spirit of the age' in Marshall's position, using the phrase coined by Edgeworth in his review of the *Principles* (Edgeworth 1890, 12). The spirit was shared by Pigou, Hobson, Cannan and the Webbs, and both the Cambridge school and the Oxford-LSE

---

[4] Otsuka, as research assistant, started to translate the recent 7th edition of the *Principles* (1916) on the advice and prompting of Fukuda and finished it except most of Book V. Then Otsuka got an order to study abroad; the draft was submitted to Fukuda, and it was published as the first Japanese translation of the *Principles* without Book V in 1919. Otsuka came back from abroad and completed the first full translation of the 8th edition of the *Principles* in 1925–26.

economists favourable towards the ethico-historical, or institutional, approach. They had much in common as regards their historical background, but their thinking rested on different intellectual foundations; while Pigou drew on Sidgwick's utilitarianism, 'the English welfare school' drew on T. H. Green, Ruskin, and Toynbee. Marshall's question 'whether it is really impossible that all should start with a fair chance of leading a cultured life, free from the pains of poverty', was probably common to Fukuda and Brentano. For Marshall the solution of economic problems was a prior condition of the exercise of man's higher faculties. For him 'economics was a handmaid to ethics, not an end itself, but a means to a further end: an instrument, by the perfecting of which it might be possible to better the conditions of human life' (Keynes 1924, 170). 'Wealth exists only for the benefit of mankind. It cannot be measured adequately in yards or in tons, nor even as equivalent to so many ounces of gold; its true measure lies only in the contribution it makes to human well-being' (Pigou 1925, 366). It was this aspect of Marshall to which Fukuda was attracted.

Fukuda soon came to emphasize the need to move 'from price struggle to welfare struggle'. What he was asking for was liberation from price economics in order to build welfare economics that was responsive to the demands of the times. Fukuda says: 'It would be the great British economist Alfred Marshall himself who should be seen as the forerunner in this trend of economic thinking outside of the German ethical school of economics. The Book I of his greatest life work, *Principles*, should be seen as a great declaration of welfare economics. But with regard to the true intention of Marshall, the apostle of welfare economics, we should look at his entire academic activity rather than this work that remained as a mere declaration' (Fukuda, V: 265, 275).

In the *Lectures on Economics*, Fukuda made the following observation in comparing the British school and the German school, where Marshall represented the former, and Schmoller the latter. British academics saw the starting point as investigating the unbound activities of individuals and they placed little importance on conceptions such as a national economy. In contrast, German scholars acknowledged the principle that the economic life was under the constraint of the society, and an individual's activities were conducted within the organizations; there was no sense of a totally free, unconstrained individual. Fukuda went on to say that the society-based German school needed to be completed, so that economics could advance as a society- or organization-based science. However, the current reality was that, in the German

style of economics, the struggle for a new way of thinking had been concluded but the serious task of constructing had barely started (Fukuda,
I: 17–18, 21–3).

Marshall's contention that economics is the research of the relationship between
man and wealth should mean that the genuine purpose of economics could be
achieved only by mastering the studies of both man and wealth. Thus, this relationship should concern not only the amount of wealth but also the possibility
of providing human beings with equal material means that would be necessary
to perform their higher developments and nobler activities. The new school, the
historical school, the ethical school, or whatever, definitely do no more than this
conception, which shows the highest, most comprehensive status in contemporary studies. (ibid., 24–5)

Fukuda criticized the German school for devoting themselves to policy,
to the compilation of facts, and losing sight of the clarity of pure reasoning (theory). Their arguments in their historical narratives might
have surprised people who did not know very much, but upon logical
dissection they were just following conventional beliefs they had inherited from elsewhere. Their original thoughts were rather few, and in
this regard the British scholars were the best. This explains Fukuda's
admiration for Marshall, who had mastered the recent research of the
German scholars, but had not neglected the purely theoretical study
of the British scholars. He represented the most advanced position in
his discipline. Pigou was succeeding his work and becoming the leading figure among the current generation of scholars in their prime
(ibid., 132–3).

According to Fukuda, Marshall's perceptions of social welfare and
welfare economics representing the 'spirit of the age' had been widely
accepted and were being gradually institutionalized, as was evident
in social legislation such as the Old Age Pensions Act, the National
Health Insurance Act – the so-called 'Liberal reforms'. The *Reports
of the Poor Law Commission* also demonstrated that these ideas had
been accepted by intelligent people. Its *Minority Report*, as well as the
Webb's *Prevention of Destitution* (1912), took on great importance for
Fukuda. One should also be directed to read Pigou's *Economics of
Welfare* (1920), which further developed Marshall's concepts. Fukuda
wished to compare them with his own ideas in 'From Price Struggle
to Welfare Struggle', which appeared in 1921 in the journal *Kaizo
(Reconstruction)* and was included in his *Social Policy and Class
Struggle (Shakai Seisaku to Kaikyu Toso)*, (1922), then in his *Collected
Works*, V.

6. 'FROM PRICE STRUGGLE TO WELFARE STRUGGLE'

Fukuda started to lecture on industrial policy (or social policy) from 1914 at Tokyo Higher Commercial School; his lectures culminated in the 'Introduction to the Social Policy' as Book I of *Social Policy and Class Struggle*. He viewed social policy (or welfare economy) as the alternative to socialism and Marxism, which was increasing its influence after 1917, as a means of overcoming the problems of capitalism. He thought that social policy should be about defending social welfare (the happiness of human life) from its infringement both by capitalism and by interventionist public policy. Fukuda had been studying Marx and advised his student to translate *Das Kapital* almost in parallel with Marshall's *Principles*. However, Fukuda, through the debates with Kawakami who favoured Marxist economics, was becoming critical of Marx's views. Welfare struggle meant legitimization of needs, humanization of labour, but not Marxian class struggle.

At that time Fukuda was contending that 'economics in the future will be social policy studies'; for social policy studies, it was crucial to discover a concept of 'the society', namely social affairs that were separate from both the state and the individual, and to develop it in the right way. Social policy should stop the state from obstructing the extension of social life, so that the state could become more flexible and could embrace the struggle of social life as much as possible (Fukuda, V: 27, 122–6). As for the discovery of 'the society', the social question, social movement, and social policy as its basic theory, Fukuda had been inspired by the pioneering works of Lorenz von Stein. Discussing welfare economy, Fukuda sought the welfare state as the 'third way', beyond the conflict between capitalism and socialism, and as an alternative to Marxism and socialism.

Under the influence of Anton Menger, Fukuda developed the theory of social rights, in particular the right to live (needs) beyond the right to labour and the right to the whole produce of labour, and made it the foundation of social policy. Authentication and assurance of the right to live (needs) was essential and should be the foundation and purpose of social policy. Fukuda thought that the 'principle of national minimum' advocated by the Webbs was basically the same in the end. Referring to Carl Fuchs's *Volkswirtschatslehre* (1905), Fukuda wrote that the art and aims of political economy would be to provide the economic or material basis necessary for the minimum human life and to make it possible for the people to lead a cultured life and that the national minimum was the prerequisite for all the cultural and moral development for the majority of the people. Investigating the actual institutions and referring to the Old Age Pensions Act in Britain, he wrote that the recent practice of social policy there would show signs to lead the current of the times, which would address one of the most important questions of the twentieth century. Legitimization of the right to live (needs), the social policy for the right to live (needs), was the root of Fukuda's welfare economic studies, which was the basis of the welfare state, as evaluated later by people like Yuzo Yamada, who followed and developed Fukuda's ideas in theory, and Ichiro Nakayama, who extended Fukuda's ideas into the practical in the post–World War II world, proclaiming 'wage doubling' as a basis of the welfare state. It is said that Nakayama's 'Proposal for Wage Doubling' was the intellectual basis of Prime Minister Ikeda's national income doubling policy (see Nishizawa 2002).

In his monumental paper 'From Price Struggle to Welfare Struggle: Especially Labour Struggles as Welfare Struggles' (1921), Fukuda divided welfare economics from price economics, saying that price economics and price struggle were based on the right to labour and the right to the whole produce of labour while welfare economics and welfare struggle were based on the right to live. In this sense, the socialist economics of Marx and William Thompson were purely price economics. Fukuda wanted liberation from this, and he thought welfare economics could be constructed on the right to live. The works he saw as creating welfare economics were all about liberation from price economics.[5]

Fukuda praised Marshall as 'the greatest authority among the contemporary economists', but in this article he became critical. Marshall, he claimed, started his *Principles* with the clear and bold statement in favour of welfare economics, but then

he gradually follows the conventional beliefs of price economics, and at the end he falls to a lowest viewpoint, one that is absolutely no different from that of his fellow price economists. In particular, Book V and Book VI which deal with price and distributional theory are the worst of all ... The critique that Marshall is wandering at the crossroads between the old price economics and the new welfare economics is no reckless slander. (V: 275–6)

In making these remarks, Fukuda referred to the arguments of an American economist in a recent issue of the *American Economic Review*. He did not mention the author's name, but it appears to be Frank A.

---

[5] In this context Fukuda referred to the works such as R. Liefmann, 'Theorie des Volkswohlstands' (not published), S. N. Patten, *The Theory of Prosperity*, 1902, and W. Mitscherlich, *Der wirtschaftliche Fortschrift*, 1910.

Fetter (see Negishi 2001). Fetter had written twice on 'Price Economics versus Welfare Economics' (1920). According to Fetter, price economics was represented by Ricardian economics, in full vigour from 1818 until 1860 in Britain. The ethical protest against it was led by Thomas Carlyle, and then Ruskin bitterly attacked the 'mercantile economy', stressing the dominance of moral over pecuniary values. This was followed by Toynbee and Hobson, and probably in some measure by all the modern social reformers of the Fabian society (Fetter 1920, 472, 476–9). Fetter then argued on 'Alfred Marshall's dilemma', saying that 'there is, indeed, a thoroughgoing inconsistency in Marshall's view as to the central aim of economics'. Marshall wanted to be a welfare economist, aspiring to make economics a study of real human life, but he also aspired to make economics an exact science with the mathematical exactness of the physical sciences. The latter led him to abandon welfare and to make money 'the centre around which economic science clusters'. However, Fetter concluded by saying that 'in his most attractive aspect Marshall is more than a Ricardian and, forgetting to be a price economist, is concerned with human welfare' (Fetter 1920, 721–3).

Liu (1934) also starts from the distinction between price economics and welfare economics in a tone very similar to Fetter's. Before proceeding to Hobson's welfare economics, Liu set forth the works of Fetter and Pigou as representing the theories of welfare economics, in contrast to those of Davenport, Mitchell, and others who represented the price economics. He argued, with Fetter, that the economist should become a social philosopher, whose task would be a deeper study of the human factor, which involves 'desires, impulses, choice, valuation' on the one hand, and 'happiness, well-being, welfare', on the other. Thus 'the larger, truer political economy is a theory of welfare and not a theory of value' (Liu 1934, 8–9, 15–16).

7. FUKUDA, HOBSON, AND THE WELFARE STATE

Fukuda continued: 'Our study of prices is not conducted for its own sake, but because we believe that it is related to economic welfare, so by studying this we hope to advance welfare studies'. His aim was 'fruit, but not light'. Fukuda sought to absorb the vision of welfare economics from Marshall and Pigou, but while he was inspired by Pigou, he believed that Pigou's analysis was not sufficient for the study of welfare. Pigou's measure of economic welfare, national dividend, was too limited in scope and he did not distinguish between utility (Fukuda meant the degree of satisfaction) and desiredness (Fukuda meant related to the price). Instead Fukuda believed that the most important thing was to deal with the degree of satisfaction, happiness, or welfare of the working people. In order to establish welfare economics scientifically, or to professionalize welfare economics, Pigou restricted the scope to economic welfare that can be brought into relation with 'the measuring rod of money'; then the non-economic welfare, such as well-being, 'the quality of life', were to be driven out. This was actually what Tsuru later warned in his 'In Place of GNP', whose original idea was expounded in his article called 'Reflections on the "National Income" Concept' (Tsuru 1943).

The human struggle (and therefore welfare struggle) included income distribution, the equity and justice of the workers' share, and related to whether the labour movement had guaranteed socially just working hours. Fukuda's welfare economic studies, like Hobson's, thus went beyond Marshall and Pigou, back to the Oxford approach or the ethico-historical thinking, involving philosophical, ethical, and policy issues. It was closer to that of the historical and ethical school that emanated from Oxford and the German historical school.

Capitalist society is an income acquisition society. What this means is that society develops by means of surplus distribution. ... J. A. Hobson's declaration that a supposed society, in which no development occurs, would have no distribution problem, even now lingers in my thinking. Insofar as the position of cost principles and utility principles are concerned, no real problems of distribution exist in economic theory.... It must be said that Marx's clear articulation of this theory was one of the penetrating insights of the ages. It is for this reason that I place Hobson, who has not the slightest connection with Marx but who reached at the same insight, in the first rank of contemporary British theorists. (Fukuda 1930, 164)

In his criticism of Pigou's welfare economics, Fukuda argued that the welfare struggle was still necessary even if Pigou's theorems were right, for they would need to be implemented. Only the labour movement and labour disputes could offer a countermeasure against labour being compelled against its own interests, against worsening income distribution, and against increasingly variable national income (Fukuda, V: 292–3).

Fukuda's tentative conclusion was the development of communal principles in capitalist society, which he stated in the chapters of his *Welfare Economic Studies* entitled '"Justice in Circulation" (justitia commutative) by Aristotle' and 'Production, Exchange, and Distribution of Surplus'. The communal principles of 'from each according to his ability' and 'to each according to his need' were 'woven into the texture of contemporary capitalist society, like the thread of fate, through the whole production, exchange, and distribution'. These principles appeared not in price theory but only in income theory, and could not be found in cost principle or utility principle, but in surplus principle. In capitalist society the struggle for surplus value develops, step by step, through class struggle, through labour contract, through minimum wage, through workers' insurance, or unemployment insurance, and further through the taxes, and through the various public corporations and public institutions (Fukuda 1930, 178–9).

Fukuda believed that the development of communal principles could be found in the progress of capitalist society and recognized its tentative advance in the progress of the British welfare state. On 10 June 1929, immediately after the inauguration of the second Labour Government in Britain, he wrote that: 'I learned from this morning's newspaper that Mr. MacDonald, in his installation ceremony speech on the evening of the 8th, stated that the major tasks of his new cabinet would be to reform the industrial system and solve the unemployment problem. The formation of this cabinet may be as much as a major "development of communal principles" in Britain, and I think it may largely affect the future of British capitalism, by which my interest has been deepened to a new degree' (ibid., 183). He went on to state:

In this chaotic arena, I perceive that the correct principle has raised its head like the thread of fate. … Most of all, I acknowledge its remarkable development among the people in the Labour Party who have formed Britain's new cabinet. How this cabinet will go forward and what kind of things it will do in the future cannot be foreseen at present. However, the plan of 'Economic General Staff' appeals to my attention. I find *The Next Ten Years in the British Social and Economic Policy* by the former guild socialist Cole as the powerful basis. This work will probably be brought out as the intellectual ledger for the new cabinet'. (ibid., 215–16)

Fukuda was also fascinated with Bertrand Russell. Highly impressed by Russell's writings, Fukuda published 'Social Policy for Liberation' in 1919 at the high tide of the democratic movement called the Taisho democracy. After the social policy for the right to live (needs), Fukuda argued for liberation (emancipation) of creativeness. He often referred to *Principles of Social Reconstruction* (1916), where Russell says, 'I consider the best life that which is most built on creative impulses, and the worst that which is most inspired by love of possession'. He was of the conviction that 'liberation of creativeness ought to be the principle of reform both in politics and economics'. Fukuda was attracted by

Russell's arguments for the creative impulses against the possessive impulses, the liberation of creativeness, more opportunity for the joy of life, and that political institutions should be such as to promote creativeness at the expense of possessiveness.

Human activity springs from two sources, impulse and desire. In the nineteenth century political philosophy and economics had been dominated by utilitarianism and almost entirely based upon desire as the source of human action. Fukuda says, it was first Schmoller and then Brentano who replaced the part played by desire with the impulses. Then, following Russell, Fukuda contended for the liberation of impulses, liberation of creative impulses, and the joy of life and joy for ever in Ruskinian words. The title of Ruskin's book, *Unto This Last* is the first half of a quotation from the Bible, "Unto this last, even as unto thee" (Matthew, ch. 20, 13–14). It meant that minimum wages should be paid 'unto this last' as much as 'unto thee'. Minimum wages are 'needs' of the workers as well as their 'right'; it should be given to each according to his needs. This is the principle of 'basic needs' or 'civil minimum', which is the foundation of the British welfare state (Tsuru 1998, 96–7, 150).

Fukuda linked the arguments of the creative impulses and the possessive impulses with his social policy for liberation, which aimed to conciliate in the conflict between the property-owning capitalist classes, whose activity was based on the possessive impulses, and the have-nots working classes, who should act based on the creative impulses. He argued for the liberation of the workers from their 'painful exertion', and more practically discussed for the 'democratic control of industry' in the factory and the company.

8. CONCLUSIONS

This study of a Japanese economist might seem far removed from discussions of British welfare economics and the welfare state. However, it establishes several important points. It helps give a new light to English welfare discussions and locate them as part of a much broader international context. Rutherford (2007) has gone part of the way towards this, focusing on the 'English connections' of American institutionalism. However, the discussion of Fukuda makes a connection to 'the English welfare school', American Walton Hamilton, Frank Fetter, and Chinese William Tien-Chien Liu and points to the strong links between the 'Oxford' approach to welfare and the German ethico-historical economics, thereby broadening our understanding of the former. Fukuda was a student of Brentano, and progressed, through close study of Marshall and Pigou, to a position closer to Hobson and what Hamilton called the English welfare school. He saw this school as working out a line of inquiry that stemmed directly from the ideas of the German historical school. Fukuda's welfare economics was not the same as that of his English counterparts. He developed his ideas in a context where Marxism was far more important than in England, and hence he presented it explicitly as an alternative. He shared with the Oxford-LSE economists both a commitment to social reform and a concept of welfare economics based on the ideas of 'no wealth but life': his welfare economic studies were inseparable from thoughts about the welfare state. His story therefore sheds fresh light on the history of welfare economics and the welfare state during this period.

References

Boulding, K. 1957. A New Look at Institutionalism. *American Economic Review* 9(2): 1–12.

Brentano, L. 1876. *Über das Verhältniss von Arbeitslohn und Arbeitszeit zur Arbeitsleistung.* 2nd ed., 1893.

Brentano, L. and Fukuda, T. 1899. *Labour Economics (Rodo Keizairon).* Tokyo: Dobunkan.

Cannan, E. 1914. *Wealth: A Brief Explanation of the Causes of Economic Welfare.* London: P. S. King & Son.

1929. *A Review of Economic Theory.* London: P. S. King & Son.

Coats, A. W. 1967. Sociological Aspects of British Economic Thought. *Journal of Political Economy* 75(5): 706–29.

1982. The Distinctive LSE Ethos in the Inter-War Years. *Atlantic Economic Journal* 10: 18–30.

Collini, S., Winch, D., and Burrow, J. 1983. *That Noble Science of Politics: A Study in Nineteenth-Century Intellectual History.* Cambridge: Cambridge University Press.

Edgeworth, F. Y. 1890. Review of *Principles of Economics* by Alfred Marshall. *The Academy* 956 (30 August 1890). In *Alfred Marshall: Critical Responses,* vol. 2. P. Groenewegen, ed. London: Routledge, 1998.

Fetter, F. A. 1920. Price Economics versus Welfare Economics. *American Economic Review* 10(3): 467–87 and 10(4): 719–37.

Fukuda, T. 1894. Report of Final Year Study Trip (Shugakuryoko Hokokusho). Tokyo: Tokyo Higher Commercial School.

1921. From Price Struggle to Welfare Struggle (Kakaku Tosoyori Kaikyu Tosoe.) In Fukuda's *Collected Works on Economics,* vol. 5, 265–341.

1925–27. *Collected Works on Economics (Keizaigaku Zenshu).* 6 vols. Tokyo: Kaizosha.

1930. *Welfare Economic Studies (Kosei Keizai Kenkyu).* Tokyo: Toko-shoin.

Groenewegen, P. D. 1995. *A Soaring Eagle: Alfred Marshall 1842–1924*. Cheltenham: Edward Elgar.

2005. A Book that Never Was: Marshall's Final Volume on Progress and His System of Ethical and Political Beliefs. *History of Economics Review* 42 (Summer): 29–44.

Hamilton, W. H. 1915. Economic Theory and 'Social Reform'. *Journal of Political Economy* 23(6): 562–84.

1919. The Institutional Approach to Economic Theory. *American Economic Review* 9(1): 309–18.

Harris, J. 1992. Political Thought and the Welfare State, 1870–1940: An Intellectual Framework for British Social Policy. *Past and Present* 135: 116–41.

1996. From Sunspots to Social Welfare: The Unemployment Problem 1870–1914. In *Unemployment and the Economists,* B. Corry, ed. Cheltenham: Edward Elgar.

Hobson, J. A. 1909. *The Industrial System: An Inquiry into Earned and Unearned Income*. London: Longmans. With a new introduction by Peter Cain. London: Routledge/Thoemmes Press, 1992.

1914. *Work and Wealth: A Human Valuation*. With a new introduction by Peter Cain. London: Routledge/Thoemmes Press, 1992.

1929. *Wealth and Life. A Study in Values*. London: Macmillan.

Hutchison, T. W. 1953. *A Review of Economic Doctrines 1870–1929*. Oxford: Clarendon Press.

1978. *On Revolutions and Progress in Economic Knowledge*. Cambridge: Cambridge University Press.

Inoue, T. 1899. *Principles of Economics (Keizaigenron)*. (Translation of Marshall's *Elements of Economics of Industry*). 1896, 7th ed. 1899. Tokyo: Tokyo Senmon-gakko Shuppanbu.

Kadish, A. 1982. *The Oxford Economists in the Late Nineteenth Century*. Oxford: Clarendon Press.

Kanai, N. 1891. Present State of Economics and the Socialists of the Chair (Keizaigaku no Kinkyo to Kodan-Shakaito). In Kawai 1939.

Kawai, E. 1939. *The Life and Works of Noboru Kanai (Kanai Noboru no Shogai to Gakuseki)*. Tokyo: Niohonhyoronsha.

Kawakami, H. 1917. *Tale of Poverty (Binbou Monogatari)*. Tokyo: Iwanami-bunko, 1947.

Keynes, J. M. 1924. Alfred Marshall, 1842–1924. *Economic Journal* 34: 311–72. In Pigou, ed., 1925.

Koot, G. M. 1987. *English Historical Economics, 1870–1926*. Cambridge: Cambridge University Press.

Liu, W. T.-C. 1934. *A Study of Hobson's Welfare Economics*. Peiping: Kwang Yuen Press.

Maloney, J. 1985. *Marshall, Orthodoxy and the Professionalization of Economics*. Cambridge: Cambridge University Press.

Marshall, A. 1873a. Lectures to Women, in T. Raffaelli, E. Biagini, and R. M. Tullberg, eds. 1995.

1873b. The Future of the Working Classes. In Pigou, ed., 1925.

1907. Social Possibilities of Economic Chivalry. In Pigou, ed., 1925.

1919. *Industry and Trade. A Study of Industrial Technique and Business Organization; and of Their Influences on the Conditions of Various Classes and Nations.* 4th ed., 1923. London: Macmillan.

1961. *Principles of Economics*, 9th (variorum) ed. C. W. Guillebaud, Vol. 1 Text. London: Macmillan.

Marshall, A. and Marshall, M. P. 1879. *The Economics of Industry.* With a new introduction by D. O'Brien. Bristol: Thoemmes Press, 1994.

Marshall, T. H. 1950. Citizenship and Social Class. In *Sociology at the Crossroads and Other Essays*, 1963. London: Heinemann.

Nakayama, I. 1978. Welfare Economics and Tokuzo Fukuda (Kosei Keizaigaku to Fukuda Tokuzo). In *Modern Economics and Japan* (Kindai Keizaigaku To Nihon), T. Minoguchi and T. Hayasaka, eds. Tokyo: Nihonkeizai-shinbunsha.

Negishi, T. 2001. Alfred Marshall in Hitotsubashi. In *Economic Theory, Dynamics, and Markets. Essays in Honour of Ryuzo Sato*, T. Negishi, R. V. Ramachandran and K. Mino, eds. Boston: Kluwer Academic Publishers.

Nishizawa, T. 2002. Ichiro Nakayama and the Stabilization of Industrial Relations in Postwar Japan. *Hitotsubashi Journal of Economics* 43(1): 1–18.

2007. *Economic Thought of Marshall and the Historical School (Marshall to Rekishigakuha no Keizaishiso).* Tokyo: Iwanamishoten.

Pigou, A. C. 1912. *Wealth and Welfare.* London: Macmillan.

1920. *The Economics of Welfare.* Fourth edition. London: Macmillan, 1932.

ed. 1925. *Memorials of Alfred Marshall.* London: Macmillan.

Raffaelli, T., Biagini, E., and Tullberg, R. M., eds. 1995. *Alfred Marshall's Lectures to Women. Some Economic Questions Directly Connected to the Welfare of the Labourer.* Aldershot, UK: Edward Elgar.

Robbins, L. C. 1932. *An Essay on the Nature and Significance of Economic Science.* Second edition. London: Macmillan, 1935.

Ruskin, J. 1860. *Unto this Last: Four Essays on the First Principles of Political Economy.* London: Routledge/Thoemmes Press, 1994.

Russell, B. 1916. *Principles of Social Reconstruction.* London: George Allen & Unwin.

Rutherford, M. 2007. Institutionalism and Its English Connections. *European Journal of the History of Economic Thought* 14(2): 291–323.

Schumpeter, J. A. 1926. Gustav v. Schmoller und die Probleme von heute. *Schmollers Jahrbuch* 50. Reprinted in *Dogmenhistorische und biographische Aufsätze*. Tübingen: J. C. B. Mohr, 1954.

1954. *History of Economic Analysis.* New York: Oxford University Press.

Sheehan, J. J. 1966. *The Career of Lujo Brentano. A Study of Liberalism and Social Reform in Imperial Germany.* Chicago: The University of Chicago Press.

Shionoya, Y. 2005. *The Soul of the German Historical School. Methodological Essays on Schmoller, Weber, and Schumpeter.* New York: Springer.

2006. Schmoller and Modern Economic Sociology. *Schmollers Jahrbuch* 126(2): 177–95.

Sidgwick, H. 1883. *The Principles of Political Economy.* Third edition. London, Macmillan, 1901.

Stedman Jones, G. 1971. *Outcast London. A Study in the Relationship between Classes in Victorian Society.* Oxford: Oxford University Press.

Tsuru, S. 1943. Reflections on the 'National Income' Concept ('Kokumin Shotoku' Gainen-eno Hansei). *Hitotsubashi Ronso* 12(6): 22–42.

1971. In Place of GNP. Presented at the Symposium on Political Economy of Environment, Paris, 5–8 July. In *Towards a New Political Economy,* S. Tsuru. Tokyo: Kodansha, 1976.

1998. *Pursuit of Scientific Humanism (Kagakuteki Hyumanizumu wo Motomete).* Tokyo: Shin-nihon Shuppansha.

Whitaker, J. K., ed. 1996. *The Correspondence of Alfred Marshall, Economist.* 3 volumes. Cambridge: Cambridge University Press.

PART THREE

WELFARE ECONOMICS IN THE POLICY ARENA

EIGHT

'The Great Educator of Unlikely People'

H. G. Wells and the Origins of the Welfare State

Richard Toye

H. G. Wells's novel *The New Machiavelli* (1911) contains some notable criticisms of the Edwardian Liberal party. The hero, Richard Remington, is elected as Liberal MP in 1906, but becomes disillusioned with the party and with 'our self-satisfied new Liberalism and Progressivism'. Of the Liberals themselves he says mockingly: 'It was tremendously clear what they were against. The trouble was to find out what on earth they were *for*'! (Wells 1911, II, pp. 31, 20). Commended as 'the equal of any political novel in the English language' (Clarke 1996, p. 40), it has also been described as 'an anti-Liberal tract' (Cowling 1985, p. 216). That interpretation might seem to be a natural one, given that, in his extensive nonfiction political writings, Wells is generally thought to have presented 'a fundamentally socialist doctrine of reform' (Hyde 1956, p. 217).[1] Believing that 'the creation of Utopias – and their exhaustive criticism – is the proper and distinctive method of sociology', he put much effort into describing the ideal society (Wells 1916). His earliest and best-known attempt at this was *A Modern Utopia* (1905a), which described an idyllic World State ruled over by 'voluntary noblemen' known as 'Samurai'. Therefore, much as Wells has been hailed for his penetrating satirical comments on the Edwardian social-sexual-political

---

[1] This assumption permeates, amongst other works, Feir 2005.

I am grateful to the editors and also to the other participants at the conference on 'Welfare Economics and the Welfare State in Britain, 1884–1951' at Hitotsubashi University in March 2006. Their comments and suggestions proved valuable. John S. Partington has given me insightful comments and has provided me with a wealth of useful information. Peter Clarke also provided helpful information. Any errors that remain are of course my own responsibility.

milieu, it might seem that he was, mentally speaking, almost on a different planet from the practical-minded men who designed the pre-1914 welfare reforms. Yet Wells undoubtedly had a significant impact on key New Liberal reformers. As will be seen, Winston Churchill's debt to *A Modern Utopia* forms the clearest instance of this, but Wells also has a claim to have influenced other politicians, including David Lloyd George and Charles Masterman, who were closely involved with the birth of the welfare state. C. P. Snow (1967, p. 57), the scientist and author, was quite right to describe Wells as 'The great educator of unlikely people'.

This chapter provides the evidence for that influence. It must be remembered, of course, that intellectual factors were only part of the stimulus to reform. Demographic, institutional, and political pressures – including the rise of the Labour Party, and the challenge posed to the Liberal government by the power of the House of Lords – were undoubtedly crucial. Equally, Wells's thought needs to be considered alongside that of a number of other figures if its true significance is to be understood. It is *not* argued here that the 'classic' New Liberal thinkers, T. H. Green, D. G. Ritchie, J. A. Hobson and L. T. Hobhouse were less influential on politicians than has been traditionally assumed. It is merely noted that, whereas the evidence for *their* influence is often circumstantial and ambiguous, it can be shown in a very concrete way that MPs and ministers were reading Wells, paying attention to his ideas, and sometimes even quoting him in speeches. This makes us realise the importance, when examining 'welfare' in the broadest sense (as in the present volume), of taking a similarly broad approach in selecting our sources. It is important not to assume – as some scholars in fact seem to have done – that Wells's imaginative works can be read as a straightforward presentation of his views on politics and society. But politicians' reactions to them can tell us much about their own attitudes, and, therefore, they deserve to be added to the repertoire of treatises, pamphlets, journalism and periodical literature on which historians of political and economic thought conventionally draw.

Expanding the range of sources on which we draw forces us to think hard about the nature of intellectual influence and the extent to which it is ever possible to prove that one thinker influenced another. Quentin Skinner suggests that, in order to demonstrate the influence of writer A on writer B, the following conditions would have to be met: '(i) that B is known to have studied A's works; (ii) that B could not have found the relevant doctrines in any other writer than A; and (iii) that B could not have arrived at the relevant doctrines independently'. (Skinner (2002, pp. 75–6) acknowledges that test (iii) could perhaps never be passed, and it might be added that test (ii) is also an extremely difficult one. Let us consider the case of Hobson's influence on Lloyd George and Churchill, which is generally accepted (see, for example, Chapter 4 by Martin Daunton). The evidence for that influence rests principally on the similarities between Hobson's arguments and those of the politicians concerned. Historians seeking to show Hobson's influence have drawn attention to the fact that some contemporaries noted these similarities at the time. Peter Clarke, for example, draws on articles published in *The Nation*. Thus Hobson's book *The Industrial System* (1909) was described by the paper as 'a theoretical exposition of the principles of democratic finance at the very moment at which Mr. Lloyd George has been administering a practical demonstration' via the People's Budget (Clarke 1978, p. 115, quoting *The Nation*, 29 May 1909). Similarly, Clarke writes that 'Churchill's Leicester speech of 5 September 1909 was almost purely Hobsonian'. He also attributes to Hobson an article in the *Nation* which described Churchill's book, *Liberalism and the Social Problem* (1909), as ' "the clearest, most eloquent, and most convincing exposition" of the new Liberalism' (ibid., p. 117, quoting *The Nation*, 27 November 1909). This evidence demonstrates *affinities* between Hobson's thinking and that of Lloyd George and Churchill. It does not, however, establish that any of Skinner's three tests have been met. This does not mean that we should reject the idea of Hobson's influence on politicians out of hand. Yet, if we are willing to accept it we should be all the more ready to take seriously the claims of authors who meet the tests in full or in part. As will be seen, this is the case with Wells.

H. G. Wells (1866–1946) was born in quite humble circumstances in Bromley, Kent. During his youth he worked for spells as a draper's apprentice, as a pharmacist's assistant and as a pupil-teacher – experiences on which he later drew in his fiction – before at last securing a place at London's Normal School of Science. There he studied for a brief period under T. H. Huxley ('Darwin's bulldog'), who was to be a great influence on his thought. However, Wells's academic career did not live up to its early promise, and he instead made his name during the 1890s as the author of 'scientific romances' or, as he preferred it, 'fantasias of possibility' (Preface to Wells 1921). Many of these works had political undertones. For example, in the future portrayed in *The Time Machine* (1895), humans have evolved into two separate species, the placid, unintelligent Eloi and the subterranean Morlocks who treat them as prey. Wells intended this as a story of the degeneration that might occur if mankind did not work together for the good of the whole species (Smith 1986, p. 49). (One might see an echo of the tale in the 1909 speech in which Churchill spoke of the 'dual degeneration which comes from the simultaneous waste of extreme wealth and extreme want' – speech of 4 September 1909, in James 1981, p. 174.)

At the turn of the century, although he did not abandon science fiction, Wells's work moved in two new directions. He published *Love and Mr. Lewisham* (1900), which he followed up with other 'social' novels including *Kipps* (1905b), *Tono-Bungay* (1909a) and *Ann Veronica* (1909b). At the same time he moved into social and political writing, beginning with *Anticipations of the Reaction of Mechanical and Scientific Progress Upon Human Life and Thought* (1901), which was followed by *Mankind in the Making* (1903) and then *A Modern Utopia*. These years also saw his involvement with the Fabian Society, which he joined in 1903 and from which he resigned in 1908, following a drawn-out battle with the Society's 'old gang'. After a brief marriage and divorce in his twenties he had wed again, but went on to have a string of affairs, with Amber Reeves and Rebecca West amongst others. This is worth mentioning because it affected his public reputation at the time and the way in which his ideas were received in Liberal circles.

There is a strong case for saying that Wells, during the Edwardian era, viewed himself as a Liberal and hoped to devise a 'new Liberalism' to 'supersede the chaotic good intentions that constitute contemporary Liberalism' (H. G. Wells to W. T. Stead, 31 October 1901, quoted in Baylen 1974, p. 61). I have laid out that case in depth elsewhere; the present chapter is primarily concerned with how Wells's ideas were received (Toye 2008). However, a few points about his attitude need to be emphasised. To begin with, he saw socialism and liberalism as compatible, indeed as two sides of the same coin. This divided him from some other socialists, such as George Bernard Shaw, who saw them as irreconcilable. It also meant that, even though he was no conventional party man, he thought it desirable for socialists to cooperate with the Liberal Party. His operating assumption before 1914 was that no labour or socialist party had any hope of gaining a parliamentary majority within the foreseeable future. Therefore, if socialists wanted to achieve anything, they needed to 'contemplate a working political combination between the Socialist members in Parliament' and the 'non-capitalist section of the Liberal Party' (Wells 1908b). This is obviously significant when trying to explain how it was that radical or 'advanced' Liberals welcomed some of his ideas. They were clearly likely to react more warmly to a socialist who deprecated 'fanatical anti-Liberalism', and who believed that Liberals should in some cases be supported against 'wild' socialist candidates at by-elections, than to one who was prepared to risk antagonising them (Wells 1908c, pp. 252, 255).

Before we look at how Liberals received Wells's work, we need to take note of the substance of his two books that proved to be particularly important. *A Modern Utopia* sought to apply the insights of biological evolution to human society. In the book, Wells rejected the idea of creating a permanent blueprint for a new society in the way that he claimed that Utopian writers had always done pre-Darwin. Much of the emphasis was on experiment and progressive development; Utopia would be 'kinetic' rather than 'static'. There was also, of course, the 'Samurai' concept. Any man or woman could be admitted to this governing elite provided they agreed to follow its self-disciplinary rules. In Utopia, moreover, many problems that were normally considered to be economic ones were to be studied instead within the field of psychology. Like Hobson and other contemporaries (see Chapter 6 by Backhouse) Wells was dismissive of conventional economics, which, he argued, was in thrall to the belief that society was composed of avaricious individuals who were only interested in maximising personal utility.

Upon such quicksands rose an edifice that aped the securities of material science, developed a technical jargon and professed the discovery of 'laws'. Our liberation from these false presumptions through the rhetoric of Carlyle and Ruskin and the activities of the Socialists, is more apparent than real. The old edifice oppresses us still, repaired and altered by indifferent builders, underpinned in places, and with a slight change of name. 'Political Economy' has been painted out, and instead we read 'Economics – under entirely new management'. (Wells 1905a, pp. 89–90)

In spite of its utopianism, the book did include a number of suggestions that were capable of practical application in the here and now. For example, in Utopia, 'the State will insure the children of every citizen, and those legitimately dependent upon him, against the inconvenience of his death [...] and it will insure him against old age and infirmity' (Wells 1905a, pp. 99–100). The book did not use the term 'welfare state', a term that was not yet in currency,[2] but it did place great emphasis on child welfare. It also envisaged a minimum wage, labour exchanges and contracyclical public works:

[2] However, the term 'Social State' was used in at least one pre-war Liberal pamphlet: R. Rea, *Social reform versus socialism* (1912), quoted in Garland 1985, p. 232.

All over the world the labour exchanges will be reporting the fluctuating pressure of economic demand and transferring workers from this region of excess to that of scarcity; and whenever the excess is universal, the World State – failing an adequate development of private enterprise – will either reduce the working day and so absorb the excess, or set on foot some permanent special works of its own, paying the minimum wage and allowing them to progress just as slowly or just as rapidly as the ebb and flow of labour dictated. (Wells 1905a, pp. 153–4)

Wells was not, of course, the first person to think of such ideas, but his proposals had some obvious similarities with the reforms implemented by the Liberal government after 1906.[3] As will be seen, this may have been more than coincidence.

Tono-Bungay, by contrast, was not a prescriptive work, but a 'Condition of England' novel, which is reckoned by some (a little implausibly) to represent the height of Wells's creative achievement (MacKenzie and MacKenzie 1973, p. 243). It is the tale of the rise and fall of Edward Ponderevo, a patent medicine king, as narrated by George Ponderevo, his nephew and sometime right-hand man; 'Tono-Bungay' is the 'slightly injurious rubbish' that they bottle and sell to a gullible public (Wells 1909a, p. 120). The follies of capitalist affluence form the book's great theme. George Ponderevo notes towards the end that he has called his story *Tono-Bungay*, 'but I had far better have called it Waste'. It was 'the story of a country hectic with a wasting aimless fever of trade and money-making and pleasure-seeking' (ibid., p. 83). (Earlier in the book a procession of the unemployed is described as 'the gutter waste of competitive civilisation'. – ibid., p. 194.) Here was Ruskin's concept of 'illth' – the opposite of wealth – writ large.[4] And this was what resonated with a number of New Liberals.

How did Wells's thinking about society, wealth and welfare fit in with the intellectual currents of the time? He had some significant affinities with many thinkers who are typically placed into the New Liberal category, although these should not be overstated.[5] Anne Fremantle has observed, in passing, that there were similarities between Green's conception of the state and Wells's (Fremantle 1960, p. 149). This is certainly true at a rather general level, given that Wells could surely have endorsed Green's view of it as 'the sustainer and harmoniser of social relations' (Green 2002, p. 105). Wells was familiar with Green's concept

---

[3] Hyde (1956, p. 227) touches on this point but does not develop it.

[4] Wells had a somewhat ambivalent attitude to Ruskin, but he did give him credit for having attacked the 'tyrannous and dogmatic' assumptions of political economy: 1908a, p. 239. See also Wells 1903, p. 156.

[5] We may also note that there are a few traces in his work of the influence of Mill: McLean 2007.

of 'positive' versus 'negative' freedom. 'Individual liberty in a community is not, as mathematicians would say, always of the same sign', as *A Modern Utopia* puts it. 'To ignore this is the essential fallacy of the cult called Individualism' (Wells 1905a, pp. 41–2). Yet the similarities between Wells and, later, more radical New Liberal thinkers – who, unlike Green, were heavily influenced by evolutionary discourse (Freeden 1978, pp. 19, 76–116) – were much more marked.

There is no evidence that Wells had any direct influence on Hobhouse or vice versa; and, unlike Wells, Hobhouse did not believe that devising utopias was a valid method of social science (Meadowcroft 1994, p. 82). Nevertheless, there were some important likenesses between the two men's ideas. They both believed that there was no necessary contradiction between individualism and collectivism, and they had similar views on social evolution. Both believed in a broad scheme of human progress, the purpose of which the human mind could grasp and thus help bring about. For Hobhouse this was 'a development of organic harmony', and for Wells it was the 'development of a common general idea, a common general purpose out of a present confusion' (Hobhouse 1913, p. 372; Wells 1929 [1908], pp. 58–9). There were also many points of overlap between Wells's ideas and those of the Oxford philosopher D. G. Ritchie, who was influenced by Green and Darwin, among others. In 1893 – the year before he was appointed to a professorship at St. Andrew's – Ritchie broke with the Fabian Society when it appeared that it might abandon permeation and create an independent party instead. This prefigured Wells's own dispute with the society. Like Wells, he argued that the theory of evolution pointed not to laissez-faire but to state action. He also criticised gender inequality, and supported the idea of world federation (den Otter 1996, chapter 3 and 2004). But there is no evidence that Ritchie engaged directly with Wells or Wells with Ritchie.

Ritchie died in 1903, which meant that, unlike Hobhouse and Hobson, he could at any rate only have read the very earliest of Wells's political and social writings. Hobson, unlike these others, undoubtedly did read Wells. Both he and Wells were notable internationalists, who welcomed the fact that, in their view, the forces of globalization were acting to unite disparate peoples by dissolving local and national identities (Iriye 2002, p. 54).[6] In 1901, Graham Wallas (whose own connections with Wells will

---

[6] In a rare comment on Hobson, Wells (1918, p. x) welcomed his book *Towards International Government* (1915) as 'a very sympathetic contribution from the English liberal left'.

be discussed below) noted having 'an interesting talk with J. A. Hobson about Wells' Anticipations' at the National Liberal Club.[7] In 1906 Hobson published an article on *A Modern Utopia* in the *Contemporary Review*. He focussed on the 'Samurai' idea, of which he was coldly dismissive: 'regarded as an experiment in speculative politics Mr. Wells' aristocratic scheme of government is defective in three respects. His aristocracy cannot acquire the power with which it is accredited, could not retain it if they got it, and could not exercise it without degrading both themselves and the subject populace'. Nevertheless, he also wrote that 'Mr. Wells possesses one of the boldest, freest, best-informed and (to adopt his own favoured term) most "poietic" [i.e. creative] minds of our age, and I know of no book which would, in the hands of a capable master, serve so well as a text-book of general politics among persons capable of free thinking and really solicitous to understand the large and tangled issues of modern progress' (Hobson 1906, pp. 497 and 487). (Hobson is likely to have approved in particular of Wells's proposal that the state should guarantee a minimum standard of living to its citizens – Partington 2003, p. 58). In 1909, Hobson thanked Wells for a copy of *Tono-Bungay*, which he had already been reading in serial form in the *English Review*. 'It is the finest piece of sociological fiction of our time', he wrote. 'You are massing many different forces against the citadel. But our amazingly cultivated obtuseness is a formidable defence'. He proposed meeting for a talk, although it is not clear if this took place, and social relations between them do not seem to have blossomed greatly, in spite of Hobson's admiration for Wells's writing.[8]

Wells's relationship with the political scientist Graham Wallas was one in which there was a much more demonstrable mutual influence. Wallas was an Oxford man, but he had not come under the sway of Green's idealist philosophy. By the end of 1900, he and Wells were acquainted, and they discussed topics such as 'what shall the agnostic teach his child'.[9] He thought *Love and Mr. Lewisham* 'a rather deeply tragical little book' and found that Wells's fiction packed an emotional punch.[10] He was also impressed by *Anticipations*. Wallas – one of the original Fabian

---

[7] Graham Wallas to Ada Wallas, 25 November 1901, Wallas Family papers, Newnham College, Cambridge, 1/1/5.
[8] Hobson to Wells, 12 February 1909, H. G. Wells Papers, University of Illinois, H–318. See also Betsy Hobson to Catherine Wells, 9 March 1909, Wells Papers, H–319.
[9] Ada Wallas diary, 1 January 1901, Wallas Family Papers, 2/1/2.
[10] Graham Wallas to Ada Wallas, 27 June 1900 and 16 March 1906, Wallas Family papers, 1/1/4 and 1/1/10.

essayists – co-sponsored Wells's Fabian membership in 1903, but himself resigned from the Society the following year, when he felt it to be taking too strong an anti-Liberal line. (It is reasonable to describe him, from at least this point on, as a New Liberal.) He and Wells took a walking holiday in the Alps in 1903. Their discussions helped provide the stimulus for *A Modern Utopia*, and the two men advised one another on the manuscripts of each other's books. In *Human Nature in Politics* (1908), Wallas paid tribute to Wells's 'sincere and courageous speculations', and the title of his book *The Great Society* (1914) may have been a nod to that of Wells's 1912 edited collection, *The Great State*. The two were agreed on the importance of education and had similar views on the waste and inefficiency of contemporary society. However, Wells came to view Wallas's approach as excessively academic, whereas Wallas was sceptical about the idea of rule by a quasi-Platonic elite, as represented by the 'Samurai' idea (Wiener 1971, pp. 5–9, 57, 77–9, 105, 107–8, 125, 130, 141–2; MacKenzie and MacKenzie 1973, pp. 168–9; Wallas 1908, p. 200).

It is also worth noting that Alfred Zimmern, who is credited with introducing the term 'welfare state' into English (in 1934), was inspired by Wells during the Edwardian period (Hennessy 1992, p. 121). Zimmern, an Oxford classical scholar, wrote to Wallas circa 1908 suggesting that Wells might be recruited to the cause of reform of the university:

An Oxford such as we want is just what he needs for the training of his samurai, and I know from what he said when he was there that he *does* believe in the future of the place (unlike [Sidney] Webb). If he could write for us and use his imagination to show people the future of Oxford at work, softening the bitternesses and reconciling the contradictions of a democratic state, it would be an immense stimulus.
    The chapter on *Culture* in his American book [*The Future in America*, 1906] suggested this to me.[11]

Nothing came of this idea, however, and Zimmern's later career, which was marked both by faith in the British Empire and antipathy to the discipline of science, shows few obvious traces of Wellsian influence (Toye and Toye 2007, Zimmern 1936). Yet this letter does demonstrate, if nothing else, that not all contemporaries were as dismissive of the Samurai idea as Hobson was. It also reinforces one's sense that Wells's Oxford links were stronger than his Cambridge ones, at least as far as Liberalism was concerned. Donald Markwell suggests that Keynes's views on 'racial

---

[11] Alfred Zimmern to Wallas, 14 July [1908?], Graham Wallas Papers, British Library of Political and Economic Science, 1/36/9.

wars, overpopulation generally, and eugenics' may have been influenced by Wells (Markwell 2006, p. 27). But the evidence for this is weak. Keynes does seem to have admired *The Time Machine*, but when he read *A Modern Utopia* in 1905 he merely observed that it 'rather peters out'.[12] Wells did have connections to young Cambridge socialists, including future Chancellor Hugh Dalton, but these are not of major significance for the history of pre-1914 welfare reform (Dalton 1953, pp. 74–5).[13]

These various intellectual similarities, interpersonal connections and hints and suggestions of influence are intriguing; but it is important not to blow them out of proportion. The main purpose of mentioning them here is to draw attention to the fact that readers of Wells would have been exposed to messages that were in important ways similar to those of the 'classic' New Liberal ideologues, at least some of whom were directly familiar with his work. This may help explain Liberal politicians' receptivity to Wells – which, as will be seen, was pronounced. Major figures within the Liberal Party found themselves in fundamental sympathy with many of his views, and at times were influenced by them. Churchill, Lloyd George, Masterman and Leo Chiozza Money are the main examples, but his opinions also attracted interest – if not always enthusiasm – in less likely quarters.

It is common knowledge that Churchill was an admirer of Wells's writings, and that the two men were friends. Their relationship has been traced in some depth, albeit with the main focus on personal rather than intellectual concerns (Smith 1989, pp. 93–116. See also Weidhorn 1992, pp. 25–30, 40–4). Paul K. Alkon (2006, pp. 167–8) does acknowledge that the men's 'views sometimes coincided', especially when it came to the impact of science on warfare, but he argues that this was 'a matter of imaginative affinities rather than influence'. Thus, although C. P. Snow was thinking of Churchill specifically when he made his remark about Wells having educated 'unlikely people', scholars do not seem to have picked up on his comment. And there has never been any explicit suggestion that Wells influenced Churchill's social thought. Yet, as will be seen, this was clearly the case. It is probable that their various public spats after World War I – most notably over British intervention in the Russian civil war – have distracted attention from Wells's earlier impact.

[12] In the 1930s, Keynes paid a generalised tribute to Wells, but made it clear that he did not think he had much worthwhile to say about economics. Keynes to G. L. Strachey, 8 July 1905, quoted in Harrod 1951, p. 106; J. Toye 2000, pp. 148–58, 160 n. 7; Keynes 1934, pp. 30–5.

[13] Interestingly, Dalton cited Wells's view on inheritance in one of his budget speeches: see Dalton 1962, p. 116.

Churchill came across Wells's early works at around the time of their first publication. As he recalled in 1931: 'when I came upon *The Time Machine*, that marvellous philosophical romance [...] I shouted with joy. Then I read all his books'.[14] At his death he had a substantial collection of Wells's novels, although *Men Like Gods* (1923), in which Churchill was satirised as 'Rupert Catskill', was missing.[15] The first personal contact between the two came in 1901, when Wells's publishers sent Churchill a copy of *Anticipations*. Churchill, who had recently been elected as a Conservative MP, sent Wells a long letter in response. 'I read everything you write', he told him, and added that there was much in the book with which he agreed, although he felt that Wells put too much faith in government by experts and argued that society would not change as quickly as the book claimed.[16] Early in 1902 the two men met at the House of Commons.

Their next significant recorded exchange was over *A Modern Utopia*. In the meantime, Churchill had joined the Liberal Party (in 1904) and had been appointed Under-Secretary for the Colonies in the new Liberal government (in December 1905). At this time, neither Churchill, nor any other minister, had a coherent, well-developed plan for state-sponsored social reform. During the general election of 1906, he spoke of the problem of poverty, and of how, paradoxically, 'great luxury' co-existed with suffering and 'waste'. He argued, though, that it 'was not possible by any mechanical state system to adequately deal with this question. The Lifeboat Service of the world was manned by the arms of men, and rescue work was voluntary'.[17] A few months later, Churchill discarded this approach, having read *A Modern Utopia* in the meantime.

Wells, or his publisher, had sent him a copy of the book soon after it was published. However, Churchill did not find time to read it until his holidays in 1906. On 9 October that year he wrote to Wells about it:

You have certainly succeeded in making earth a heaven; but I have always feared that heaven might be a v[er]y dull place *à la longue*. Still there is so much in your

---

[14] Winston Churchill, 'H. G. Wells', *Sunday Pictorial*, 23 August 1931, in *The Collected Essays of Sir Winston Churchill*, ed. Michael Wolff, 4 vols. (London: Library of Imperial History, 1976) III, pp. 50–4 at 52–3.

[15] Martin Gilbert to Randolph Churchill, 27 July 1967, Randolph Churchill Papers, Churchill College, Cambridge, 1/2/30.

[16] Winston Churchill to H. G. Wells, 17 November 1901, Wells Papers, C-238–3a.

[17] 'In Angel Meadow', *Manchester Guardian*, 8 January 1906, reproduced in Randolph S. Churchill, *Winston S. Churchill, vol. II: Young Statesman, 1901–1914*, London: Heinemann, 1967, pp. 123–4. It should, however, be noted that Churchill had shown some interest in social reform during his earlier Conservative period.

writing that stimulates my fancy that I owe you a great debt, quite apart from the courtesy & kindness of your present. Especially did I admire the skill and courage with which the questions of marriage & population were discussed.[18]

Two days after writing to Wells, Churchill gave a speech in Glasgow (11 October 1906, in James 1981, pp. 105–11). In it he declared boldly that 'The cause of the Liberal Party is the cause of the left-out millions', and spoke of the need of the state to concern itself with the care of children, the sick and the aged. Like Wells, he used the terminology of evolution: 'The existing organisation of society is driven by one mainspring – competitive selection'. There were also direct verbal similarities with Wells's work. Some of these may have been no more than commonplaces. For example, Wells (1905a, p. 92) argued that 'To the onlooker, both Individualism and Socialism are, in the absolute, absurdities [...] the way of sanity runs, perhaps even sinuously, down the intervening valley'. Churchill likewise noted that 'It is not possible to draw a hard-and-fast line between individualism and collectivism'. There were also more striking similarities. Wells wrote: 'The State will stand at the back of the economic struggle as the reserve employer of labour' (ibid., p. 141). Churchill said: 'I am of the opinion that the State should increasingly assume the position of the reserve employer of labour'. Wells argued: 'Whatever we do, man will remain a competitive creature [...] no Utopia will ever save him completely from the emotional drama of struggle, from exultations and humiliations, from pride and prostration and shame. [...] But we may do much to make the margin of failure endurable' (ibid., p. 139). Churchill said: 'I do not want to see impaired the vigour of competition, but we can do much to mitigate the consequences of failure'. Furthermore, it may be significant that Churchill explicitly used the term 'Utopia':

I am sure that if the vision of a fair [i.e. beautiful] Utopia which cheers the hearts and lights the imagination of the toiling multitudes, should ever break into reality, it will be by developments through, and modifications in, and by improvements out of, the existing competitive organisation of society; and I believe that Liberalism mobilised, and active as it is to-day, will be a principal and indispensable factor in that noble evolution.

The Glasgow speech is generally seen as a landmark in Churchill's thinking on social questions. Paul Addison has written that 'Churchill had stumbled into a declaration of support for the New Liberalism' (Addison

---

[18] Winston Churchill to H. G. Wells, 9 October 1906, Wells Papers, C-238–2.

1992, p. 57). But he had not stumbled into it at all. He had been led into it, albeit by Wells rather than by one of the usual New Liberal suspects. As for Skinner's tests, the first is met, in that Churchill had read Wells. If Churchill's own testimony is accepted, then the second and even third conditions are also met insofar as we may infer from his letter that he found the ideas concerned in Wells and not elsewhere and did not arrive at them independently.[19]

Given Churchill's explicit approval of Wells's treatment of 'marriage & population' questions, it is possible that *A Modern Utopia* played a part in his becoming 'a strong eugenist' (Blunt n.d., p. 399).[20] Wells had suggested that in Utopia people would only be allowed to have children if they met certain conditions, including physical fitness and financial independence. He implied that those who broke the rules would be subject to compulsory sterilisation, especially if 'if it is disease or imbecility you have multiplied' (Wells 1905a, pp. 182–3). Churchill was, of course, open to a wide array of intellectual influences and political pressures, and it is important not to overstate Wells's impact on him. All the same, on the evidence presented here, there seems to be a strong case for saying, at the very least, that Wells's ideas did have a significant direct effect on the way that he articulated his views on social reform during this formative period. If so, Wells's subsequent decision to support Churchill, rather than the socialist candidate, in the 1908 North-West Manchester by-election, is rendered more explicable. This is usually seen as a typically 'maverick' act on Wells's part, and personal considerations doubtless did play a role in it.[21] Yet, as has been seen, he had good grounds for his claim that Churchill's mind was 'active and still rapidly developing and broadening' in line with his own views, even if his apparent hope that his ministerial friend would mutate into a socialist was far-fetched.[22]

Lloyd George presents an equally interesting case, although a less clear-cut one. It is well known that Frances Stevenson, with whom he began a thirty-year affair in 1913, was much influenced by Wells, and perhaps especially by *Ann Veronica*, the story of an (at least ostensibly) liberated young woman. (Lloyd George, obviously, was not one to condemn

---

[19] Of course, one might argue that Churchill could have exaggerated the book's influence on him in order to flatter Wells.

[20] Churchill's eugenic beliefs are well documented. See Addison 1992, pp. 123–6.

[21] Smith 1989, p. 99. See also Radice 1984, p. 178, and Foot 1996, pp. 88–9. Anthony West (1984, p. 315), however, correctly notes Wells's view that Churchill was 'open-minded and educable'.

[22] Wells, 'An Open Letter to an Elector in N. W. Manchester', *Daily News*, 21 April 1908.

Wells's private life.) As she wrote in her memoirs, 'I was exceedingly interested [...] in the emancipation of women, and Wells's contribution towards the breaking of the barriers which hitherto had hemmed us in and discriminated between the sexes appealed to me inevitably' (Lloyd George 1967, p. 36. See also Campbell 2006, pp. 7–8). Lloyd George was, of course, the beneficiary of this, in that, like Ann Veronica, Stevenson exercised her 'emancipation' by dedicating her life rather slavishly to the service of a Great Man. However, he undoubtedly had an independent interest in Wells's work. This is demonstrated by an entry in the diary of Lucy Masterman (wife of Charles Masterman) from December 1910, the year before Lloyd George met Stevenson. 'Wells came up into the conversation in connection with the many rumours about him lately, and Charlie described a party at Taplow where the whole company had cut him except [Arthur] Balfour'. She added: 'George admires Wells's writings tremendously. "He is the only writer whose opinions on politics interests me in the least", he said, "I think he is the greatest writer of today' ".[23] (Skinner's first test is thus passed, even if the others are not.) Other evidence suggests that this was more than a chance remark. In 1912, Charles Masterman told Wells that Lloyd George was continually reproving him for not arranging a meeting with him.[24] In November 1914, Stevenson recorded in her diary that 'We have both been reading Wells' last book *The Wife of Sir Isaac Harman* and C. [i.e. Lloyd George] thinks it is his most brilliant work' (Taylor 1971, p. 13, entry for 30 November 1914). (The lovers may have been attracted by the book's negative portrayal of the institution of marriage.) Wells and Lloyd George shared some views on policy, moreover. For example, they both favoured a census of national production; although, when Wells called for this in 1912, he overlooked the fact that Lloyd George had successfully introduced a bill for this purpose six years earlier (Wells 1912a, p. 25; Tooze n.d.).

The two men did meet, although it is not clear precisely when.[25] According Lloyd George's son Richard:

I remember a wonderful little passage of arms between my father and H. G. Wells at home, with the great novelist and sociologist baiting L. G. over what he

---

[23] Lucy Masterman diary, 8 December 1910, Masterman Papers, University of Birmingham Special Collections, CFGM 29/2/2/2.

[24] C. F. G. Masterman to H. G. Wells, 'Sunday 25th' [1912], Wells Papers, M-228.

[25] Smith is a little vague, but appears to suggest that they met prior to 1914. Masterman, however, claimed to have introduced Wells to Lloyd George when the latter was Minister of Munitions (i.e., in 1915–16). Smith 1986, p. 114; Masterman, 1922, p. 595.

called the 'patchwork' economic policy of those former times – 'cutting a piece of the tail of the shirt to mend the hole in the collar'. H. G. was an excitable debater, and his thin pugnacious voice rose to a squeak of triumph as he out-Lloyded George in his own method of argument. (Lloyd George 1961, p. 86)

They had some further contacts, particularly after the latter's fall from power in 1922.[26] Wells wrote that he had 'a strong but qualified affection' for Lloyd George (Wells 1923, p. 71). But, as Stevenson noted in 1934, they never seemed 'really to hit it off when they meet. There is a clash of intellects, which is disappointing' (Taylor 1971, p. 286 – entry for 31 October 1934. See also Masterman 1922, p. 595). All the same, there seems no real reason not to take Lloyd George's remark to Lucy Masterman at face value. Given what we know of the latter's reading habits – he attracted the sobriquet 'the illiterate Prime Minister' because 'he never reads or writes' (Hendrick 1925, p. 371) – it is not difficult to believe that he should have preferred Wells's vivid style to that of, say, Hobson and Hobhouse. (Of course, he may well have picked up on these other men's ideas indirectly through conversations with his officials and others.) In other words, we should take seriously the evidence of Lloyd George's sympathy with Wells's ideas, even if we cannot trace their impact on him in detail. One might even say that his later record as Minister of Munitions (1915–16) – which demonstrated a belief that private businessmen could collaborate selflessly with the government in order to maximise production for the common good – was evidence that he shared Wells's vision of a 'Great State', distinct from conventional socialism, that would undertake national economic planning.

The man who introduced Wells to Lloyd George was Charles Masterman, who is himself generally seen as a significant New Liberal thinker. Masterman rose to prominence as a journalist and commentator and in 1903 became literary editor of the *Daily News*. He was elected to Parliament in 1906 and, as a junior minister after 1908, played an important role in the drafting of the National Insurance Bill. His enthusiasm for Wells, personally and ideologically, was manifest, as Wells scholars have noted (MacKenzie and MacKenzie 1973, p. 243; Smith, 1986, pp. 99, 113–14, 132, 202–4). However, the possible significance of this for the study of New Liberalism has been overlooked. Eric Hopkins's recent biography

---

[26] Wells to Lord Northcliffe, n.d., 1916, Northcliffe Papers, British Library, MS Add.62161, f. 95. For the later contacts see the correspondence in the Lloyd George Papers, Parliamentary Archives, London, LG G/19/19 and, in particular, Wells to Philip Guedalla, 7 February 1929, in Smith, *Correspondence 3*, pp. 288–9.

of Masterman mentions his friendship with Wells, but there is little suggestion in it of a significant intellectual relationship between them (even
though Lucy Masterman's earlier book on her husband provides some
important clues). Samuel Hynes, albeit only in passing, has emphasised the
men's dissimilarity (Hopkins 1999; Hynes 1991; Masterman 1939, p. 68).
Yet Masterman's and Wells's world-views overlapped to a great extent, as
the former's advocacy of 'government by an aristocracy of intelligence'
suggests (Masterman 1920, p. 213, quoted in Jackson 2007, p. 28).

Masterman read *Love and Mr. Lewisham* on first publication, and
found it 'Good especially in some parts' and 'Sordid enough' (diary entry,
30 June 1900, in Masterman 1939, p. 34). His response to *Anticipations*
was similarly ambivalent: he acknowledged Wells's 'profound insight'
but, as a committed Christian himself, thought the book underrated the
strength and value of religious forces in society (Masterman 1902, pp. 25).
(That November, Beatrice Webb invited Wells to join the Co-Efficients,
a cross-party dining club of which Masterman was a member – Seymour-
Jones 1992, p. 260.) The following year, he made a first, unsuccessful,
attempt at getting into the Commons, fighting a by-election campaign
at Dulwich. In the course of doing so, he spoke to a group of local parents. He told Wells afterwards: 'I quoted freely in my lecture from your
new book [...] and urged all the unhappy parents to read it'.[27] This book
was *Mankind in the Making*, much of which focussed on the problem of
education. Clearly, a poorly reported meeting with a tyro candidate was
not as seminal as Churchill's Glasgow speech. But here was another clear
example of a New Liberal politician absorbing parts of Wells's message
and relaying them to the public.

By 1905 Masterman was describing Wells as 'that most courageous
and individual of all social prophets' (Masterman 1905a, p. 320). He
told him directly that he was one of the few men whose opinion he valued: 'I believe we have an enormous amount in common: and have felt
again and again in reading your work – this is exactly what I have been
wanting to say – and unable to say it'.[28] He found *A Modern Utopia* to
be 'eloquent, provocative, and stimulating' (Masterman 1905b). A few
months later he wrote: 'I have read – and I suppose all sensible men
have read – all Mr. Wells's novels and social prophecies; and I should
unhesitatingly affirm "Kipps" to be the best story he has yet given us'
(Masterman 1905c). *Tono-Bungay* struck an even greater chord. In

[27] Masterman to Wells, 4 November 1903, Wells Papers, M-228.
[28] Masterman to Wells, 11 May 1905, Wells Papers, M-228.

1922, Masterman recalled reading the proofs on the train after visiting Wells at Folkestone: 'I could scarcely refrain from shouting out and brandishing it in the faces of the bewildered passengers, as I realised I had got hold of a masterpiece. I doubt if a year passes in which I do not read it again'.[29] Masterman wholly endorsed the book's satire of modern commercial values. His own work *The Condition of England* (1909), which criticised 'public penury, private ostentation', was peppered with references to Wells's work. (One commentator noted that 'The style of the book will often remind the reader of Mr. Wells; but Mr. Wells writes with more freedom and more enjoyment'.) Wells, in Masterman's view, successfully depicted a world that, although calm on the surface, was exhibiting fractures that portended cataclysmic change (Masterman 1909, pp. 25, 150, 234–7, 282–3; Kennedy 1912).

Wells later recalled that Masterman was one of those who stuck by him during the uproar provoked by *Ann Veronica*, which was denounced for its alleged immorality in *The Spectator* and elsewhere (Wells 1984 [1934], p. 471). Masterman wrote to him of *The New Machiavelli*: 'Whether in agreement or not, it is amazingly stimulating and interesting'.[30] All in all it was natural that, when Masterman was put in charge of British wartime propaganda, Wells was one of the authors he recruited.[31] In a laudatory post-war assessment, Masterman said that he knew of no other modern writer who was 'so passionately disturbed by the fate of future generations'; Wells was listened to 'because men believe in his transparent sincerity and honesty'. By now, although his own religious faith was still firm, Masterman did not view Wells's scientific humanism as a major barrier to mutual understanding. He wrote: 'Mr Wells has seemed to have struggled towards a Gospel – clutching desperately at a faith by which a man can live [...]. He has refused to "put by" the burden of human destiny'.[32] Masterman may sometimes have fallen short of the utterly slavish reaction to his books that Wells often seemed to require. But he was surely right to tell him – when he reacted badly to some mild criticisms – 'I think I have written more of praise and attempted interpretation of your work for nearly 20 years than any man alive'.[33]

---

[29] Masterman 1922, p. 590.
[30] Masterman to Wells, 10 September 1910, Wells Papers, M-228.
[31] Masterman 1939, p. 272.
[32] Masterman, 1922, p. 597. For Wells's views see Glover 1972, pp. 117–35.
[33] Masterman to Wells, 10 December 1922, Wells Papers, M-228. Wells had objected to passages (pp. 178–83) in Masterman's book *England After War: A Study*, London: Hodder and Stoughton, n.d. (1922).

Of course, in his role as a journalist, Masterman read a lot of books and commended many of them, including, notably, those of E. M. Forster.[34] His praise of Wells was therefore not exactly unique, but its significance went beyond a merely literary judgement. As the episode of the 1903 Dulwich speech shows, Wells's views did have a direct impact on his public political message. Again, some of Skinner's tests are met, in whole or in part.

Another New Liberal figure with significant connections to Wells was Leo Chiozza Money, a radical author and journalist elected in 1906 as Liberal MP for North Paddington. Though neglected today, Money was a seminal figure in Edwardian political economy.[35] He did not hold office until World War I; his chief services to the Edwardian Liberal Party were as a publicist, but were none the less significant for that. He influenced Churchill's thinking on trade, and in 1912 Lloyd George thanked him for his 'magnificent service to the National Insurance Scheme'.[36] Asquith cited him as the foremost authority on the fiscal question.[37] His best-known work was *Riches and Poverty* (1905). This book provided a vivid statistical illustration of the stark inequalities of income distribution in Britain and impressed Wells as being 'extraordinarily valuable and suggestive' (Wells 1905c, p. 413). After its publication, the two men struck up a warm friendship, and Wells successfully urged Money to join the Fabians.[38] Money did not feel able to join Wells's agitation for the Society's reform; and, surprisingly for a Liberal MP, he was keener than Wells was on the idea of it organising a socialist political party.[39] But in 1908 – not long before his own resignation from the Society – Wells nominated him as a candidate for the executive; he was elected, and served for three years.[40] In 1909 Money told Wells that *Tono-Bungay* had 'delighted' him – although he criticised the scene in which

---

[34] Masterman's early reviews of Forster are regarded as insightful and important by a number of modern critics. He is also seen by some as an important influence on Forster. See, for example, Born (1992, pp. 141–59).

[35] A useful introduction to his career is Daunton 2004. However, Chiozza Money has not received the attention he deserves in the wider historiography.

[36] Toye 2007, pp. 27–9; Lloyd George to Leo Chiozza Money, 29 January 1912, Leo Chiozza Money Papers, Cambridge University Library, MS Add 9259/IV/37.

[37] 'The Coalition', *The Times*, 23 November 1912.

[38] Money, 'On the Brink', f. 378; Wells to Chiozza Money, 10 October 1906, Chiozza Money Papers, Add. 9259/IV/61.

[39] Money to Wells, 20 May 1907, Wells Papers, M-409.

[40] Wells to Edward Pease, 14 March 1908, Fabian Society Papers, A9/3/29; Pease, *History*, p. 286. Money served again in 1919–22.

George Ponderevo finally parts from Beatrice, his childhood sweet-heart.[41] (Masterman, by contrast, approved highly of the book's female characters.)[42] In 1912 he contributed an essay to Wells's book *The Great State*. Like him, he feared that 'Without culture of a kind which is not now possessed even by our ruling classes' there was a risk that a social-ist society would turn out to be nothing more than a 'Servile State'.[43] At the same time, he endorsed Wells's idea of 'The Great State', which, in Money's words, meant that 'the whole of the adult population should be organised to produce a high minimum standard of life, and that such organisation would yield to the whole community not only the materials of such a standard but a quality and degree of leisure and liberty at pres-ent undreamed of' (Money 1914, p. v).

Wells applauded Money's decision to resign from the coalition gov-ernment at the end of the war, in protest at its decision to discontinue state control of the shipping industry.[44] Money fought the ensuing elec-tion as a Labour candidate but was defeated, and never sat in parlia-ment again. During the 1920s he fell out with Wells, who disapproved of his outspoken support for Mussolini.[45] In his memoirs, he compared himself to Wells: 'It is ever those who delight in organizing society who are themselves the least amenable to discipline. For others, like H. G. Wells [does], I make far-reaching arrangements, but again like H. G., I do not love to be arranged!'[46] This may have been an oblique reference to Money's own chaotic private life. In 1928 he was acquitted of commit-ting an indecent offence with a young lady in Hyde Park, but five years later he was convicted of indecently assaulting a woman in a railway carriage.[47] 'There was a time when our ideas were much in common', he wrote to Wells ruefully in 1934. 'Since then your voice has become a trumpet and mine a whisper.'[48] Again, there is a case for saying that Skinner's tests are met to some degree.

Another radical MP who liked Wells's work was Charles Trevelyan. Trevelyan was a member of the Rainbow Circle, a progressive discussion

---

[41] Money to Wells, 18 February 1909, Wells Papers, M-409.
[42] Masterman to Wells, n.d., 'Tuesday', c. 1909, Wells Papers, M-228.
[43] Money 1912, p. 101. Wells and Money owed the term 'servile state' to Hilaire Belloc. For Belloc's influence on Wells, see Toye 2008.
[44] Wells to Money, n.d., 1918, Chiozza Money Papers Add. 9259/IV/63.
[45] Money, 'On the Brink', f. 378; Money to Wells, 18 and 24 February 1927, Wells Papers, M-409.
[46] Money, 'On the Brink', f. 11.
[47] Daunton 2004.
[48] Money to Wells, 6 November 1934, Wells Papers, M-409.

group that counted many New Liberals among its number. In 1905 he told Wells, whom he had previously met at the Webbs', that he had been reading *Anticipations* 'with a good deal of agreement and immense interest'.[49] Prior to 1914, Wells also received quite a warm reception from *The Nation*, a weekly paper that was one of the bastions of the New Liberalism. During his dispute with the Fabian Society, the paper praised the 'gallant endeavour of Mr. H. G. Wells and his reforming friends to pump oxygen into the body of Fabianism', whilst attacking the 'anti-democratic attitude' of Shaw and the Society's other leaders.[50] When Wells left the society, H. W. Massingham, the paper's editor, wrote to him: 'I'm sorry for progress and glad for literature you're out'.[51] (Massingham had himself left the Fabians in 1893, at the same time as Ritchie.)[52] Although *The Nation* declined to serialize *Tono-Bungay*, Massingham read it 'with great interest & sympathy' and thought it provided a 'very remarkable' portrait of modern English life.[53] *The New Machiavelli* got a rather mixed review in the paper, but the reviewer did acknowledge that 'for a sketch of a profoundly uneasy society, conscious of its muddles and unable to see a way out', the book 'would be hard to beat'.[54] Wells's policy proposals also received serious consideration. In *The Great State* he proposed, in order to avoid one class of the community being condemned to act as a servile labouring class, 'a general conscription and a period of public service for everyone'.[55] *The Nation*'s reviewer expressed 'profound sympathy' with much of Wells's overall message, and found this solution to the labour question highly desirable: 'It is just, honest, and, on the face of things, technically feasible'.[56] Wells, prickly as ever, was not grateful for the review, as he thought it gave a misleading account of his earlier ideas.[57] Relations do not seem to have been permanently soured, though, as Wells attended the

---

[49] C. P. Trevelyan to H. G. Wells, 1 May 1905, Wells Papers, M-409.

[50] 'The Career of Fabianism', *The Nation*, 30 March 1907.

[51] H. W. Massingham to Wells, n.d., 1908, quoted in Smith 1986, p. 110; Clarke 1978, p. 43.

[52] Clarke 1978, p. 43.

[53] Massingham to Wells, 16 May 1907, H. W. Massingham Papers, Norfolk Record Office. It may have been Massingham who provided the paper's enthusiastic review: 'The Town of Vanity', *The Nation*, 13 February 1909.

[54] 'An Odyssey of Discontent', *The Nation*, 21 January 1911.

[55] He anticipated that this period would be short, perhaps a year: Wells 1912, p. 39.

[56] 'Pot-Shots at Utopia', *The Nation*, 15 June 1912. H. G. Wells to the editor of *The Nation*, published 12 June 1912, reproduced in Smith, *Correspondence 2*, pp. 327–8.

[57] Wells to the editor of *The Nation*, published 12 June 1912, reproduced in Smith, *Correspondence 2*, pp. 327–8.

paper's regular weekly lunch on at least one subsequent occasion (in 1913) (Havighurst 1974, p. 153).

Wells's belief that socialism was not 'a fundamentally different thing from Progressive Liberalism' may not have been wholly philosophically plausible.[58] But it clearly was true in practice that many progressive Liberals found Wells's own liberal version of socialism to be interesting and in many ways appealing. None of them accepted his policy plans lock, stock and barrel but, at the very least, he was recognised as a powerful social critic. In 1916, Wells told Lord Northcliffe that he had decided to write on the war in *The Daily News*, *The Daily Chronicle* and *The Nation* 'as I think those papers reach the doubtful "liberal" public which I can best influence'.[59] This belief may well have had some basis in his pre-war reception in some Liberal quarters.

Wells's views even won admiration from individuals within the Liberal Party whom one would not normally think of as 'progressive'. In May 1910, Wells endorsed Hilaire Belloc's harsh criticisms of the Prevention of Destitution Bill, which, although it had no hope of being passed, had been designed to implement Sidney and Beatrice Webb's proposals for the break-up of the poor law. 'It might be only too easy for such a measure to be used to replace the present pauper classes by classes of State labourers with an essentially servile status', he declared.[60] The same week he contributed a letter to the first issue of the official journal of the National League of Young Liberals, in which he emphasised that although he was known as a socialist he had 'never ceased to be a Liberal'[61] John Burns, the insufferably complacent President of the Local Government Board, congratulated him on these 'first rate' interventions. 'The new helotry in the Servile State run by the archivists of the [London] School of Economics means a race of paupers in a grovelling community ruled by uniformed prigs', Burns wrote. 'Rely upon me saving you from this plague.'[62] It was not only Wells's thinking on social problems that won him an audience in government. In 1913, J. E. B. Seely, the Secretary of

---

[58] H. G. Wells to Mr. Making (unidentified), 30 March 1907, in Smith, *Correspondence 2*, p. 144.

[59] Wells to Lord Northcliffe, n.d., 1916, Northcliffe Papers, British Library, MS Add.62161, f. 95.

[60] S. D. Shallard, 'Mr. H. G. Wells on the Prevention of Destitution Bill', *The Labour Leader*, 13 May 1910.

[61] Wells's letter to *The Young Liberal* was reproduced in *The Manchester Guardian* on 14 May 1910.

[62] John Burns to Wells, 16 May 1910, Burns Papers, British Library, MS Add. 46301, f. 121.

State for War, publicly commended a 'very interesting' series of articles by Wells, which opposed conscription and argued for more research to devise new military technology: 'Mr. Wells pointed out, and he [Seely] believed truly[,] that victory in the future was not only going to be with those who produced great numbers of men, but with those who applied the best brains to the problem of war'.[63]

One of the most interesting, and ambivalent, responses to Wells's thinking came from J. A. Pease, the President of the Board of Education and an Asquith loyalist, in 1912. Wells had published a series of articles on 'The Labour Unrest' in the *Daily Mail*. He sought to diagnose the then-current wave of industrial discontent, which he attributed to the workers' growing awareness of economic inequalities, spectacularly symbolized by the recent *Titanic* disaster, in which the Third Class passengers perished disproportionately. The articles called for a 'National Plan', 'co-partnery' between labour and employees in industry, 'a compulsory period of labour service for everyone', and argued for proportional representation for Westminster elections.[64] Pamela McKenna, the wife of the Home Secretary Reginald McKenna, sent the articles to Pease, and he read them whilst laid up after an accident. He wrote to thank her:

I read Wells' articles this morning from 4.30 to 5.30 in bed. – I have a nasty feeling about him from his books & his views on your sex, – but I read all he says very carefully & my first impression was, a wonderfully brilliant diagnosis of the cause & reason of unrest – but I was awfully disappointed at his conclusions & his remedies.

He also cast doubt on Wells's radicalism: 'He claims to be a socialist, yet he realises men must have a self-interest in their own work for themselves, he even asks for royalties to be given them for further specialization by improvements in labour saving machinery'. Pease was unenthusiastic about the idea of proportional representation. And he criticised Wells's argument for 'co-partnery' in industry not because the idea was too radical but because he himself, as an employer, had already tried such a scheme and found his employees indifferent to it.[65] (In some respects, Pease's reaction

---

[63] 'Colonel Seely on Mechanical Science in War', *The Times*, 18 April 1913. The articles had been published in the *Daily Mail* on 7, 8 and 9 April.

[64] Wells 1912, pp. 21–7.

[65] Some other Liberal politician-employers promoted such schemes, although sometimes (as in the case of the shipping magnate Sir Christopher Furness) also without success. By contrast, the Labour politicians George Barnes and Keir Hardie were opposed to co-partnership. Pease to Pamela McKenna, 30 May 1912, Reginald McKenna Papers, Churchill College, Cambridge, MCKN 9/4; 'The Failure of Co-Partnership', *The Labour Leader*, 8 April 1910.

was similar to that of Masterman, who wrote to Wells that the articles were
'D – – d good in criticism – quite the best stuff you have been doing – [...] but
yr. remedies leave me cold'.)[66] It is intriguing that Pease – who has no great
reputation as a radical – was apparently already familiar with Wells's work,
and that he found his diagnosis 'wonderfully brilliant'. It is also interesting
that Pamela McKenna thought he would find them worth reading, which
raises the possibility that her husband had read them and thought so too.

Pease's comment about Wells's attitude to women was also significant,
because this issue undoubtedly did have a negative influence on how some
Liberals received the latter's ideas. Herbert Samuel, who held a variety of
ministerial posts after 1905, later recalled the social ostracism to which
Wells was subjected once his affair with Reeves became known. After
that, Wells was no longer asked to Samuel's dinner parties at the House of
Commons or at his house, 'and if one saw Wells in the street one passed
him by'.[67] Nor did Samuel much relish the depiction of himself (as 'Lewis')
in *The New Machiavelli*, though he thought the attack 'quite mild'.[68]
Presumably, though, he would not have been inviting Wells to dinner parties in the first place, or accepting his invitations in turn, unless he had
thought that he had some worthwhile things to say.[69] As for Lloyd George,
we may deduce that Wells's critique of the constricting nature of conventional sexual values was an important part of the appeal of his work.

There is plenty of evidence, then, that many Liberals, and particularly 'advanced' ones, read Wells and engaged with his ideas. The level of
that engagement varied substantially, from Churchill's actual borrowing
of phrases to Pease's slightly puzzled interest. Of course, there were also
some who were indifferent to Wells's thinking, or who at least left no record
of their views. Asquith – an obviously important example – was introduced
to Wells in 1902, but we do not know if he ever read any of his work.[70] Yet,
although Wells's ideas clearly did not pervade the Liberal Party utterly, his

[66] C. F. G. Masterman to H. G. Wells, 'Sunday 25th' [1912], Wells Papers, M-228.

[67] Frank Singleton, record of a conversation with Herbert Samuel, 6 February 1939,
Herbert Samuel Papers, Parliamentary Archives, London, SAM A/161.

[68] Herbert Samuel to Clara Samuel, 12 and 19 February 1911, Herbert Samuel Papers,
SAM A/156/368–9.

[69] Herbert Samuel to Catherine Wells, 13 January 1908, Wells Papers S-028.

[70] MacKenzie and MacKenzie 1973, p. 171. In 1907, Asquith asked Pamela McKenna
about Amber Reeves, who, he had heard, was 'much the cleverest & also the most beautiful' of her student cohort, '& like the majority of the best undergraduates, male &
female, a strong Socialist'. We cannot be certain, though, that he ever learned of
Reeves's affair with Wells. H. H. Asquith to Pamela McKenna 7 December 1907,
McKenna Papers, MCKN 9/3.

influence does need to be taken seriously. In order to conclude this, we do not have to rely on inference, as is often the case, for example, when looking at the impact of Hobson and Hobhouse. It is certainly true that the ideas of these men and those of the politicians coincided closely.[71] In the case of Wells, however, we can not only detect such intellectual similarities but also trace his direct influence with some precision.

What, then, was Wells's significance? It has always been difficult to show how shifting patterns of thinking amongst the 'opinion-forming intellectuals' actually translated into concrete political action on social reform.[72] This applies to Wells as much as it does to the 'classic' New Liberals. Although we can sometimes demonstrate how he influenced the way particular politicians expressed themselves, we cannot attribute to him any given piece of legislation. Wells's true importance, then, may lie in his role as a populariser. Even if his ideas about welfare and social organisation were not themselves profoundly original, he communicated them brilliantly, often using innovative methods of presentation. Busy ministers may well have been disinclined to read heavy, theoretical works in their spare time. Although even Wells was sometimes too dry for them – Churchill's one criticism of *A Modern Utopia* was that he wanted 'more *story*' – he set out ideas in a highly accessible way.[73] Nor was Wells the only source of literary influence on New Liberal ministers. We might note, for example, Masterman may have been influenced by Forster; and that Churchill, when Home Secretary, had his interest in prison reform stimulated in part by John Galsworthy's play *Justice*.[74] (It might be interesting to consider the possible influence of George Bernard Shaw's plays too.)[75] Such writers may have tended to influence politicians' broad visions of society rather than their detailed policies, but they were not the less important for that. The lesson for the history of welfare may be that, in trying to explain how ideas were diffused, we need to look closely at society's informal public 'educators' as much as at its technically specialised intellectuals.

---

[71] Clarke 1978, pp. 115, 117.

[72] Freeden 1978, p. 2.

[73] Churchill to Wells, 9 October 1906, Wells Papers, C-238–2.

[74] Addison 1992, p. 113.

[75] Margery Morgan suggests that '*Major Barbara* and the policy of the (Royal) Court Theatre, where it was first staged [...] must be counted among factors in the climate of thought and feeling that led to a landslide vote for the Liberals in the 1906 General Election' (Introduction to the Penguin edition, London, 2000, vii). The play received its premiere in November 1905, days before the fall of Arthur Balfour's Conservative government. A line in Act I anticipates Churchill's oft-quoted remark that he was 'easily satisfied with the best'.

References

Addison, P. 1992. *Churchill on the Home Front 1900–1955.* London: Pimlico.

Alkon, P. K. 2006. *Winston Churchill's Imagination.* Lewisburg: Bucknell University Press.

Baylen, J. O. 1974. W. T. Stead and the Early Career of H. G. Wells, 1895–1911. *Huntingdon Library Quarterly* 38(1): 53–9.

Blunt, W. S. n.d. *My Diaries: Being a Personal Narrative of Events 1888– 1914: Part Two [1900–1914].* London: Martin Secker.

Born, D. 1992. Private Gardens, Public Swamps: 'Howards End' and the Revaluation of Liberal Guilt. *NOVEL: A Forum on Fiction* 25(2): 141–59.

Campbell, J. 2006. *If Love Were All ... The Story of Frances Stevenson and David Lloyd George.* London: Cape.

Churchill, W. S. 1909. *Liberalism and the Social Problem.* London: Hodder and Stoughton.

Clarke, P. 1978. *Liberals and Social Democrats.* Cambridge: Cambridge University Press.

1996. *Hope and Glory: Britain 1900–1990.* London: Allen Lane.

Cowling, M. 1985. *Religion and Public Doctrine in Modern England, Vol. II: Assaults.* Cambridge: Cambridge University Press.

Dalton, H. 1953. *Call Back Yesterday: Memoirs 1887–1931.* London: Frederick Muller.

1962. *High Tide and After: Memoirs 1945–1960.* London: Frederick Muller.

Daunton, M. 2004. Money, Sir Leo George Chiozza (1870–1944). *Oxford Dictionary of National Biography.* Oxford: Oxford University Press. [http://www.oxforddnb.com/view/article/55929, accessed 21 May 2009]

den Otter, S. M. 1996. *British Idealism and Social Explanation: A Study in Late Victorian Thought.* Oxford: Clarendon Press.

2004. Ritchie, David George (1853–1903). *Oxford Dictionary of National Biography.* Oxford: Oxford University Press. [http://www.oxforddnb.com/view/article/35763, accessed 21 December 2006]

Feir, G. D. 2005. *H. G. Wells at the End of His Tether: His Social and Political Adventures.* New York: iUniverse Inc.

Foot, M. R. D. 1996. *H. G.: The History of Mr. Wells.* London: Doubleday.

Freeden, M. 1978. *The New Liberalism: An Ideology of Social Reform.* Oxford: Clarendon Press.

Fremantle, A. 1960. *This Little Band of Prophets: The Story of the Gentle Fabians.* London: Allen and Unwin.

Garland, D. 1985. *Punishment and Welfare: A History of Penal Strategies.* Aldershot: Gower.

Glover, W. B. 1972. Religious Orientations of H. G. Wells: A Case Study in Scientific Humanism. *Harvard Theological Review* 65: 117–35.

Green, T. H. 2002. *Thomas Hill Green: Lectures on the Principles of Political Obligation.* Ed. D. Bagnoli. London: Cambridge Scholars Press Ltd.

Harrod, R. F. 1951. *The Life of John Maynard Keynes.* London: Macmillan.

Havighurst, A. F. 1974. *Radical Journalist: H. W. Massingham (1860–1924).* Cambridge: Cambridge University Press.

Hendrick, B. J. 1925. *The Life and Letters of Walter H. Page. Vol. III.* London: Heinemann.

Hennessy, P. 1992. *Never Again: Britain 1945–1951.* London: Vintage.

Hobhouse, L. T. 1913. *Development and Purpose: An Essay Towards a Philosophy of Evolution.* London: Macmillan.

Hobson, J. A. 1906. The New Aristocracy of Mr. Wells. *Contemporary Review* 89(Apr.): 487–97.

   1909. *The Industrial System.* London: Longmans and Co.

   1915. *Towards International Government.* London: George Allen and Unwin.

Hopkins, E. 1999. *Charles Masterman (1873–1927), Politician and Journalist: The Splendid Failure.* Lampeter: Edwin Mellen Press.

Hyde, W. J. 1956. The Socialism of H. G. Wells in the Early Twentieth Century. *Journal of the History of Ideas* 17(2): 217–34.

Hynes, S. 1991. *Edwardian Turn of Mind.* London: Pimlico. [First published 1968.]

Iriye, A. 2002. Internationalizing International History. In *Rethinking American History in a Global Age,* ed. T. Bender. Berkeley, CA: University of California Press.

Jackson, B. 2007. *Equality and the British Left: A Study in Progressive Political Thought, 1900–64.* Manchester: Manchester University Press.

James, R. R., ed. 1981. *Churchill Speaks: Winston S. Churchill in Peace and War: Collected Speeches, 1897–1963.* Leicester: Windward.

Kennedy, J. M. 1912. Eupeptic Politicians, II – Mr. Masterman's Diagnosis. *The New Age* 14(March).

Keynes, J. M. 1934. Mr. Keynes Replies to Shaw. *The New Statesman and Nation,* 10 November 1934. Reprinted in *The Collected Writings of John Maynard Keynes,* Vol. 28: *Social, Political and Literary Writings,* ed. D. Moggridge. London: Macmillan for the Royal Economic Society.

Lloyd George, F. 1967. *The Years that Are Past.* London: Hutchinson.

Lloyd George, R. 1961. *My Father, Lloyd George.* New York: Crown.

MacKenzie, N., and J. MacKenzie. 1973. *The Time Traveller: The Life of H. G. Wells.* London: Weidenfeld and Nicolson.

Markwell, D. 2006. *John Maynard Keynes and International Relations: Economic Paths to War and Peace.* Oxford: Oxford University Press.

Masterman, C. F. G. 1902. Review of *Anticipations. The Commonwealth* 7(1): 25–7.

   1905a. *In Peril of Change: Essays Written in Time of Tranquillity.* London: T. Fisher Unwin.

   1905b. The Day of Better Things (review of *A Modern Utopia*). *Daily News,* 11 April.

   1905c. Book of the Day (review of *Kipps*). *Daily News,* 25 October.

   1909. *The Condition of England.* London: Methuen & Co.

   1920. *The New Liberalism.* London: Leonard Parsons.

   1922. H. G. Wells. Review of Reviews, no. 390, 15 June: 589–98.

Masterman, L. 1939. *C. F. G. Masterman: A Biography.* London: Nicholson and Watson.

McLean, S. 2007. 'The Fertilising Conflict of Individualities': H. G. Wells's *A Modern Utopia*, John Stuart Mill's *On Liberty* and the Victorian Tradition of Liberalism. *Papers on Language and Literature* 43(2): 166–89.

Meadowcroft, J. (ed.) 1994. *L. T. Hobhouse: Liberalism and Other Writings*. Cambridge: Cambridge University Press.

Money, L. G. C. 1905. *Riches and Poverty*. London: Methuen & Co.

    1912. Work in the Great State. In *The Great State: Essays in Construction*, H. G. Wells et al. London: Harper & Brothers.

    1914. *The Future of Work and Other Essays*. London: T. Fisher Unwin.

Partington, J. S. 2003. *Building Cosmopolis: The Political Thought of H. G. Wells*. Aldershot: Ashgate.

Radice, L. 1984. *Beatrice and Sidney Webb: Fabian Socialists*. London: Macmillan.

Seymour-Jones, C. 1992. *Beatrice Webb: Woman of Conflict*. London: Allison and Busby.

Skinner, Q. 2002. *Visions of Politics, Vol. 1: Regarding Method*. Cambridge: Cambridge University Press.

Smith, D. C. 1986. *H. G. Wells: Desperately Mortal: A Biography*. New Haven, CT: Yale University Press.

    1989. Winston Churchill and H. G. Wells: Edwardians in the Twentieth Century. *Cahiers Victoriens et Edouardien* 30: 93–116.

Snow, C. P. 1967. *Variety of Men*. London: Macmillan.

Taylor, A. J. P., ed. 1971. *Lloyd George: A Diary by Frances Stevenson*. New York: Harper & Row.

Tooze, A. n. d. Marshallian Macroeconomics in Action: The Industrial Statistics of the Board of Trade, 1907–1935. Unpublished manuscript.

Toye, J. 2000. *Keynes on Population*. Oxford: Oxford University Press.

Toye, J. and R. Toye. 2007. Alfred Zimmern, Julian Huxley et le leadership initial de l'UNESCO. In UNESCO *60 Ans d'histoire de l'UNESCO*.

Toye, R. 2007. *Lloyd George and Churchill: Rivals for Greatness*. London: Macmillan.

    2008. H. G. Wells and the New Liberalism. *Twentieth Century British History* 19(2): 156–85.

Wallas, G. 1908. *Human Nature in Politics*. London: Archibald Constable & Co.

    1914. The Great Society: A Psychological Analysis. London: Macmillan.

Weidhorn, M. 1992. *A Harmony of Interests: Explorations in the Mind of Sir Winston Churchill*. Cranbury, NJ: Associated University Presses.

Wells, H. G. 1895. *The Time Machine: An Invention*. London: Heinemann.

    1900. *Love and Mr. Lewisham*. Leipzig: Bernhard Tauchnitz.

    1903. *Mankind in the Making*. London: Chapman & Hall.

    1905a. *A Modern Utopia*. London: Chapman & Hall.

    1905b. *Kipps: The Story of a Simple Soul*. London: Macmillan.

    1905c. This Misery of Boots. *The Independent Review* 7(27): 396–413.

    1908a. *New Worlds for Old*. London: Archibald Constable & Co.

    1908b. About Chesterton and Belloc. *The New Age:* 11 January.

    1908c. Socialism and Politics. *The Socialist Review:* 250–6.

    1909a. *Tono-Bungay*. London: Macmillan.

1909b. *Ann Veronica: A Modern Love Story.* London: Fisher Unwin.

1911. *The New Machiavelli.* Leipzig: Bernhard Tauchnitz.

1912a. H. G. Wells, 'The Labour Unrest', in *What the Worker Wants: The Daily Mail Enquiry.* London: Daily Mail.

1912b. 'The Past and the Great State', in *The Great State: Essays in Construction,* H. G. Wells et al., London: Harper & Brothers, 3–46.

1916 [1914]. *An Englishman Looks at the World: Being a Series of Unrestrained Remarks upon Contemporary Matters.* London: Cassell.

1918. *In the Fourth Year: Anticipations of a World Peace.* London: Chatto & Windus.

1921. *War in the Air, and Particularly How Mr. Bert Smallways Fared While It Lasted.* London: George Bell & Sons.

1923. *A Year of Prophesying.* London: T. Fisher Unwin.

1929 [1908]. *First and Last Things.* London: Watts & Co.

1964 [1909b]. *Ann Veronica.* London: Pan Books.

1984. *An Experiment in Autobiography: Discoveries and Conclusions of a Very Ordinary Brain (since 1866),* Vol. II. London: Faber and Faber. [First published 1934].

1999 [1901]. *Anticipations of the Reaction of Mechanical and Scientific Progress Upon Human Life and Thought.* Mineola, NY: Dover. [Originally published in serial form in 1901 and in volume form in 1902].

West, A. 1984. *H. G. Wells: Aspects of a Life.* London: Hutchinson.

Wiener, M. J. 1971. *Between Two Worlds: The Political Thought of Graham Wallas.* Oxford: Clarendon Press.

Zimmern, A. E. 1936. Letter to *The Times*: 1 May.

NINE

Whose Welfare State? Beveridge versus Keynes

Maria Cristina Marcuzzo

[Keynes] told me that he no longer believed in the importance of economic reconstruction: what we wanted was more culture and beauty and noble motive, and some sort of creed and code of conduct. But he so sorrowfully admitted that he had no definite social creed and did not see the emergence of a new code of conduct. (B. Webb to W. Beveridge, 13 July 1936)

[Your general scheme] leave[s] me in a state of wild enthusiasm ... I think it a vast constructive reform of real importance and I am relieved to find that it is so financially possible. (J. M. Keynes to W. Beveridge, 17 March 1942)

I. INTRODUCTION

There is a widespread tendency to portray Keynes as the founding father of the Welfare State and to claim that the Keynesian revolution provided the justification for the need of a large public sector in the economy.[1] As the literature has amply shown, there are scant grounds for these claims.

---

[1] There is a vast literature containing such claims, an extreme example being Buchanan and Wagner (1977): see, for instance, the following assertion: 'The legacy or heritage of Lord Keynes is ... political bias toward deficit spending, inflation, and the growth of government' (ibid.: 24).

Earlier drafts of this chapter were presented at Hitotsubashi University, London School of Economics, Federal University of Rio de Janeiro, and Storep Conference in Lecce; I benefited from comments by the participants to these occasions, in particular to A. Komine, who was very helpful in correcting inaccuracies and omissions in the first draft. I am also indebted to Alex Saunders for excellent research assistance and to an anonymous referee. An abridged version of the chapter is published in Italian in Marcuzzo (2006), where a tentative list, together with a selection of the correspondence between Keynes and Beveridge, can be found.

Keynes's criticism of *laissez-faire* policy and disbelief in the smooth working of market forces is antecedent[2] to the *General Theory*, where the case for intervention is made when faced with aggregate demand failure. The policy message in the *General Theory* is to sustain the level of investment, but this should be interpreted more in the sense of 'stabilizing business confidence' (Bateman 1996: 148) than as a plea for debt-financed public works (Kregel 1985). His reliance on 'social-izing investment' rather than a fiscal policy aimed at smoothing out consumption levels over the cycle shows his concern for the size of the deficit, and the importance ascribed to market incentives to bring about the desired level of employment. In the *General Theory* he made it very clear: 'If the State is able to determine the aggregate amount of resources devoted to augmenting the instruments and the basic rate of reward to those who own them, it will have accomplished all that is nec-essary' (Keynes CWK VII: 378). Thus, the implication that Keynes was in favour of large and growing public expenditure such as we have expe-rienced since World War II – as a consequence of so-called Keynesian policies – simply cannot be drawn.[3]

Keynes's role in the foundation of the Welfare State as far as his actual contributions are concerned both in theoretical and practical terms has not, however, been investigated in detail. This chapter sets out to pro-pose some further thoughts on the matter, focusing on two aspects in particular. The first is an assessment of Keynes's views vis-à-vis what we now understand as the Welfare State; the second is a comparison between these views and those of Beveridge, the twin founding-father of the system, as they emerge in the exchange Beveridge and Keynes had on the subject. As a sideline, it may also shed some light on the nature of their relations, from the years that saw them playing leading roles in shaping contemporary economics, respectively, at Cambridge and at the London School of Economics, to the time when their com-mitment to a high and stable level of employment and to spreading the benefits of higher standard of living widely found acceptance amongst the general public and was endorsed by the British government.

---

[2] 'Keynes challenged laissez-faire as a *policy* well before he had developed a critique of the orthodox economic *theory* of the self-adjusting tendencies of the free market' (Meade 1990: 21).

[3] 'It is simply unreasonable to claim that [the] growth in government is the *logical* conse-quence of Keynes's views on the functions of government, as distinct from those of his followers' (Peacock 1993: 28); 'Keynes was concerned that expansionary fiscal policies should not give rise to mounting budget deficit' (Dimsdale 1988: 334).

Section 2 reviews the main issues faced today in defining the Welfare State; Section 3 compares Keynes's and Beveridge's ideas on unemployment and social insurance; Section 4 examines some aspects of their relations as they emerge from the extant correspondence.

2. THE GENESIS OF THE WELFARE STATE

Shionoya (Chapter 5, pp. 91–113) maintains that debates on welfare issues have had 'a longer history' than the rise of so-called welfare state in the 20th century and the underlying ideas 'had been in circulation under different labels'. Moreover, according to a popular textbook entirely dedicated to this topic (Barr 2004), the Welfare State 'defies precise definition'. The main reasons are that welfare derives from other sources besides state activity, and there are various modes of delivery of the services made available to citizens. Some are funded but not produced by the State, some publicly produced and delivered free of charge, some bought by the private sector, and some acquired by individuals with the money handed on to them by the State. Although its boundaries are not well defined, the Welfare State is used as 'shorthand for the state's activities in four broad areas: cash benefits; health care; education; and food, housing, and other welfare services' (Barr 2004: 21).

The objectives of the Welfare State can be grouped under four general headings. It should support living standards and reduce inequality, and in so doing it should avoid costs explosion and deter behaviour conducive to moral hazard and adverse selection. All these objectives should be achieved minimizing administrative costs and the abuse of power by those in charge of running it.

The road leading to endorsement of the above goals in Britain started with the liberal reforms of 1906–14, but full commitment to them was only sealed with the legislation of 1944–48, favourable conditions for which derived from the experience of World War II and the aftermath.

In the first decade of the 20th century the 'new liberalism' was an ideology based on the premise that, in order to advance individual freedom, the state must adopt an active role in social reform; the new measures resulted in the simultaneous introduction of old-age pensions, unemployment insurance, sickness benefits and progressive taxation. However, 'the reforms were relatively minor and had limited coverage' (Barr 2004: 13). Even less was achieved in the interwar period, apart from housing and unemployment insurance. Unemployment benefits were in constant danger of outgrowing contributions as unemployment levels soared. By the late 1920s two lines of policy were dominating the political arena: one concerned the financing of unemployment benefits, the other the challenge of reducing unemployment. In 1931 the screws were tightened on eligibility for benefits, and in 1934 the Unemployment Act separated unemployment benefits from measures supporting the long-term unemployed. So 'in the 1930s the Welfare State was in abeyance, and new measures were little more than crisis management ... When intervention came, in the form of rearmament and war production, the unemployment problem disappeared – an unhappy way of ending an unhappy period in British social policy' (Barr 2004: 26).

In this setting a major breakthrough came with the Beveridge Report (Beveridge 1942).[4] It was based on three pillars: (a) family allowances; (b) comprehensive health care; (c) full employment policy. The social insurance scheme was 'all-embracing in scope of person and of needs ... Every person ... will pay a single security contribution by a stamp on a single insurance document each week ... Unemployment benefit, disability benefit [and] retirement pensions after a transitional period ... will be at the same rate irrespective of previous earnings' (Beveridge 1942: 9–10). The system was to be centrally administered, and financed by equal contributions from employers, employee and the state, with equal benefits set at a physical subsistence level.[5]

Since the publication of the *General Theory* in 1936 Keynes had been arguing in favour of control over total investment[6] – the bulk of it ought to be carried out or influenced by public or semi-public bodies – as the viable solution to maintain a steady level of employment.[7] He saw the 'curse of unemployment' (Keynes CWK XXVI: 16) as the root of the evil of market economies, driving the risk of being overwhelmed by totalitarian solutions – whether of right-wing or left-wing inspiration – to alarmingly high levels in the 1930s. As he wrote to the editor of *The New Statesman and Nation*, 11 August 1934 'Marxists are ready to sacrifice the political liberties of individuals in order to change the existing economic order. So are Fascists and Nazis ... My own aim is economic reform by the methods of political liberalism' (Keynes CWK XXVIII: 28–9).

---

[4] The background to it is given in Harris [1977] 1997.

[5] The 1944 White Paper, *Social Insurance*, accepted most of these recommendations.

[6] This was just the final and mature stage of Keynes's thinking on this matter. On the earliest stage, mainly his contribution to *Britain's Industrial Future*, see Moggridge 1992: 458–60.

[7] The 1944 White Paper, *Employment Policy*, committed the government to 'the maintenance of a high and stable level of employment'.

The question arises of the relationship between two approaches taken by Beveridge and Keynes, respectively, to counteract the instability and insecurity deriving from a market economy, in terms of their source of inspiration, design and implementation.

3. THE CASE FOR FULL EMPLOYMENT AND NATIONAL INSURANCE: KEYNES AND BEVERIDGE

It has been argued (Cutler, Williams, and Williams 1986) that the Beveridge Report and the *General Theory* 'share a common political a priori'. I find the argument not entirely convincing, since the comparison between the two approaches brings us up against certain paradoxes, which have baffled both Keynes's and Beveridge's biographers.

The first paradox is noted by Skidelsky: 'Keynes's incuriosity about this battle [Beveridge and Social Security] is itself curious. The truth seems to be that he was not interested in social policy as such, and never attended to it. The sole question in his mind was whether the Exchequer could 'afford' Beveridge' (Skidelsky 2000: 270). Skidelsky's conclusion, which in the light of the common view taken of Keynes is itself paradoxical, is that 'Keynes was never a passionate social reformer' (ibid.: 265). This evaluation takes Keynes off the Cambridge path as followed by the 'good-doers', such as Sidgwick, Marshall and Pigou, and has him in fact more attuned to a vision of society in which 'freedom from the economic problem' would create the conditions for transforming human nature and thereby society. Thus Keynes made his plea for government intervention on the grounds of a more 'conservative' social theory than Beveridge's.

On the other hand, Keynes's limited involvement in domestic issues during the years in which the Beveridge proposals were being formulated is explained by Moggridge 'in part by his absences in the United States and Canada for long periods in 1941, 1943, 1944 and 1945; and in part he was probably deliberately excluded by the permanent Treasury officials from some of the key Committees and discussions' (Moggridge 1992: 695). Be this as it may, it is true that 'there never was a comprehensive Keynes plan for maintaining full employment after the war. Keynes's contribution to the famous White Paper on Employment Policy, issued in May 1944, was mainly by way of encouragement, commentary and criticism, even though parts of it clearly reflected his theories' (Skidelsky 2000: 270–1). Evidently, therefore, Keynes's involvement in the design of the two milestones of the Welfare State in Great Britain, national social insurance and full employment government policy, was rather limited.

The case of Beveridge is also interesting since he developed his ideas independently and, in the case of full employment, in opposition to Keynes.[8] The paradox here is that Beveridge made his proposals on social reforms rest on the orthodox theory that Keynes was attacking. Beveridge taught himself economics studying Jevons and Marshall above all, and was drawn towards applied economics (facts and figures) rather than pure theory (concepts and vision).

In this respect, it is interesting to examine Beveridge's comments on the *General Theory*, written while he was on holiday in Majorca with Sydney and Beatrice Webb in March 1936, recovering from a distressful period fraught with personal and professional anxieties (Harris 1997: 298–9).[9] His comments, examined in conjunction with his farewell address as Director of the London School of Economics (LSE) (Beveridge 1937), show how little sympathy he had for Keynesian theory. Indeed, his hostility to the 'new theory' was such that at the end of 1937 he came to the decision to engage in a study on unemployment, 'purposely designed to correct the methodological heresies of Keynes's *General Theory*' (Harris 1997: 351).

On reading Beveridge's comments on the *General Theory*, one is astonished to see how difficult that book appeared to someone who had taught himself economics on the basis of Jevons and Marshall, and until then had been close to the ideology (although much less to the theory) of the LSE free market devotees, namely Robbins and Hayek. What strikes the reader is how little he understood of the basics of the multiplier and of Keynes's argument against trusting in the effects of a fall in money wages in bringing about full employment.

A few quotations will suffice. Commenting on the passage where Keynes demonstrates that if the propensity to consume is 9/10, the multiplier is 10, so that for any given increase in public works the secondary employment will prove 10 times the primary employment, Beveridge writes:

because out of a given increment of income the community will generally choose to consume nine-tenths and *invest one-tenth*, therefore with a given increment of investment however caused, the community will find its income increased by

---

[8] 'Beveridge in the late 1930s had scornfully rejected Keynes's analysis of unemployment and there is no documentary evidence to suggest that he had changed his mind by 1941–42' (Harris 1997: 427).

[9] Beveridge presented his comments at the Hayek seminar at the London School of Economics, but he was disappointed by its reception, as he wrote to Beatrice Webb in a letter of 9 July 1936: 'I did not myself get quite as much as I had hoped out of the seminar discussion in the way of telling me whether my criticisms were right or wrong' (BEV 2/B/35/3).

ten times the *amount of the new investment* ('Employment Theory and the Facts of Unemployment' in BEV 9/B/23/4–5, emphasis added).[10]

Noteworthy here is the confusion between propensity to save and investment, and between income and investment. A few paragraphs on, Beveridge again misses the point, accusing Keynes of holding that 'investment enriches, irrespective of the object of expenditure' (BEV 9/B/23/5) and once more he fails to see why 'a rise in the rate of interest must always and in all circumstances reduce the volume of savings, because it discourages investment' (BEV 9/B/23/6). As for Keynes's point that a reduction in money wages is unlikely ever to increase employment, Beveridge accuses Keynes of endowing labour 'with some mystical quality making the demand for it in a market economy independent of the price asked for it' (BEV 9/B/23/10).

From these premises it is not surprising that his assessment is that 'the *General Theory* does not in itself explain the actual phenomena of the economic system as we know it. ... involuntary unemployment is not a proved fact but either an unproven assumption or a confusion of terms' (BEV 9/B/23/14).

Harris rightly describes Beveridge's reading of the *General Theory* as 'a shattering experience' (Harris 1997: 331). The key to his rejection, apart from the fact that – as we have seen – his command of economics was entirely self-taught, is revealed by one of his closing remarks: 'If economics is a science, the answer to this question must be sought not by general reasoning but by analysis of the facts of unemployment and reasoning about the facts' (BEV 9/B/23/17).

This is the theme of his farewell address to the LSE, which can be taken as Beveridge's manifesto against contemporary economics, whether Keynesian or of the LSE brand. His methodological stance is very much in the positivist vein:

It is the duty of the propounder of every new theory ... to indicate where verification of his theory is to be sought in facts – what may be expected to happen or to have happened if his theory is true, what will not happen if it is false (Beveridge 1937: 464).

It had, however, a tinge of Robbins in it: 'economics is concerned with human behaviour in the disposal of scarce resources' (Beveridge 1937: 462).[11]

---

[10] Reference to the Beveridge papers (BEV), held at British Library of Political and Economic Science, is given according to their archival classification.

[11] However, Beveridge did not entirely endorse Robbins's formalistic programme. See his comments to *The Nature and Significance of Economic Science*: 'To be content with

Robbins (1932) had claimed that arguments pertaining to ethics and political philosophy should be banned from economics. The message was that, while moral sciences deal with what ought to be, economics is concerned with what is. Keynes fought for the opposite view. Indeed, he was challenging economics to abandon the 'modernist claim' to be a scientific study of society and become an investigation 'into problems which seek to bring about defined or desired end states (or solutions) and clarify values' (see Marcuzzo 2004).

The premise of Keynesian economics, as we find it in the *General Theory*, is that 'we cannot hope to make completely accurate generalisations' (Keynes CWK VII: 257) because the economic system is not ruled by 'natural forces' that economists can discover and order in a neat pattern of causes and effects. The implication of this assumption is that the task of economics is rather to 'select those variables which can be deliberately controlled and managed by central authority in the kind of system in which we actually live' (Keynes CWK VII: 257).

The goal is to change the environment within which individuals operate, so that moral and rational motives become the spring of action of the collectivity as a whole (Keynes CWK XVII: 453). Keynes's approach, based on the categories of knowledge, ignorance and rational belief, is chosen as the appropriate method for a 'moral science' such as economics that deals with complexity and judgement.

We may therefore take the profound methodological differences in their approach to economics to underlie both Beveridge's inability to come to grips with the *General Theory* and Keynes's conviction that it was a case of 'two minds which have not truly met',[12] since he reacted to Beveridge's comments, by pointing out to him 'how very remote we are'.[13]

However, in the making of his scheme, Beveridge sought help and assistance from Keynes – who responded readily and liberally – and soon afterwards he became a convert to Keynesianism, possibly under

---

deducing the implications of scarcity, is to reduce economics either to the formality of one-dimensional geometry or (if we choose to multiply hypothesis as to data in preference to collecting data) to the futility of a parlour game' (BEV II/B/39/5).

[12] Keynes was keen to have his ideas tested 'in conversation' with others. However, his interlocutors had to be attuned to his thinking or show a critical but sympathetic attitude. See Marcuzzo and Rosselli (2005).

[13] We have a glimpse of Keynes's pessimistic mood in general about the reception of his book, in the letter Beatrice Webb sent to Beveridge after reading the latter's comments to the *General Theory*, 'I lunched [...] with Keynes's the other day, and found him very depressed about the reception of his book, and the hopeless disunity of opinion among abstract economists' (BEV 2/B/35/3).

the influence of the group of progressive economists of Keynesian faith – including Joan Robinson, N. Kaldor, E. Schumacher – that he had brought together to assist him in an inquiry into full employment, which eventually became *Full Employment in a Free Society* (Beveridge 1944).

The story of Keynes's advice and help has been carefully reconstructed by Harris, Skidelsky and Moggridge, and is only outlined here. In March 1942 Beveridge wrote to Keynes suggesting a talk on how his scheme could be financed. Keynes reacted very enthusiastically and offered suggestions to make it financially more viable.[14] According to Harris, 'the co-operation of Keynes was to be of great importance to Beveridge over the next few months, both in enhancing the financial viability of his report and in smoothing the way for its reception in official circles' (Harris 1997: 400). This is borne out by Lady Beveridge's memoir: '[The Beveridge Plan] was scrutinized and approved by the unquestioned authority of William's close but highly critical friend in such matters, J. M. Keynes' (J. Beveridge 1954).

On substantive issues Keynes was not in favour of high taxes to pay for social benefits and pensions, the costs of which ought to be borne out by employers: 'Should not the employer,' he wrote, 'meet the total cost of providing him with a healthy worker? If the unemployed were allowed to starve what would employers do when the demand for employment, seasonally or cyclically, increased again? Why should the general taxpayer pay for a pool of available dock labour?' (Keynes CWK XXVII: 224).

Secondly, he was in favour of making the State accountable to the taxpayer for the goods and services provided, associating 'as closely as possible the cost of particular services with the sources out of which they are provided', since he believed that 'this is the only way by which to preserve sound accounting, to measure efficiency, to maintain economy and to keep the public properly aware of what things cost' (Keynes CWK XXVII: 225).

So while Keynes was appreciative of the 'new features' of Beveridge's Plan, namely 'the extension of the social security benefits and contributions to the whole of the population, and not merely to the present contributory classes' (Keynes CWK XXVII: 252), he was concerned with the budgetary aspects of it. From the strictly economic point of view he

---

[14] Keynes's suggestions were heavily dependent on contemporary estimates of post-war national income, which were at their infancy and largely controversial. For a discussion of the gap between the 'pessimistic' (Henderson's and the Treasury) versus the 'optimistic' side (Stone and Keynes), see Moggridge (1992: 707–8).

was keener to make 'public investment a counterweight to fluctuations of private investment' (Keynes CWK XXVII: 381), seeing 'narrow limitations' in any plan aimed 'to stabilize consuming capacity in dealing with depressions' (Keynes to James Meade, 8 May 1942, Keynes CWK XXVII: 206).

Both Keynes and Beveridge were concerned with the moral and social problems deriving from unemployment, but while Beveridge stressed the need to ensure everybody against the vagaries and fluctuations of economic activity, Keynes believed that 'to provide an adequate material standard of life' was not the 'real problem of the future'. He saw it rather as 'how to organize material abundance to yield up the fruits of a good life'. For Beveridge, it was the human fight against scarcity, the plague of cycles in production and business confidence – as unpredictable as weather and natural calamities, as he saw them. Social insurance was meant to disjoint individual coverage from general economic performance. For Keynes it was the fight 'to persuade [his] countrymen and the world at large to change their traditional doctrines' (Keynes CWK XXVI: 16). By making the future dependent on the economic success of an active social investment policy it would free individuals from the deprivations deriving from unemployment.

The two pillars of the Welfare State – distrust of market forces and, with it, reliance on government intervention to bring about full employment on the one hand, and lack of confidence in the power of liberalism to achieve economic security and social stability on the other, again making the case for government intervention – were formulated independently and, perhaps, even in opposition to one another. Beveridge, the Fabians' heir, relied on neoclassical economic theory while Keynes, the revolutionary economist, relied on reformed liberalism for his social policy.

4. THE KEYNES–BEVERIDGE CORRESPONDENCE

The excellent and extremely well-documented biography of Beveridge by Jose Harris (1977) was being written when the edition of Keynes's *Collected Writings* was under way; the revised edition was published (Harris 1997) and indeed makes use of the new evidence available, in particular on Keynes's attitudes and reaction to the Beveridge Report. I feel, however, that a comprehensive assessment of the relationship between Keynes and Beveridge and a comparison of their contribution to the Welfare State is perhaps still wanting.[15] Studying their correspondence sheds light on their personalities and intellectual environment and may take us a step further in that direction.

The earlier extant letters between them go back to the eve of World War I, when Keynes – in his capacity as editor – was dealing with Beveridge's requests to have his work published in the *Economic Journal*. The first is 'A Seventeenth-Century Labour Exchange' (EJ September 1914), which Keynes found 'exceedingly interesting' (JMK to WHB, 25 March 1914, BEV 2/B/13/18), in a letter also including praise of Beveridge's review of Pigou's *Unemployment* (EJ, June 1914), which appeared in the same issue. 'I am glad', Keynes wrote, 'you criticise Pigou's treatment of the plasticity of wages theory. I entirely agree with what you say about it. I do not think he commits himself to an actual recommendation to the working classes to allow greater plasticity. But the natural suggestion of what he says is misleading'.

Pigou wrote – in advance of Keynes's *General Theory* – the first theoretical treatise on systematic unemployment (Pigou 1913, 1933). In the extant correspondence between Keynes and Pigou, we have five letters on their collaboration concerning *Wealth and Welfare* in 1913 (Bridel and Ingrao 2005).

Again, in 1919 Beveridge submitted an article, 'The Agricultural Factor in Trade Fluctuations', about which he was very excited: 'I am inclined to think', he said in the accompanying letter, 'that I have made something in the way of a small discovery in connection with cyclical fluctuation' (WHB to JMK, 20 December 1919, BEV 7/42/144). Keynes immediately replied that he would be 'delighted to print' it, and eventually the article was published in two instalments, in the March and June issues of 1920.

In February 1920 he sent in another article, 'British Exports and the World Crops', (WHB to JMK, 3 February 1920, BEV 7/42/147): in this case Keynes came up with some reservation (JMK to WHB, 7 February 1920, BEV VII/42/149), which Beveridge was prepared to accept (WHB to JMK, 9 February 1920, BEV 7/42/150).

Again, three years later, after agreeing to print Beveridge's Presidential Address to the Royal Economic Society ('Population and Unemployment') Keynes had some criticism to make, proposing to print rejoinder of his

---

[15] The excellent paper by Dimand (1999) is somehow more focused on Beveridge than Keynes; while Komine (Chapter 10) addresses the issue of the integrated perspective on the welfare state by Beveridge, rather than comparing the two approaches, thus leaving perhaps room for the present investigation.

own. Again Beveridge reacted very positively: 'I certainly hope you will make a rejoinder so that truth may ultimately emerge from controversy' (WHB to JMK, 27 September 1923, BEV 7/37/8).

Throughout the period from 1914 to 1924, then, their relationship can be seen to have been friendly and collaborative; they seem to have been in general agreement on the issues involved, although it was mostly Keynes who came up with advice and comments on Beveridge's works rather than the other way around. Things changed in 1931. In the late 1920s Beveridge had come around to wage-rigidity as explaining unemployment, possibly as a consequence of his work in the Coal Commission of 1925, whose members had persuaded him that the miners' wages were too high, and certainly under the influence of Lionel Robbins he was converted to a belief in the self-regulating virtues of a market economy. During the 1929 crisis he wrote to Robbins: 'The first essential is to restore the price-machine – in wage fixing and elsewhere' (Harris 1977: 321, 323).

It is of course a well-known fact that at The Economic Advisory Council's Committee of Economists and at the Macmillan Committee, Keynes made a plea for protectionism to reduce unemployment, finding himself in a minority position and in contraposition with Lionel Robbins (Howson and Winch 1977; Eichengreen 1984). A group of people (among others, Beveridge, Hicks and Robbins) joined together under Beveridge's chairmanship (Keynes CWK XX: 513) and opposed Keynes's view, defending the free trade position. The collective effort produced a book (*Tariff: The Case Examined*)[16] including a contribution by Beveridge, which he announced to Keynes with an interesting declaration of intent: 'I am naturally anxious to make any public difference between economists appear to be as much as possible a difference of judgement as to what is expedient (as indeed I think it to be) rather than a difference as to scientific truth' (WHB to JMK, 14 January 1931, BEV 2/B/63/K). In March, six chapters of the book in the proof stage were sent to Keynes, who unsurprisingly criticized them in a letter of 23 March 1931 (Keynes CWK XX: 513–4). The next serious confrontation arose between them in 1936, when another interesting exchange occurred.

---

[16] The book (Beveridge 1931) included contributions by Benham, Bowley, Gregory, Hicks, Layton (the only one not a member of the staff of the School), Plant, Robbins and Schwartz. A substantial contribution was made by Dennis Robertson, who pulled out of the project only in August 1931. (I am indebted to a referee for pointing this out.)

Since 1919 Beveridge had been Director of the LSE,[17] making an enormous effort to manage transformation from a small academic endeavour into an international institution, with more than 3,000 students, and 120 members of staff. In the field of economics, Robbins and Hayek were the key figures, attracting foreign scholars and determined to make it the intellectual centre of free market culture. Hicks recalled of himself and his LSE colleagues that,

we seemed, at the start, to share a common view point, or even a common faith. The faith in question was a belief in the free market, or 'price mechanism' that a competitive system, free of all 'interferences', by government or monopolistic combinations, of capital or of labour, would easily find an 'equilibrium'. (...) Hayek, when he joined us, was to introduce into this doctrine an important qualification – that money (somehow) must be kept 'neutral', in order that the mechanism should work smoothly. (Hicks 1982: 3)

Besides the natural rivalry with Cambridge, as a competing academic centre with an outstanding record of excellence in many fields, LSE economics was also opposed to the heritage of Marshall, Pigou and partial equilibrium, endorsing the Austrian and the general equilibrium approach in the tradition of continental authors such as Walras and Pareto. The controversy between Hayek and Keynes during 1931–33 seemed to have stretched these differences to the extreme notwithstanding the efforts of the younger and less 'embattled' (J. Robinson 1951: viii) members of the two groups to find a common ground (Marcuzzo and Sanfilippo 2008). The situation came to a climax with the publication of the *General Theory*. A line was drawn between those who felt themselves in total agreement with Keynes and those who felt either misrepresented or alienated by it. In Cambridge, Kahn, Joan and Austin Robinson belonged to the former category, Pigou and Robertson to the latter. Sraffa was secretly sceptical. At the LSE, Durbin, Lerner and Kaldor converted to it, Hicks found a compromise, while Hayek, Robbins and Beveridge resisted, although only Hayek remained unconvinced to the end.

Keynes admitted to Beveridge in June 1936 that 'the general nature of your points is such as to convince me that I have really had a total failure in my attempt to convey to you what I am driving at' (Keynes CWK XIV: 56).

---

[17] The position had first been offered by Sydney Webb to Keynes, who turned it down. See McCormick (1992: 13).

Beveridge responded that by that time, thanks to Hicks's article, he thought he had understood what Keynes 'was driving at' and the matter was not discussed further. In September 1936 we see Keynes resuming his role of soliciting articles for the *Economic Journal* (JMK to WHB, 22 September 1936). In this case it was the 'Analysis of Unemployment', read at the *British Association for the Advancement of Science*, which Beveridge had already committed to *Economica* (WHB to JMK, 24 September 1936).

At the outbreak of the war Beveridge and Keynes, together with other veterans of World War I ('Old Dogs'), shared anxiety over the ability of government to tackle the problems of the war (Keynes CWK XXII: 15–16). They met at Keynes's house in London and put forward strategies and policies (Harris 1997: 354) and it is likely that these discussions reverberated in Keynes's *How to Pay for the War*.

The correspondence of those months in 1939–40 witnesses these concerns. On one occasion there was a minor diplomatic incident. In July 1940 Beveridge sent Keynes a memo, wishing to discuss how industry and government ought to be re-organized if the war was to be won. He went so far as to argue that state socialism and the service motive must be substituted universally for capitalism and the motive of personal gain (JMK/W/1/54–8). Keynes took him seriously and forwarded the memo to the Treasury's Second Secretary, R. Hopkins (JMK to WHB, 1 August 1940, JMK/W/1/59–60),[18] much to Beveridge's alarm, who did not wish 'to make too many enemies' (WHB to JMK, 2 August 1940, JMK/W/1/63).

The correspondence of March–October 1942 is entirely devoted to the Beveridge Plan. Keynes's main objection to it was that it made pensions conditional only on retirement, which he found politically unacceptable. Beveridge resisted, made small concessions and in the end Keynes acquiesced: 'After reading this further instalment', Keynes wrote to Beveridge on 14 October 1942, 'I feel confirmed in the feeling I expressed the other day, that it is a grand document. You can scarcely expect it will be adopted just as it stands, but it seems to me that you have got it into an extremely workable shape, and I should hope that the major and more essential parts of it might be adopted substantially as you have conceived them' (Keynes CWK XXVII: 255).

Keynes had wished to make his maiden speech in the Lords debate on the Beveridge Report on February 24; he was prevented from doing

---

[18] Reference to the Keynes papers (JMK), held at King's College Cambridge, is given according to their archival classification.

so by the political sensitivity of the issues involved, which made him fearful of 'disobliging' the Treasury, which had got itself 'into a hideous mess over this Report', as he explained to his mother on the eve of the appointed date (Keynes CWK XXVII: 256). The draft of his speech is, however, extant, and it reveals Keynes's whole-hearted commitment and political support. The main point stressed there is (a) 'there is no cheaper scheme on the map'; (b) [it] 'is a relatively cheap scheme for the early period' (Keynes CWK XVII: 258). The crucial question for Keynes was whether the country could afford the future commitments which the scheme entailed. And his answer once again stressed the view that in the future 'the economic problems of the day ... will lie in solving the problems of an era of material abundance not those of an era of poverty' (ibid.: 261).

The extant letters of the last two years of Keynes's life are interesting because they show their attitudes towards the *White Paper on Employment Policy* (1944), which later became known as being inspired by Keynes and Beveridge. Keynes was organizing a meeting at the Royal Economic Society to discuss it and invited Beveridge to contribute to the subject in the *Economic Journal* (JMK to WHB, 31 May 1944, BEV 9/B/30). Beveridge accepted and added, 'As regards what I think about the White Paper ... I do most heartily congratulate you and the economists on the distance to which you have moved the government. I shall do what I can to help to move them still further' (WHB to JMK, 5 June 1944, BEV 9/B/30).

On his return voyage from the United States, Keynes read *Full Employment in a Free Society* and reported to Beveridge that he found it 'extremely good' (JMK to WHB, 16 December 1944, Keynes CWK XXVII: 380). Beveridge had hopes to be able to discuss points Keynes raised (WHB to JMK, 8 January 1945, BEV 2/B/44/1), but the extant letters do not reveal whether they ever did.

Finally, we have the last exchange relative to nominations to the British Academy, section IX, Economic Science. In 1942 Beveridge had suggested Robbins and Cole (WHB to JMK, 17 January 1942, BEV/BA/1/80); in 1944 he agreed to put forward Hayek, but with scant enthusiasm since he felt he should have proposed Joan Robinson, who was 'really much better than Hayek' (WHR to JMK, 28 February 1944, BEV/2/B/43/1).

Beveridge had really made a full turnabout and as far as economic ideas were concerned he had become closer to the most radical amongst the Keynesians than to the holder of the torch of free market and liberalism.

5. CONCLUSION

In December 1942, a few days after the Beveridge Report was published, Beveridge married Juliet (Jessie) Mair, the controversial Secretary of the LSE and his cousin's widow, who had been a close friend for many years. In a volume of recollections, she recorded that Keynes's wedding present was the 1691 edition of W. Petty's *Political Arithmetic*, with the following inscription: 'To Sir William Beveridge this book by the founder of his (and my) craft on the occasion of his contriving social security for the rest of us and *not forgetting himself*' (J. Beveridge 1954: 127).

The playful tone of Keynes's inscription seals the understanding reached between Keynes and Beveridge after their disagreement over free trade and the *General Theory*.[19]

While Keynes was able to be in tune with Beveridge's proposals at the time of his Report, Beveridge was unable to do the same with Keynesian theory when the *General Theory* appeared. I surmise that this was due to the revolutionary aspect of Keynes's theory, which took quite a long time to be accepted and absorbed. His path-breaking ideas were unacceptable to anyone accustomed to viewing questions of economics with the lenses of scarcity and allocative constraints. This may explain why Keynes was not too much bothered by the financial burden of a generalized insurance scheme since he believed that it would force the country to adapt its attitude to the future. 'If we approach it with cringing and timidity, we shall get what we deserve. If we march on with confidence and vigour the facts will respond' (Keynes CWK XXVII: 260). This, it seems to me, is the intellectual and political legacy of Keynes: building the future on confidence, rather than deficit spending.

References

Barr, N. 2004. *The Economics of the Welfare State*. 4th ed. Oxford: Oxford University Press.

Bateman, B. 1996. *Keynes's Uncertain Revolution*. Ann Arbor: University of Michigan Press.

---

[19] It is worth recalling here how in September 1931 in her diary Beatrice Webb contrasted Keynes and Beveridge: 'In London, we lunched with Beveridge, who heartily dislikes Keynes and regards him a quack in economics. These two men are equally aloof from the common man, but they have little appreciation of each other; Keynes, the imaginative forecaster of events and speculator in ideas, his mind flashing into the future; Beveridge bound down to the past, a bureaucratic statistician, intent on keeping intact the inequality between the few who could govern and the many who must be governed, and believing in the productivity of the acquisitive instinct.' (Quoted in Caldwell 2004: 174n).

Beveridge, J. 1954. *Beveridge and His Plan.* London: Hodder and Stoughton.
Beveridge, W. B., ed. 1931. *Tariffs: The Case Examined.* London: Longman.
  1937. The Place of the Social Science in Human Knowledge. *Politica* 2: 459–79.
  1942. *Social Insurance and Allied Services.* London: HMSO.
  1944. *Full Employment in a Free Society.* London: Allen and Unwin.
Bridel, P. and Ingrao, B. 2005. Managing Cambridge Economics: The Correspondence between Keynes and Pigou. In M. C. Marcuzzo and A. Rosselli (eds.), *Economists in Cambridge: A Study Through Their Correspondence, 1907–1946.* London: Routledge.
Buchanan, J. and Wagner, R. 1977. *Democracy in Deficit.* New York: Academic Press.
Caldwell, B. 2004. *Hayek's Challenge: The Intellectual Biography of F. A. Hayek.* Chicago: The University of Chicago Press.
Cutler, T., Williams, K., and Williams, J. 1986. *Keynes, Beveridge and Beyond.* London: Routledge.
Dimand, R. 1999. The Beveridge Retort: Beveridge's Response to the Keynesian Challenge. In L. Pasinetti and B. Schefold (eds.), *The Impact of Keynes on Economics in the 20th Century.* Cheltenham: Edward Elgar.
Dimsdale, N. H. 1988. Keynes on Interwar Economic Policy. In W. Eltis and P. Sinclair (eds.), *Keynes and Economic Policy: The Relevance of the General Theory after Fifty Years.* Basingstoke: Macmillan Press.
Eichengreen, B. 1984. Keynes and Protection. *Journal of Economic History* 44: 363–73.
Harris, J. 1997 [1977]. *William Beveridge. A Biography.* 2nd ed. Oxford: Clarendon Press.
Hicks, J. R. 1982. Introductory: LSE and the Robbins Circle. In J. R. Hicks (ed.), *Money Interest and Wages,* vol. 2. pp. 3–10.
Howson, S. and Winch, D. 1977. *The Economic Advisory Council 1930– 1939: A Study of Economic Advice During Depression and Recovery.* Cambridge: Cambridge University Press.
Keynes, J. M. 1971–1989. *The Collected Writings of John Maynard Keynes* (CWK). Managing Editors E. A. G. Robinson and D. Moggridge. London: Macmillan.
CWK VII, The General Theory of Employment, Interest, and Money.
CWK XIV, The General Theory and After: Defence and Development (ed. D. Moggridge).
CWK XVII, Activities 1920–22. Treaty Revision and Reconstruction (ed. E. Johnson).
CWK XX, Activities 1929–1931. Rethinking Employment and Unemployment Policies (ed. D. Moggridge).
CWK XXII, Activities 1939–1945. Internal War Finance (ed. D. Moggridge).
CWK XXVI, Activities 1940–1946. Shaping the Post-War World: Bretton Woods and Reparation (ed. D. Moggridge).
CWK XXVII, Activities 1940–1946. Shaping the Post-War World: Employment and Commodities (ed. D. Moggridge).
CWK XXVIII, Social, Political and Literary Writings (ed. D. Moggridge).

Kregel, J. 1985. Budget Deficits, Stabilisation Policy and Liquidity Preference: Keynes's Post-War Policy Proposals. In F. Vicarelli (ed.), *Keynes's Relevance Today*. London: Macmillan.

Marcuzzo, M. C. 2004. From Market 'Imperfections' to Market 'Failures': Some Cambridge Challenges to Laissez-Faire. *Annals of the Society for the History of Economic Thought* 45: 1–10.

2006. Una nota su Keynes e Beveridge, Lettere e Commenti, 1910–1946. *Economia & Lavoro* 39: 51–64.

Marcuzzo, M. C. and Rosselli, A. 2005. Introduction. In M. C. Marcuzzo and A. Rosselli (eds.), *Economists in Cambridge: A Study Through Their Correspondence, 1907–1946*. London: Routledge.

Marcuzzo, M. C. and Sanfilippo, E. 2008. Dear John, Dear Ursula (Cambridge and LSE, 1935): 88 Letters Unearthed. In R. Scazzieri, A. K. Sen and S. Zamagni (eds.) *Markets, Money and Capital: Hicksian Economics for the 21st Century*. Cambridge: Cambridge University, pp. 72–91.

McCormick, B. J. 1992. *Hayek and the Keynesian Avalanche*. London: Harvester Wheatsheaf.

Meade, J. 1990. *The Cabinet Office Diary, 1944–46*. In S. Howson (ed.), *Collected Papers of James Meade*. Vol. IV. London: Unwin Hyman.

Moggridge, D. 1992. *Maynard Keynes: An Economist's Biography*. London: Routledge.

Peacock, A. 1993. Keynes and the Role of the State. In D. Crabtree and A. P. Thirlwall (eds.), *Keynes and the Role of the State*. London: Macmillan.

Pigou, A.C. 1913. *Unemployment*. London: Williams and Norgate.

1933. *The Theory of Unemployment*. London: Macmillan.

Robbins, L. 1932. *An Essay on the Nature and Significance of Economic Science*. London: Macmillan.

Robinson, J. 1951. *Collected Economic Papers*, Vol. I. Oxford: Blackwell.

Skidelsky, R. 2000. *John Maynard Keynes, III: Fighting for Britain, 1937–1946*. London, Macmillan.

TEN

Beveridge on a Welfare Society

An Integration of His Trilogy

Atsushi Komine

I. INTRODUCTION

It is generally accepted that the Beveridge Report, formally entitled the *Social Insurance and Allied Services* (1942), was 'regarded as the main blueprint for the creation of the post-war welfare state and his "scheme" affected the development of British social policy for a generation after 1945' (Harris 2004 p. 289). During the Atlee government, basic acts, such as the National Insurance Act and the National Health Service Act of 1946, were passed. Through such measures, some of Beveridge's ideas were put into practice.

In this chapter we shall look at the broader picture, considering three works that can be seen as trilogy providing an integrated perspective on the welfare state. There are two reasons why it is valuable to see these three works as a whole. First, this brings out a more coherent understanding of Beveridge's ideas on welfare. Beyond both his unquestioning belief in price mechanism in the early 1930s and his fierce attack on economists' methodology, including that of *Keynes's General Theory*, in the late 1930s (see Chapter 9 by Marcuzzo), Beveridge came to embrace a comprehensive vision of an ideal future world, encompassing the roles of government, market, and community. Second, the notion of a welfare society with citizenship helps defend Beveridge against some of the criticisms that have been levelled against the welfare state. The second section of this chapter deals with social security, the third section discusses full employment, and the fourth section considers voluntary action. The final section then brings these three themes together, showing that they form a unified whole.

This research was supported by a grant from JSPS. KAKENHI (20530174).

2. THE BEVERIDGE REPORT

In his report, Beveridge designed a system of social security to meet two goals: (1) securing a minimum level of income for those who encountered interrupted income, the loss of working capability, or exceptional expenditures and (2) ensuring that losses of earnings were brought to an end as soon as possible (Beveridge 1942 p. 120, para. 300). Social security as a whole, Beveridge argued, involved three elements.

The first and most important component of social security was social insurance for basic needs, based on the principle of compulsory contributions. All citizens had a right to be guaranteed a minimum standard of living. His scheme embodied six fundamental principles: 'flat rate of subsistence benefit; flat rate of contribution; unification of administrative responsibility; adequacy of benefits; comprehensiveness; and classification' (Beveridge 1942 p. 9, para. 17). The first principle meant that the state should ensure a minimum level of subsistence, regardless of citizens' incomes. The second principle implied that all citizens had to pay the same contribution, irrespective of their wealth.[1] Under a social insurance system following the first and the second principles, revenue and expenditure would be apparently balanced for both an individual and a state[2]: people had a right to benefits in exchange for the payment of contributions. The social insurance system subsumed a standard citizen who was industrious and independent to some degree.

Nevertheless, not all citizens could afford to contribute fully. Some physically or mentally handicapped persons would fall through the mesh of any insurance scheme (Beveridge 1942 p. 12, para. 23). Accordingly, the state had to establish a second and subordinate component, that is, public aid for exceptional contingencies. This was a transfer in cash out of the National Treasury. Traditionally, from the age of the poor laws, people in Britain had strongly resisted any type of means test (Beveridge 1942 p. 11, para. 12). 'Doles' in poor laws were always accompanied by a 'stigma of pauperism'. Under Beveridge's proposals, this public assistance was to be subjected to a strict means test because it had to 'be felt to be something less desirable than insurance benefit' (Beveridge 1942 p. 141, para. 369). The National Treasury was no infinite cash dispenser,

---

[1] The weekly contribution rate was four shillings and three pence (except for people between age 16 and 20) (Beveridge 1942 p. 152, para. 403).

[2] As Keynes pointed out and agreed, the social security budget was a fiction. However, the 'more socialized we become, the more important it is to associate as closely as possible the cost of particular services with the sources' (Keynes 1980 p. 224).

so the state was duty-bound not to let members of society be extravagant and lazy. The second component needed certification and means testing, with provisions to avoid engendering stigma.

The third and complementary component was related to the guiding principle that implicitly permeated the entire report: 'Social security must be achieved by co-operation between the State and the individual'. Complementarity meant encouraging private insurance in addition to the state's basic provision (Beveridge 1942 p. 143, para. 375). The state had to leave room for self-help efforts, so that people would plan out their own life freely, based on the level of income they could achieve. The state should not stifle incentive, opportunity, or responsibility. In 'establishing a national minimum, it should leave room and encouragement for *voluntary action* by each to provide more than that minimum for himself and his family' (Beveridge 1942 p. 7, para. 9, emphasis added). This system included not only rights for every citizen but also duties. There was no guarantee that the state would provide its citizens with benefits beyond the minimum (Beveridge 1942 p. 121, para. 302). Instead, there remained ample room for private insurance. People had to work for an abundant living. Up to the minimum, there was a protection by the state, but beyond that you had to survive in competition.

The basic idea of the welfare state, which was clear in the report, can be traced back to Beveridge's earlier years and the pioneering works by Beatrice Webb and her husband, Sidney Webb. In 1906, Beveridge declared that 'every place in free industry, carrying with it the rights of citizenship ... should be ... a "whole" place involving substantially full employment and average earnings up to a definite minimum' (Beveridge 1907 p. 327). As early as 1909, Beveridge had clearly combined the idea of a national minimum with full employment. In *Insurance for All and Everything* (1924), he proposed a contributory flat-rate national insurance. Although his writings at that time had non-negligible differences[3] with the 1942 scheme, it is clear that his idea on social security had gradually developed from the 1900s. This line also followed the Webbs's initial concept of a national minimum.[4]

However, the report also referred to citizens' duties, at least as a complement to what was provided by the state. Beveridge was worried about

[3] In 1906, Beveridge excluded from the category of citizens the unemployable, who should exit from the industry and fall under the control of the Poor Laws. In 1924, he regarded 'All' as persons with incomes below a certain level.

[4] Refer to the following phrase: 'a definite quota of education, sanitation, leisure and wages for every grade of workers in every industry' (Webb and Webb 1898 [1897] p. 817).

Table 10.1. *Estimated Cost of Social Security (million pounds)*

	Actual, 1945		Proposed, 1945	
Nation	265	61.3%	351	50.3%
Insured	69	15.9%	194	27.8%
Employers	83	19.2%	137	19.6%
TOTAL	342	100.0%	697	100.0%

Note: Made according to Beveridge (1942 p. 112, Table 13). The rates do not include interest, so the sum of the three elements does not match 100%.

creating free riders, those who might become overly dependent upon the state.[5] In fact, the respective rates of contribution were 28 per cent for individuals, 20 per cent for employers, 50 per cent for the state, and 2 per cent for interest. Those figures indicated a burden for the programme that would be larger than that of the system that was actually put in place (see Table 10.1). In this sense, Beveridge's idea of the welfare state, by its nature, presupposed mutual efforts between individuals and the state.[6]

The first report had dual elements: a national minimum embodied in a major part of social security, which had a long history, on the one hand, and the industriousness of individuals, on the other. This dual structure pointed to the subsequent final report.

3. FULL EMPLOYMENT

The second book in the trilogy, *Full Employment in a Free Society*, was published in November 1944. There has been much controversy over its interpretation. On the one hand, Robbins (1971 p. 158) and Hayek (1994 pp. 83–6) have claimed that Beveridge understood so little of economics that he had to be learning from Keynesian ideas.[7] On the other hand, as Marcuzzo (Chapter 9) implies, it can be argued that his conversion to Keynesianism was superficial, on the grounds that he had previously relied on the orthodox economic ideas and could not understand the

---

[5] In particular, see Beveridge (1942 p. 170, para. 455): 'The plan is not one for giving to everybody something for nothing and without trouble, or something that will free the recipients for ever thereafter from personal responsibilities'.

[6] Unlike popular criticisms about the welfare state, sincere studies of the Beveridge Report do not overlook this point. For instance, see Ohmae (1983 p. 226), Mouri (1990 p. 217), and Jinushi (1995 p. 46).

[7] For instance, see Harris (1997 p. 434) and Jinushi (1995 p. 39).

essence of Keynes's revolutionary economics. Our view is that in order to appreciate the contribution of his book, we need to place it in a broader context, namely Beveridge's overall vision of an ideal world.

Beveridge took important ideas about unemployment from Keynes, notably the idea that there was a tendency towards insufficient effective demand. 'There will be unemployment if effective demand is not sufficient at total to require use of the whole labour force', where effective demand is defined as 'desire for goods or services backed by willingness to pay the price' (Beveridge 1945/1944 p. 25, para. 24, and p. 404). He also accepted that the economy had no propensity to return automatically to equilibrium, denying that the rate of interest would equilibrate savings with investment or that the rate of wages would balance demand for labour against the supply. Beveridge also accepted Keynesian policies. He wrote, 'It must be a function of the State[8] in future to ensure adequate total outlay and by consequence to protect its citizens against mass unemployment' (Beveridge 1945/1944 p. 29, para. 31). He also advocated socialization of effective demand, echoing Keynes's claim that 'the only way to secure full employment is socialisation of investment' (Keynes 1973/1936 p. 378). Beveridge hoped to establish a national investment board that had 'powers of obtaining intelligence, of giving assistance and of regulating investment by public and private enterprise alike' (Beveridge 1945/1944 p. 177, para. 241). This board would use the credit of the state to ensure that borrowers could obtain funds on suitable terms (Beveridge 1945/1944 p. 178, para. 241). Finally, his proposal for a 'double budget' echoed Keynes, who had argued for 'the separation between the normal Budget for expenditure out of income and the so-to-speak capital budget', the former being balanced at all times, and the latter fluctuating with employment.[9]

Beveridge combined these with his own ideas on unemployment, reflecting his earlier experience. His definition of full employment differed subtly from that provided in *Keynes's General Theory*: full employment, to Beveridge, means that there are 'more vacant jobs than unemployed men', and that 'unemployment in the individual case need not last for a length of time exceeding that which can be covered by unemployment insurance without risk of demoralization' (Beveridge 1945/1944 pp. 19–20, para. 7). This reflected his observation that the

---

[8] 'I expect to see the State … taking an ever greater responsibility for directly organizing investment' (Keynes 1973/1936 p. 164).

[9] Keynes (1980 p. 275), Keynes to Hopkins, 15 April 1942.

'number of vacancies notified to the employment exchanges always exceeds considerably the number filled by them and the difference is greater in good years than in bad years' (Beveridge 1945/1944 p. 88, para. 113).[10] Beveridge also attached importance to the location of industry and hence to labour mobility (Beveridge 1945/1944 p. 24, para. 20). This led him to propose that a minister of national development should carry out a plan for land, housing, and transport (Beveridge 1945/1944 p. 170, para. 228). Effective demand was thus a vector rather than the single magnitude found in Keynesian theory. Beveridge's approach saw effective demand as a vector (size and direction), whereas Keynes only paid attention to one dimension (size). Beveridge also advocated provision of job training for younger workers and stiffening 'the conditions of unemployment benefit as regards individuals whose unemployment continues for any length of time' (Beveridge 1945/1944 p. 173, para. 232). One of the main ideas permeating *Full Employment in a Free Society* is the protection of fundamental liberties. This is reflected in the change of its title from *Full Employment in a Progressive Society*[11] to *Full Employment in a Free Society*. Beveridge, who was then banned from exchanging views with top government officials, felt himself unjustly oppressed and deliberately selected the word 'free' to mount a strong protest against those in power. Indeed, a free society was 'subject to the proviso that all essential citizen liberties are preserved' (Beveridge 1945/1944 p. 21, para. 11). Furthermore, he discussed these liberties in detail, ranking them in order of importance. Ranked most highly were nonaggressive liberties: freedom of worship, speech, writing, study, and teaching. Next came 'freedom of assembly and of association for political and other purposes, ... freedom in choice of occupation[,] and freedom in the management of a personal income' (Beveridge 1945/1944 p. 21, para. 11). There were several reasons why rights in this second group were less clear-cut than those in the first. It was important to prevent a rising spiral of wages and prices, raising the question of whether the right to strike should be limited. Freedom of choice in occupation made it harder to ensure that all workers were employed continuously. Finally, free disposal would sometimes lead to under-consumption. Beveridge claimed that full employment could be achieved by restricting some of those rights temporarily to accomplish permanent benefits for society. 'All liberties carry their responsibilities' (Beveridge 1945/1944 p. 23, para. 16).

---

[10] Echoes of this can be found in modern U-V analysis.
[11] PRO, BT 64/3393, Beveridge to Watkinson, 11 October 1943.

What is needed for creating a managed economy towards full employment was not an abolition of rights to freedom but their restriction for a higher purpose. However, stating that 'society exists for the individual', Beveridge described his own view as individualistic liberalism, arguing that 'a restoration of all essential citizen liberties ... is the essence of what is proposed here' (Beveridge 1945/1944 p. 191, para. 271).

To sum up, Beveridge, in *Full Employment in a Free Society*, showed that he had absorbed the core of Keynes's theories and policies (especially the *General Theory*). He advocated the socialization of investment, based on a simplified concept of effective demand. Beveridge shared Keynes's view that investment managed by the state was indispensable for full employment. Thus, Keynes wrote a letter to Beveridge, relating his very 'warm congratulations on it. I thought it extremely good and found myself in general agreement with by far the greater part of it'.[12] However, Beveridge's analysis of unemployment contained original features. His main prescription was sufficient effective demand, but that had to be supplemented by controlled location of industry and organization of the labour market.[13] Beveridge addressed the supply side as well as the demand. This was all rooted in respect for a free society.

Thus, although Beveridge acceded to Keynes's economics, he did so because he fully understood that Keynes's economics could strengthen – and could be integrated with – his own economics of unemployment and could serve as a means of protecting a free society. In this sense, Beveridge was bringing to completion his own theory of unemployment.

4. VOLUNTARY ACTION

The last book of the trilogy, *Voluntary Action: A Report on Methods of Social Advance*, was published in April 1948. Unlike previous reports, the book did not arouse a public response and was neglected by the government (Harris 1997 p. 460). The book's title itself reveals its contents. The term 'voluntary action' meant private action, not action performed under the direction of any authority. Voluntary action represented independence from public control, regardless of whether that action was paid or unpaid. 'Co-operation between public and voluntary agencies was one of the special features of British public life' (Beveridge 1948 p. 8).

---

[12] Keynes (1980 p. 380), Keynes to Beveridge, 16 December 1944.

[13] Those supplementary elements (controlled location of industry and organization of the labour market) were the main prescription in *Unemployment* (1909). Beveridge was aware of the shift of emphasis. See Beveridge (1945/1944 p. 86, para. 111; p. 90, para. 115).

The report excluded business motives and personal thrift, however voluntary, because the study was confined to voluntary action for a public purpose. Moreover, it was concerned specifically with action inspired by two main motives: mutual aid and philanthropy. The first meant that all those involved might have helped themselves because they had a need for security against misfortune. The second arose from 'the feeling which makes men who are materially comfortable, mentally uncomfortable so long as their neighbours are materially uncomfortable' (Beveridge 1948 p. 9). This can be called social conscience.

Agencies based on mutual aid included trade unions, cooperative unions, housing unions, and private savings companies. Among them, friendly societies were representative. The Rose Act (1793) regulated these societies in detail and encouraged them to work well. Friendly societies were voluntary agencies that worked to save funds to cover against various misfortunes. In 1911, when the National Insurance Bill was passed, 'the State made the fatal decision of using existing friendly societies to administer the new benefits and of avoiding any direct State administration' (Beveridge 1948 p. 74). However, in 1946, in contrast to a proposal in the Beveridge Report, friendly societies and the state were split. Beveridge judged the divorce undesirable and was on the side of the friendly societies. These adhered to the contribution principle; namely, citizens had a minimum duty of contributions and a right to provide benefits from pooled funds. Beveridge submitted a proposal to the Labour government to expand the functions of friendly societies, but it was turned down.[14]

Beveridge believed that even when the social service state[15] had been established, problems would remain. There was a need to address good use of the rising amount of time available for leisure activities and to provide guidance regarding the complexities of modern life. Industrialization made it possible to shorten daily working hours by two hours. Accordingly, commercial activities cut into workers' leisure time: cinema, football pools, and gambling became rampant. Beveridge was not complacent about the current usual way of sparing time, because the attack 'on wasteful or harmful use of leisure cannot, in a free society, be made by direct action of the State' (Beveridge 1948 p. 286). Voluntary

[14] There was at the time an enormous patchwork of philanthropic agencies – so many that the Royal Commission of 1871–74 classified them into no fewer than 17 categories.

[15] Beveridge preferred this term to the welfare state (Beveridge 1948 p. 217). He did not like the word 'welfare state', which insinuates generous gifts from the state. See also Harris (1997 p. 452).

action should substitute for state action. Citizen's advice bureaux could provide guidance on modern life; this idea was first mooted in the report of the National Council of Social Service for 1935–36. In September 1939, 200 bureaux were opened. In 1948, there were about 600 functioning. Any citizen could go to a citizen's bureau to seek information and advice related to their rights and duties. Each adviser in an office should be a volunteer, paid or unpaid. The adviser should be sociable and friendly like a neighbour, not a bureaucrat. Each bureau was autonomous, dependent on local authorities, but all bureaux were linked. As members of local communities moved away from religious organizations, they had been left without sources of help and advice, a gap the Citizen's Advice Bureau was intended to fill. 'A public authority may provide the material means for Citizen's Advice Bureaux but should no more control them than it controls universities' (Beveridge 1948 p. 287).[16]

It was also necessary to watch over people with special needs – atypical minorities such as abandoned or abused children, physically or mentally handicapped people, chronically sick people, unmarried mothers and their dependants, discharged prisoners, and so on (Beveridge 1948 p. 226). Unhappiness was related not simply to a shortage of money but rather to a shortage of 'services of a kind which money often cannot buy' (Beveridge 1948 p. 266). It was, therefore, necessary to provide physical resources, such as suitable houses, hospitals, and training facilities. Naturally, there had to be full use of voluntary action. The role of the state was thus to prepare infrastructures, to subsidize, and to encourage private original ideas.

This described explicitly Beveridge's view of society, something that was only implicit in his two previous works. This involved two types of balance. The first balance was between state and individual. Although private savings and business motives were driving forces towards economic development, the incentives facing individuals were private and should be kept within bounds: 'The business motive is a good servant but a bad master, and a society which gives itself up to dominance of the business motive is a bad society' (Beveridge 1948 p. 322). On the other hand, if there were problems with the inventives facing individuals, there were also problems with the state, which exhibited a tendency towards centralized and unified control, even in a democracy. There was a need for co-ordination to bring together individual intentions and state

---

[16] In Britain, universities were autonomous bodies and, unlike in some continental countries, academics were not civil servants.

powers. In modern society, it was not possible to rely on personal bonds so voluntary action springing from individuals' social conscience (public purposes) would be a buffer zone between the two. Friendly societies, for instance, would come to replace religious communities. This would rectify the balance between the state and individuals.

The second balance was between the state and markets. Markets had brought people immense wealth, guided by individuals' business motives. However, as was shown by in the behaviour of the labour market, market economies had weaknesses such as large fluctuations of demand and supply. State interference had increased in the first half of the 20th century, and the introduction of social insurance and a target for full employment were great advances. Nevertheless, they were merely a first step. There remained a sphere in which neither the state nor the market could solve problems.[17] That sphere required voluntary action: a third way that was neither business nor control. Spontaneous voluntary action connects the state and markets, restoring their balance.

5. CONCLUSIONS

In *Social Insurance and Allied Services*, Beveridge drew on contemporary progressive ideas, such as the Webbs's national minimum, to propose a social insurance system. Though he saw citizens as having duties that stood alongside the duties of the state, he did not develop this notion. In *Full Employment in a Free Society*, he went on to face the problem of full employment, maintenance of which was the duty of the state. Like Keynes, he sought to use state intervention to develop the market economy, though he brought in his own ideas on unemployment. Beveridge was clearly conscious of the close connections between these two works: the plan for social security assumed full employment, and the system of social security would help maintain full employment through income redistribution. Thus he wrote that 'The decision to destroy Want [to establish social insurance] ... would deliver at the same time the first blow in the war against Idleness [unemployment]' (Beveridge 1945/1944 p. 255, para. 379). He concluded: 'The redistribution of income that is involved in abolishing Want by Social Insurance and children's allowances will of itself be a potent force in helping to maintain demand for

---

[17] 'It would be a pity if the whole field of security against misfortune, once the domain of voluntary Mutual Aid, became divided between the State and private business conducted for gain' (Beveridge 1948 p. 296).

the products of industry, and so in preventing unemployment' (Beveridge 1945/1944 pp. 255–6, para. 379).

Finally, in *Voluntary Action*, Beveridge took up the duty of citizens, something discussed only very briefly in his previous works. 'Emphasis on duty rather than assertion of rights presents itself to-day as the condition on which alone humanity can resume the progress in civilization which has been interrupted by two world wars' (Beveridge 1948 p. 14). Voluntary action offered a way into communities that, in a free society, the state could not provide. This return to ideas of civic humanism brought him back, at least in part, to the Oxford idealistic tradition of Benjamin Jowett, Edward Caird, and T. H. Green that he had encountered in his youth (see Chapter 5 by Shionoya).

Beveridge's three later writings can thus be seen as a trilogy. Each successive volume was premised on the work of the others but developed new concepts. He achieved a synthesis through articulating a vision of welfare, rather than through constructing a logically consistent system of economics. This vision included not only economic concerns (the first two works), but also social commitments (the third work). In articulating it, he employed and absorbed various ideas, integrating ideas taken from Keynes with ones from his own earlier work.

Beveridge's achievement hints at modern arguments about the welfare state. From the start of the 'cradle to grave' system, there was criticism. A state that provides benefits imposes burdens on people to provide welfare services that are provided unilaterally as rights. 'Large government' gives rise to what may be seen as irresponsible financial policies. A 'centralized state' provides only unified services. However, if we take his books together, we find that he addressed all of these criticisms. In his social service state, each citizen had an external duty (contribution of insurance) and an internal duty (voluntary action). The state was not a monopolist in the provision of welfare. Rather, the 'State was to do that which the State alone can do: manage money so as to maintain spending. Subject to that, the State should leave as much as possible to the initiative and enterprise of the citizens' (Beveridge 1948 p. 319).[18] The role of the state lay in the construction and maintenance of social security. The role of citizens was situated in the support of their fellows by voluntary action. The roles were sharply defined and complementary.

---

[18] Keynes shared the same recognition: 'The enlargement of the functions of government ... [is] both as the only practicable means of avoiding the destruction of existing economic forms ... and as the condition of the successful functioning of individual initiative' (Keynes 1973/1936 p. 380).

Without either of them, society would not have worked. Moreover, as Keynes assumed, the structure of welfare 'was by far the cheapest we ever had' (Keynes 1980 p. 263). It would not bankrupt the budget, so long as the principle of contribution remained. 'The welfare society' is a suitable term for a society in which the state, markets, and citizens are mutually dependent and continue to develop. As Beveridge (1948, p. 324) put it, 'Ultimately, human society may become a friendly society – an Affiliated Order of branches, some large and many small, each with its own life in freedom, each linked to all the rest by common purpose and by bonds to serve that purpose'.

References

Beveridge, W. H. 1907. 'The Problem of the Unemployed', *Sociological Papers 1906*, vol. 3. London: Macmillan, pp. 323–31.

Beveridge, W. H. 1942. *Social Insurance and Allied Services.* Cmd. 6404. London: HMSO.

1945. *Full Employment in a Free Society.* New York: W. W. Norton & Company Inc. (London: George Allen & Unwin, 1944).

1948. *Voluntary Action: A Report on Methods of Social Advance.* London: George Allen & Unwin.

1955. *Power and Influence.* New York: The Beechhurst Press. British version. London: Hodder & Stoughton, 1953.

British Library of Political and Economic Science, the Beveridge Papers in the Archive Section, British Library of Political Science, London School of Economics and Political Science.

Cockett, R. 1995. *Thinking the Unthinkable: Think-Tanks and the Economic Counter-Revolution, 1931–1983.* London: Fontana Press.

Durbin, E. 1985. *New Jerusalems: The Labour Party and the Economic of Democratic Socialism.* London: Routledge.

Harris, B. 2004. *The Origins of the British Welfare State: Social Welfare in England and Wales.* Hampshire, UK: Palgrave Macmillan.

Harris, J. 1997 [1977]. *William Beveridge: A Biography.* Revised edition. Oxford: Oxford University Press.

Harrod. R. 1982 [1951]. *The Life of John Maynard Keynes.* London: W. W. Norton & Company.

Hayek, F. A. 1994. *Hayek on Hayek: An Autobiographical Dialogue.* Ed. S. Kresge and L. Wenar. London: Routledge.

Jinushi, S. 1995. William Beveridge: A Pioneer in the Field of Unemployment and Social Security. In: Research Institute for Social Security (ed.) *New Stream of Social Security* (Tokyo: Yuhikaku), pp. 27–49. (In Japanese).

Johnson, N. 1987. *The Welfare State in Transition.* Brighton, UK: Wheatsheaf Books.

Keynes 1973 [1936]. *The General Theory of Employment, Interest and Money. Keynes CW.* Vol. VII.

1980. *Activities 1940–1946: Shaping the Post-War World: Employment and Commodities. Keynes CW.* Vol. 27.

Komine, A. 2004. 'The Making of Beveridge's Unemployment [1909]: Three Concepts Blended'. *The European Journal of the History of Economic Thought*, 11(2): 255–80.

2007. *W. H. Beveridge in Economic Thought: A Collaboration with J. M. Keynes et al.* Kyoto: Showa-do. (In Japanese).

Marcuzzo, M. C. 2004. Keynes and the Welfare State, a paper presented at the Workshop: Cambridge School of Economics; Welfare Economics and the Welfare State, 26–27 February 2005, Hitotsubashi University, Japan, pp. 1–18.

Moggridge, D. 1980. *Keynes.* 2nd ed. London: Macmillan.

1992. *Maynard Keynes: An Economist's Biography.* London: Routledge.

Mouri, K. 1990. *A Study on British Welfare State.* Tokyo: University of Tokyo Press. (In Japanese).

Ohmae, S. 1983. *Social Security and National Minimum.* Revised version. Kyoto: Minerva Shobo. (In Japanese).

Ohsawa, M. 1999. Social Security Policy: A Trail to Gender Analysis. In M. Kenzo (ed.) *A Modern History of British Social Policy 1945–1990.* Tokyo: Minerva Publishing Co.

Pierson, C. 1991. *Beyond the Welfare State?* Oxford: Basil Blackwell.

PRO, Public Record Office (The National Archives). Kew: London.

Robbins, L. 1971. *Autobiography of an Economist.* London: Macmillan.

Skidelsky, R. 1983. *John Maynard Keynes I: Hopes Betrayed 1883–1920.* London: Macmillan.

1994. *John Maynard Keynes II: The Economist as Saviour 1920–1937.* London: Macmillan.

2000. *John Maynard Keynes III: Fighting for Britain 1937–1946.* London: Macmillan.

Toye, J. 2000. *Keynes on Population.* Oxford: Oxford University Press.

Webb, S. and B. Webb 1898 [1897]. *Industrial Democracy.* 2nd ed. London: Longmans, Green and Co.

PART FOUR

POSTSCRIPT

ELEVEN

Welfare Economics, Old and New

Roger E. Backhouse and Tamotsu Nishizawa

I. INTRODUCTION

In the 1930s, economists turned to the task of developing welfare economics on non-utilitarian foundations. This was both narrowing and broadening. It narrowed welfare economics in that the assumptions underlying the 'New welfare economics' of Hicks, Kaldor and their colleagues made it hard to go beyond the extremely restrictive confines of what became known, after Little (1950), as Pareto-efficiency or Pareto-optimality. The attempt to go beyond this using compensation tests was a failure. However, though this was not immediately apparent, certain ideas within the New Welfare Economics had the potential to broaden the study of welfare, through providing frameworks within which alternative ethical frameworks could be analysed. Abram Bergson (1938) introduced the concept of a social welfare function, writing social welfare as a completely general function of goods and services supplied or consumed by all agents – we might say, as a function of a complete description of the state of the world. In itself, such a social welfare function had no content, for it was too general, but it provided a framework for exploring the implications of different value judgements.

An even more formal approach was introduced by Kenneth Arrow (1951), whose social welfare function took a different form. It was a mapping from the set of individuals' orderings of all possible states of the world to a social ordering. As with Bergson's social welfare function, it was possible to explore restrictions stemming from different ethical judgements. However, Arrow went further in that, having access to more powerful mathematical techniques, he was able to demonstrate a startling result – that, given certain apparently plausible judgements about the form that his social welfare function could take, there was no ethically acceptable way to move from a set of individual preferences to a social preference. This negative result contributed significantly to the pessimism that emerged in the 1950s about the possibility of doing welfare economics. However Arrow's paradoxical result had another effect. His theorem, unacceptable to many, provided both the motivation and the techniques for opening up new ways of looking at the problem of welfare, through the field that came to be known as social choice theory. Paretian welfare economics might continue in the textbooks, with the concept of Pareto efficiency and its associated conditions becoming the workhorse of economists' everyday welfare analysis, but there was also a group of economists who were exploring very different approaches. John Harsanyi (1955) made the case for utilitarianism, whilst others argued the case for partial inter-personal comparability of utilities. Amartya Sen (1970) became famous for demonstrating that the seemingly innocuous Pareto criterion might conflict with the idea of Liberalism. The 'maximin' criterion proposed by John Rawls (1971), that welfare should be measured by the ability of an economic system to provide for the needs of the worst off in society, was taken up as an alternative to both utilitarianism and the Pareto criterion. For years, social choice theory was seen as something exotic – abstract mathematical theorizing that was removed from the concerns of most economists. However, as economists became technically more proficient, social choice theory came to merge more and more with welfare economics (exemplified by the journal *Social Choice and Welfare*), providing an alternative approach to welfare economics that had relevance to the analysis of economic life, a transition symbolized by the award of the Nobel Memorial Prize to Amartya Sen.

This work goes beyond the concerns of Parts I to III of this book, which is concerned with an earlier period. There are, however, significant connections. To economists brought up on the very narrow welfare economics of the 1950s and 1960s, unable to see beyond the criterion of Pareto efficiency (close to vacuous because virtually every conceivable policy change implies making someone worse off), the attempts by Pigou, Hobson and their contemporaries to bring in additional ethical criteria involve an illicit intrusion of values into economic science. In contrast, from the perspective of Harsanyi, Rawls, Sen and modern social choice theory, it makes good sense to argue that welfare judgements require some set of ethical criteria. By the standards of modern social choice theory, many of the economists discussed in this book were anything but rigorous, and their ethical judgements may have done little more than echo the prejudices of their time. However, it no longer makes sense to say that they were wrong in claiming that ethical judgements were needed to draw conclusions about welfare. The result is that the attempt to exclude value judgements from economics, the defining feature of the New Welfare Economics, should be seen in a new light. In the remainder of this chapter we argue, that in the 1920s, British welfare economics was pluralist, the subject being tackled in very diverse ways, and that this background casts a different light on what happened to welfare economics in the 1930s and 1940s.

2. PLURALISM IN WELFARE ECONOMICS

In the period from around the 1880s to the 1920s, ideas on welfare economics were being developed by economists working in a variety of overlapping contexts. There were academic economists, anxious to give economics the authority of a science. There were also academics who were studying welfare as part of a political analysis that could provide a framework for transforming British society. There were also political activists working outside, or on the fringes of academia, and administrators seeking administrative solutions to social problems. This heterogeneous group of scholars based their arguments about welfare on a wide variety of philosophical positions, which included utilitarianism, idealist philosophy, the ethics of G. E. Moore, the moralism of Ruskin and moral values taken straight from religious beliefs. Clearly, much of the resulting literature did not meet the academic standards laid down by Marshall and Pigou, let alone those of modern economics, and does not look much like welfare economics as it is understood today. However, it would be anachronistic to use modern standards to demarcate part of this literature as welfare economics and the rest as something else (such as political or religious tracts). If welfare economics is interpreted broadly to mean systematic reflection on the implications of economic activity for human welfare, these people should be considered as contributors to a pluralistic welfare economics, echoing the pluralism that Morgan and Rutherford (1998) have found in American economics during the inter-war period.

Hobson offers the clearest example of a thinker who needs to be taken more seriously as a welfare economist. His writing on welfare (see Chapter 6) does not usually appear in histories of welfare economics: when the subject is viewed retrospectively, he does not fit into any lines running from Pigou and Pareto to the New Welfare economics. His work is passed over, appearing to be unscientific journalism by someone whose political commitments were paramount. Yet he was taken seriously by his contemporaries as a welfare economist, notably in the United States. Wesley Mitchell chose Hobson as the representative of 'welfare economics' in his lectures on the history of economics, devoting a long chapter to his work (Mitchell 1969). Paul Homan (1928) characterized him the same way almost a decade later. It is highly significant that the Americans who endorsed Hobson as a welfare economist were Institutionalists, but the significance of their endorsement should not be minimised for that reason. Institutitionalism was a major (perhaps even the dominant) strand in American economics before the Second World War.

It was not just Hobson who was appreciated by Mitchell and the Institutionalists. Walton Hamilton (1919: 318), instrumental in the establishment of Institutionalism, went so far as to write of an 'English welfare school', comprising Webb,[1] Hobson, Edwin Cannan, R. H. Tawney and Henry Clay.[2] (Pigou was not mentioned, even though *Wealth and Welfare* (1912) had been published just a few years earlier.)

Henry Clay, who came through the Oxford classics school, wrote a well-received textbook, *Economics: An Introduction for the General Reader* (1916), based on his Workers Educational Association lectures. He started from the observation that welfare depended on ethical views and argues that welfare depends not only on material causes (the external cause of welfare) but also on internal causes – the factors internal to the individual that determine wants. In neglecting the internal causes of welfare, conventional economics was materialistic. 'Materialism is the subordination of the internal sources of satisfaction to the external; most religions exalt the internal over the external, and teach that welfare lies in the former, to which the latter must be sacrificed: "The Kingdom of Heaven is within you" (Clay 1916: 447–8). This critique of materialism had much in common with Tawney's critique of ' "the acquisitive society" ' (Tawney 1920, 1921).[3] An acquisitive society was one where a priority was given to protecting economic rights, in particular property rights, whilst leaving economic functions to fulfil themselves (except under exceptional circumstances). Tawney argued that goods and

---

[1] He does not specify whether Sidney or Beatrice.

[2] See Backhouse (2008) for a more detailed discussion of the religious context of the work of Hobson, Clay and Tawney.

[3] Though they use different terminology, this similarity may not be accidental, for Tawney was described by Clay (1916: ix) as one of the friends who had read a substantial part of his manuscript.

activities had to be judged according to the contribution made to the public purpose. People were not isolated individuals but parts of societies that had common goals and purposes, or moral principles, and such principles were needed to determine what goods should be produced.

These theoretical arguments were developed into critiques of contemporary capitalist society. Individualism had, Tawney claimed, destroyed the moral principles and the sense of a common purpose, without which society could not exist. His arguments for greater equality (Tawney 1931) proved highly influential in the Labour Party and elsewhere. Clay focused not so much on equality as on the failure of capitalism, or as he called it, 'the business system' to reflect the values of the time. A system of free enterprise took account of demands and not needs; inequality in the distribution of income caused these to diverge, and those 'who subordinate everything else to money-getting will exercise the greatest influence' whereas those who 'devote themselves to altruistic objects and neglect the pursuit of private wealth' will have little influence (Clay 1916: 452). Furthermore, economic organisation affects moral standards (455–60). Under free markets many receive incomes for which no service has been provided (for example, the unearned increment of land values) which 'obliterates' the distinction between 'social and anti-social effort': 'wealth is respectable however won, and great wealth is honoured, because it is powerful, whatever its source' (460). The economic organisation of his day strengthened materialistic tendencies at the expense of idealistic ones.

Another approach contributing to the pluralism of the 1920s was that of Ralph Hawtrey, better known as one of the period's leading monetary economists. He stood apart from Hobson, Tawney and Clay (he came from Cambridge, not Oxford), and was not seen by Hamilton as part of the 'English welfare school'. His work was, however, picked out for detailed criticism by Robbins (1927, 1932). Though a Cambridge-trained economist,[4] his views on welfare were very different from those of Marshall and Pigou. They are found towards the end of a general treatise on economics, *The Economic Problem*, where he argued that 'economics *cannot* be dissociated from ethics' (Hawtrey 1926: 184). His ethics came not from religion but from the philosopher G. E. Moore, who had argued that utilitarianism was flawed, for it presumed that pleasure or happiness was the right end to pursue. This was not necessarily true, and to think so was to participate in the 'cult of individualism'

---

[4] His career was spent in the Treasury, though with a brief, but influential period visiting Harvard.

(Hawtrey 1926: 182). Welfare was, for Hawtrey, not an aggregate of satisfactions: 'The aggregate of satisfactions is not an aggregate of welfare at all. It includes good satisfactions which are welfare, and bad satisfactions, which are the reverse' (Hawtrey 1926: 215). Different individuals' satisfactions are compared through feelings of approval and disapproval, 'which the course of evolution has planted in our nature in regard to certain classes of objects. ... In so far as other people have similar feelings of approval and disapproval, he and they will find common ground in the search for a solution' (Hawtrey 1926: 187). Welfare judgements, therefore, had to be based on 'the common ethical judgements of mankind' – on those judgements that are common to all ethical systems (Hawtrey 1926: 188). If mankind could not agree, then Hawtrey had little to offer.

Though others would no doubt have differed from Hawtrey over the details, Hawtrey's argument against utilitarianism would have been shared by his Cambridge friends and fellow Apostles. Pigou's attempts to distance himself from utilitarianism no doubt reflected, if not Moore's direct influence, then the climate fostered by Moore at Cambridge. Keynes, though he had clear attitudes relating to problems of welfare (see Chapter 9), did not write on the theory of welfare, but he shared the ideas Hawtrey took from Moore, in particular his rejection of utilitarianism.[5] The good was an end in itself: activities were not good because they yielded utility. This perspective would completely justify his drawing policy conclusions directly from his economic theories: the value of maintaining a high and stable level of employment was something that could be perceived directly, especially after the Great Depression, not something derived from a criterion such as the utilitarian one. The same was true of Beveridge's scheme for social insurance. Unlike Pigou, he did not see the need to offer utilitarian or other arguments as to why it was good to protect people from poverty. In his discussions with Beveridge relating to the institutions of the welfare state (see Chapter 9), he focused on the affordability of schemes for social insurance without adopting a Pigovian approach of weighing its social costs and benefits against each other.

Thus a case can be made that, in the 1920s, British welfare economics was highly pluralistic. Cambridge might have been dominated by Pigou, but outside Cambridge a wide range of approaches was being pursued. This is the background to Robbins's *Essay* and the emergence in the 1930s of the New Welfare Economics.

---

[5] Daunton (in Chapter 4) discusses his views on taxation.

3. ROBBINS AND THE SCIENCE OF WELFARE

The canonical statement of the methodological basis for the New Welfare Economics was made in Lionel Robbins's *Essay on the Nature and Significance of Economic Science* (1932).[6] He argued vigorously that value judgements should be excluded from economic science. His younger colleagues at the London School of Economics took this injunction seriously and sought to develop a scientific welfare economics on the basis of ideas taken from the Italian economist, Vilfredo Pareto. Its basis was the so-called Pareto criterion, that if a change makes some people better off without making anyone worse off, it raises the welfare of the society as a whole. This is, of course, a value judgement, but it was considered so innocuous as not to contravene Robbins's injunction.[7]

The conventional view of this development, which came to be known as the New Welfare Economics, is that it was a reaction against Pigovian welfare economics. Pigovian welfare economics rested on interpersonal utility comparisons and hence on value judgements that were thought to go beyond ones that economists could make in their capacity as economists. In deciding whether or not an economic policy was beneficial, one might have to form a judgement as to whether one person's gain outweighed another person's loss, but this could not be part of economic science. The New Welfare Economics was thus scientific, in contrast to the Pigovian muddling of value judgements with economic analysis.

However, once it is accepted that welfare economics was highly pluralist in the 1920s, Robbins's *Essay* appears rather differently. In comparison with Hobson, Clay, Tawney and Hawtrey, Robbins appears much closer to Pigou than the conventional view implies: they were both arguing for welfare economics to be confined to what could be said scientifically.[8] To see this, it is helpful to look at the difference between Pigou and Hobson. Their main difference did not lie in utilitarianism, but in the greater importance Pigou attached to being scientific, even though this meant narrowing the scope of welfare economics. At the beginning of *Wealth and Welfare*, Pigou argued that welfare comprised more than simply economic welfare:

Economic welfare, however, does not contain all welfare arising in this connection [the earning and spending of the national dividend]. Various good and bad

---

[6] This section draws on ideas that are though focused on Robbins, this section uses material on Hobson taken from Chapter 6.

[7] Subsequent work by Sen and others has shown that it is far less innocuous than it might seem.

[8] Backhouse (2009) goes further in arguing that Hobson and Hawtrey, along with the approaches they represented, not Pigou, were Robbins's primary target in his *Essay*.

qualities indirectly associated with income-getting and income-spending are excluded from it. It does not include the whole psychic return, which emerges when the objective services constituting the national dividend have passed through the factory of the body; it includes only the psychic return of *satisfaction*. Thus economic welfare is, as it were, a part of welfare. (Pigou 1912: 3–4, emphasis in original)

These were sentiments that Hobson (and many others influenced by Ruskin) endorsed wholeheartedly: much of *Work and Wealth* (1914) and *Wealth and Life* (1929) was an exploration of precisely these differences between what Pigou here calls 'the whole psychic return' and 'the psychic return of satisfaction'. However, after recognising these differences, Pigou goes on to minimize their importance, arguing that economic welfare will generally be a good proxy for overall welfare. In other words, Pigou drastically narrows the scope of his inquiries in order to tackle them scientifically, making a much narrower range of value judgements than those that Hobson, Clay, Tawney, Hawtrey and others thought it necessary to make.

Though he took it a stage further, this is exactly what Robbins was doing, a point that Hobson saw very clearly.

Supporters of Pigou contend that, if we introduce distinctively ethical criteria, we and ourselves in a region not merely outside measurable facts, but outside agreed facts. This is clearly put by Mr. Lionel Robbins [1927: 176]. 'It is not because we believe that our science is exact that we wish to exclude ethics from our analysis, but because we wish to confine our investigations to a subject about which positive statement of any kind is conceivable.' (Hobson 1929: 128)

Pigou and Robbins were both guilty of narrowing economics to what could be quantified and stated exactly, which forced them to play down the differences between wealth and welfare.

Thus when Robbins argued for confining economic science to matters that did not rest on value judgements, he was continuing along a path already taken by Pigou. He may have considered that Pigou had gone too far towards allowing value judgements into economic science, but that was nothing when compared with the way in which Hobson, Hawtrey and (though he did not cite them) Clay and Tawney mounted comprehensive critiques of capitalism on the basis of ethical judgements that were allegedly shared by most of mankind. They had no basis for making such claims. It was legitimate for them to apply their own ethical judgements, but they could not claim for them any scientific authority. Their arguments were therefore dangerous in a way that Pigovian welfare economics, based on the much narrower and less specific value judgements that underlay utilitarianism, was not.

4. WELFARE ECONOMICS, MARKETS AND THE STATE

The choice between Cambridge welfare economics, Greenian ideal-ism, Moorean intuitionism and the Paretianism of the New Welfare Economics had dramatic implications for what could be said about social welfare and hence on how easy it was to justify moving towards a wel-fare state. In arguing against those inspired by Green's idealism (notably Hobson) and Moore's intuitionism (Hawtrey), and as well as by provid-ing arguments that undermined Cambridge welfare economics, Robbins helped to determine the path that was taken by welfare economics in the 1930s and 1940s. Of course, he did not do this alone. There were others (e.g., Myrdal 1953) who were protesting at the illicit intrusion of values into economics. Even more important are the broader intellectual devel-opments, represented by (though not encompassed by) the philosophies of 'Logical positivism' and 'operationalism', and the rise of formal and axiomatic methods in mathematics, the natural sciences and economics.[9] The movement away from pluralistic welfare economics to a narrower, more overtly scientific welfare economics occurred in part because of the same intellectual developments that made Institutionalism fall out of favour. Yet there is another dimension.

Economists are sometimes accused of providing an apologia for capitalism – for demonstrating that free markets are the solution to all economic ills. In the period considered by this volume, that was emphatically not the case. As the three chapters in Part I show, even the 'orthodox' economists of the Marshallian Cambridge school did not argue that. Marshall did develop a theorem about the maximization of satisfaction in a competitive market but did not draw the conclusion that capitalism was the ideal system. He and his successors constructed care-ful arguments relating to the need for components of what later came to be known as the welfare state. They developed theoretical tools with which the functioning of a market economy could be analysed scientifi-cally. However, these theoretical tools did constrain the conclusions they could reach (not that they wished to draw more radical conclusions, for as has been shown, utilitarianism would have justified more radical con-clusions concerning distribution, had they wished to do so).

In contrast, those who developed welfare economics coming out of Oxford developed far more radical perspectives on the capitalist system and social welfare. They were able to justify these conclusions because

---

[9] See Weintraub (1998) and Backhouse and Medema (forthcoming).

their way of arguing about welfare allowed a wide range of ethical judgements to be brought to bear on capitalism. The study of welfare was the arena in which ethical judgements from Christianity, humanism or other sources were brought to bear on the analysis of capitalism. Unlike Cambridge utilitarianism, Oxford idealism served as an inspiration for social involvement and provided a framework for discussing ethics and social welfare. It was both a strength and a weakness that it was consistent with approaches to welfare as varied as Hobson's Ruskin-inspired analysis of life-giving activities, Tawney's Christian socialist communitarianism and Beveridge's practical reformism. Appeal to shared human values could have tremendous rhetorical force, as Green's example showed. However, without a procedure for establishing more rigorously what values, if any, were universally shared, the analytical power of Greenian idealism was weak. The theoretical freedom it implied, much greater than that facing their Cambridge counterparts who were constrained by their commitment to scientific analysis, could cut both ways.

It is thus perhaps not surprising that the links between ideas about welfare and the policies that were introduced were complex. Hobson and Wells were both social theorists who may have influenced policy early in the century, but, though Hobson was justifiably recognised as a welfare economist in a way that Wells was not, it is not certain that his direct influence on the Liberal reforms was any greater than that of Wells. A vision of what needed to be achieved, combined with common sense in working out the details (which in different proportions describes the Webbs, Beveridge and Keynes) was a powerful instrument for reform. Economic theory, whether Keynesian macroeconomics or Cambridge welfare economics, could be important in forming opinions but 'scientific' arguments were no substitute for the energy of committed reformers prepared to become engaged in the practical details of policy.

This is the background to Robbins's critique of inter-personal comparisons and the reorientation of welfare economics that it stimulated. The authority of economic science (and to call something science was to give it authority) should not be conferred on ethical judgements that were matters of individual belief. In a world where, not only had the Great Depression shaken confidence in capitalism, but Marxist theory was being used to justify Communism and Corporatist arguments were being used to justify Fascism and National Socialism, analyses that incorporated such beliefs into what pretended to be a systematic analysis of welfare were highly dangerous. The narrowing of economics, to which Robbins's essay made a significant contribution, thus had apparently clear political implications.

Narrowing economics in this way could foster a more favourable attitude towards markets and a more sceptical attitude towards state intervention, more sceptical than that of either socialists or practical liberal reformers such as Beveridge.[10] Robbins himself saw more virtues in free markets than did many of the Cambridge economists, though in practice he was a utilitarian in his approach to questions of policy. However, there was still no simple relationship between welfare economics and policy, for some of the most prominent proponents of the New Welfare Economics were advocates of market socialism and others were highly critical of capitalism.[11] However, it can be argued that the effect of this narrowing of welfare economics was eventually (by the 1980s) to lead economists in a direction that was more favourable towards a market economy and more sceptical towards the welfare state.[12] As long as economists saw capitalist market economies as far from what became the ideal of a perfectly competitive equilibrium to which the so-called fundamental theorems of welfare economics of Arrow and Debreu applied, welfare economics provided a technique for diagnosing their limitations. But once they began to accept, as did the Chicago school under Milton Friedman and George Stigler, that markets approximated perfect competition, this exclusion of value judgements served to foster a much more favourable view of markets and a more critical view of the welfare state.[13]

5. CONCLUDING REMARKS

To read thinkers of an earlier age, who did not think in terms of modern disciplinary boundaries, in the light of those boundaries, can be profoundly misleading. Not least, it makes a profound difference whether we view the welfare economics of this period from the standpoint of welfare economics, circa 1960, or from the standpoint of welfare economics after Rawls, Sen and modern social choice theory. Thinking on welfare in the first part of the 20th century concerned both ideas that, from a modern perspective, look like welfare economics and ideas that do not. The latter included not only different theoretical approaches but also ideas that arose out of implementing practical measures to

---

[10] The word 'liberal' is deliberately written without a capital. It is not Beveridge's membership of the Liberal Party, but his liberal views that are relevant here.

[11] The debate over socialist calculation has been widely discussed elsewhere. See, for example, Lavoie (1985).

[12] See Tribe (2009).

[13] This does not express a view on the merits of these developments.

alleviate problems identified in contemporary society and which led, years later, to what came to be known as the welfare state. It is debatable whether some of these approaches merit being called welfare economics, for they comprised approaches that were very different from what subsequently came to be understood by that phrase. But that is the point: Pigovian welfare economics formed part of a set of conversations, within which boundaries between economic analysis and political philosophy were neither clear-cut nor drawn in the same places as they are in modern economics.[14] To consider Cambridge welfare economics apart from its Oxford-inspired counterparts is seriously to distort the context in which it arose. Given that the New Welfare Economics was responding to the state of the subject in the 1920s, this distorts, in turn, our view of the context out of which modern welfare economics emerged.

References

Arrow, K. J. 1951. *Social Choice and Individual Values*. New York: Wiley.

Backhouse, R. E. 2008. Faith, Morality and Welfare: The 'English School of Welfare Economics', 1901–29, *History of Political Economy* 40 (Annual supplement): 312–36.

2009. Robbins and Welfare Economics: A Reappraisal. *Journal of the History of Economic Thought* 31(4): 68–82.

Backhouse, R. E. and Medema, S. G. 2009. The Robbins Definition and the Axiomatization of Economics. *Journal of the History of Economic Thought* 31(4): 57–67.

Bergson, A. 1938. A Reformulation of Certain Aspects of Welfare Economics. *Quarterly Journal of Economics* 52(2): 310–34.

Blaug, M. 1997. *Economic Theory in Retrospect*. 5th ed. Cambridge: Cambridge University Press.

Clay, H. 1916. *Economics: An Introduction for the General Reader*. London: Macmillan.

Hamilton, W. H. 1919. The Institutional Approach to Economic Theory. *American Economic Review* 9 (1): 309–18.

Harsanyi, J. C. 1955. Cardinal Welfare, Individualistic Ethics, and Interpersonal Comparisons of Utility. *Journal of Political Economy* 63: 309–21.

Hawtrey, R. G. 1926. *The Economic Problem*. London: Longmans, Green.

Hobson, J. A. 1914. *Work and Wealth*. London: Macmillan.

1929. *Wealth and Life*. London: Macmillan.

Homan, P. T. 1928. *Contemporary Economic Thought*. New York: Harper.

---

[14] Given the political concerns of those influenced by the Oxford approach, it is worth noting that Blaug (1997: 583) describes Pigou's *Economics of Welfare* (1920) as not a theoretical treatise 'but a tract for the times'.

Lavoie, D. 1985. *Rivalry and Central Planning.* Cambridge: Cambridge University Press.

Little, I. M. D. 1950. *A Critique of Welfare Economics.* Oxford: Clarendon Press.

Mitchell, W. C. 1969. *Types of Economic Theory.* New York: Kelley.

Morgan, M. S., and Rutherford, M. 1998. American Economics: The Character of the Transformation. In *From Interwar Pluralism to Postwar Neoclassicism,* M. S. Morgan and M. Rutherford, eds. Annual Supplement to *History of Political Economy.* Durham, NC: Duke University Press, pp. 1–26.

Myrdal, G. 1953. *The Political Element in the Development of Economic Theory.* P. Streeten, trans. London: Routledge.

Pigou, A. C. 1912. *Wealth and Welfare.* London: Macmillan.

1920. *Economics of Welfare.* London: Macmillan.

Rawls, J. 1971. *A Theory of Justice.* Cambridge, MA: Harvard University Press.

Robbins, L. C. 1927. Mr. Hawtrey on the Scope of Economics. *Economica* 20: 172–78.

1932. *An Essay on the Nature and Significance of Economic Science.* London: Macmillan.

Sen, A. K. 1970. The Impossibility of a Paretian Liberal. *Journal of Political Economy* 78(1): 152–7.

Tawney, R. H. 1920. *The Sickness of an Acquisitive Society.* London: Fabian Society/George Allen and Unwin.

1921. *The Acquisitive Society.* London: G. Bell and Sons.

1931. *Equality.* London: Allen and Unwin.

Tribe, K. 2009. Liberalism and Neoliberalism in Britain, 1930–1980. In *The Road from Mont Pelerin: The Making of the Neoliberal Thought Collective,* P. Mirowski and D. Plehwe, eds. Cambridge, MA: Harvard University Press.

Weintraub, E. R. 1998. Axiomatisches Verständnis. *Economic Journal* 108: 1837–47.

INDEX